JURISPRUDENCE: CAMBRIDGE ESSAYS

JURISPRUDENCE
Cambridge Essays

EDITED BY
HYMAN GROSS
AND
ROSS HARRISON

CLARENDON PRESS · OXFORD
1992

Oxford University Press, Walton Street, Oxford OX2 6DP
Oxford New York Toronto
Delhi Bombay Calcutta Madras Karachi
Petaling Jaya Singapore Hong Kong Tokyo
Nairobi Dar es Salaam Cape Town
Melbourne Auckland
and associated companies in
Berlin Ibadan

Oxford is a trade mark of Oxford University Press

Published in the United States
by Oxford University Press, New York

British Library Cataloguing in Publication Data
Data available

Library of Congress Cataloging in Publication Data
Jurisprudence: Cambridge essays / edited by Hyman Gross and Ross
Harrison.
Includes index.
1. Jurisprudence. I. Gross, Hyman. II. Harrison, Ross.
K235.J85 1992 340—dc20 92–5714
ISBN 0–19–825289–7

Typeset by Hope Services (Abingdon) Ltd.
Printed in Great Britain by
Bookcraft Ltd.
Midsomer Norton, Avon

PREFACE

These essays reflect an unorthodox conception of jurisprudence. Ideas about the law come from many different quarters, and some of the law's most perplexing features are illuminated from perspectives which are not immediately familiar to lawyers. Conceived along these lines, jurisprudence turns out to be less a discipline in its own right and more an area of common concern for people working in diverse disciplines.

With this conception in mind we have brought together in this volume original essays by Cambridge academics whose subjects include law, philosophy, criminology, intellectual history, and political theory.

H.G. and R.H.

CONTENTS

CONTRIBUTORS

T. R. S. Allan is a Lecturer in Law and Fellow of Pembroke College.

Philip Allott is a Lecturer in Law and Fellow of Trinity College.

Thomas Baldwin is a Lecturer in Philosophy and Fellow of Clare College.

Richard Bellamy was a Fellow in History at Jesus College and is now a member of the Department of Politics, University of Edinburgh.

Hyman Gross is a Fellow of Corpus Christi College and sometime Arthur Goodhart Professor of Legal Science.

Ross Harrison is a Reader in Philosophy and Fellow of King's College.

David Howarth is a Lecturer in Land Economy and Fellow of Clare College.

Peter Lipton lectures in the Department of the History and Philosophy of Science.

Onora O'Neill is Principal of Newnham College.

N. E. Simmonds is a Lecturer in Law and Fellow of Corpus Christi College.

Quentin Skinner is Professor of Political Science and Fellow of Christ's College.

Nigel Walker was formerly Wolfson Professor of Criminology and Fellow of King's College.

I

Bluntness and Bricolage

N. E. SIMMONDS

IDEALISM

Whatever their differing views on the respective roles of reason and fiat in law, the classical philosophies of law have generally concurred in attaching importance to the determinate and ascertainable character of positive law. For natural law theories, positive law may be seen as a concretization of the more abstract requirements of reason, reducing for the individual the extent of wisdom and judgement that must bridge the divide between the general demands of reason and the decision of specific instances. For theories of a more Hobbesian cast, law is a pure product of will, creating order out of a moral vacuum. But for all such theories, positive law exhibits a degree of certainty and specificity not to be found in the requirements of reason apart from law: their differences turn on whether law is seen as creating new requirements on conduct, or as channelling and redirecting pre-existing requirements.

In this century, philosophy of law has exhibited a closer attention to the detailed structure and character of legal arguments than ever before. This has had the salutary effect of producing theories which challenge the picture of law as determinate and ascertainable. It has had the less salutary effect of somewhat detaching such legal theories from more general accounts of the bases of social order, and the way in which law contributes to social order. The heterogeneous group of writers usually called the American Realists seemed (in so far as one can generalize about them) to exhibit this tendency. They assaulted with vigour and insight the crude picture of law as a discrete body of rules yielding mechanical answers. But the assault, at least in its more extreme versions, left in doubt the question of how the ordering of conduct and the stabilization of expectations was achieved in a world where law exhibited such radical uncertainty.

For there is undoubtedly a great deal of force in the argument, most recently presented by H. L. A. Hart, that a society of any complexity requires rules which are ascertainable by publicly available criteria, such as source of enactment.[1] Whether we are moral subjectivists or believers in moral truth, we are bound to acknowledge that moral issues are sources of intense and prolonged disagreement. Yet, at the same time, it is necessary that our conduct should be regulated by some shared set of rules, both to provide a solution to problems of co-ordination, and to enable one to form reliable expectations about the conduct of others outside of the context of pure co-ordination problems. A theory of law can quite properly allow for a considerable amount of leeway and openness in the law, but it seems reasonable to stipulate as a requirement of adequacy in any such theory that it should be capable of explaining how law exhibits a degree of determinacy and certainty not exhibited by moral debate; or, in the event that the theory denies the existence of such determinacy, it should offer a convincing account of the bases of social order that shows law to be dispensable even in the context of a modern differentiated society.

All of this suggests that the role of law is important but somewhat mundane. A legal system is unlikely to be viable for any length of time if it cannot depend upon widespread support. Given that (on this account) the major point of law is to provide a set of rules which can be shared even in the presence of moral disagreement, support for law must take the form of a willingness to comply even when the rules do not precisely reflect one's own moral beliefs. Support for law will be most widespread, therefore, when the law can occupy to maximal extent the ground of convergence between rival moral positions, or when it can achieve compromises between rival positions. This makes it unlikely that the law will be found to be implementing some highly refined and elevated moral or political theory. It is more likely to reflect the humdrum median positions that can expect some support from a great diversity of persons or groups.[2]

---

[1] H. L. A. Hart, *The Concept of Law* (Oxford, 1961), 89–96, 189–95.

[2] Stability and order are themselves of great moral importance. Any theory which values liberty (understood as the capacity and opportunity to formulate and execute projects) must value order, for it is only in an ordered world, where one can form stable expectations about the conduct of others, that genuine liberty can exist. The ability of law to stabilize expectations is therefore of great moral importance; but this capacity to stabilize expectations may be eroded if the law is seen as a rigorous expression of elevated but controversial conceptions of justice.

The legal theory of Ronald Dworkin seems hard to reconcile with these assumptions. Dworkin suggests that law is not a body of rules ascertained by reference to some determinate criteria such as a basic rule of recognition. Rather, the law is that body of rights which results from applying to the extant governmental decrees and decisions the moral requirement that government should treat its citizens as equals.[3] To determine the content of the existing law, a judge must draw on his own moral judgement in order to construct the best interpretation of the existing law. The correct interpretation is that reconstruction of a moral theory underpinning the law which, while exhibiting an adequate degree of 'fit' with the text of statutes and cases, possesses the highest degree of moral appeal. One's view of the law is soundly based when it both satisfies the 'constraints of fit' and makes the law the best that it can be, from a moral point of view.

It may at first be thought that this theory preserves an acceptably high degree of determinacy in the law. Interpretations must 'fit' the text and are, to that extent, constrained by the text. The problem here is that, for Dworkin, the fit need not be absolute (some rules or cases can be treated as 'mistakes') and we are offered no independent criteria for the tightness of the constraints of 'fit'. The criteria of fit employed by the Dworkinian judge are derived from his or her own political theory.[4] What are we to say of an interpretation that treats 20 per cent (or 30, or 49 per cent?) of the cases as 'mistakes'? Simply that

[3] Ronald Dworkin, *Law's Empire* (London, 1986); *A Matter of Principle* (Cambridge, Mass., 1985); *Taking Rights Seriously* (London, 1977).

[4] Dworkin's theory relies on a distinction between two stages or levels in the process of adjudication. At stage 1, the judge must interpret the practices of law and choose a conception of law (conventionalism, pragmatism, or 'law as integrity'). At stage 2, the judge must formulate conclusions of law, employing the conception of law selected at stage 1. It is important for us to distinguish the two stages, because we may (for example) agree with Dworkin's characterization of stage 1, but not with his selection of 'law as integrity' as the best conception of law. Confusion results from any preparedness to underplay the distinction between these two levels of argument, e.g.:
(i) When Dworkin discusses the constraints of fit in adjudication, he tells us that the judge's commitment to 'law as integrity' will be expressed in convictions about substance and fit that, by mutual opposition or tension, constrain his interpretation (*Law's Empire*, 257). But what constrains interpretation at stage 1? 'Law as integrity' is the theory selected at stage 1, and cannot guide its own selection. See N. E. Simmonds, 'Imperial Visions and Mundane Practices', *Cambridge Law Journal*, 46 (1987), 477–80.
(ii) It is easy to fall into the trap of defending 'law as integrity' by pointing out the extent to which every judge must begin the process of adjudication from the standpoint of the judge's own political convictions. This will not serve as a defence, however, for it only gets us to stage 1. The judge's political convictions may lead to the selection of conventionalism as the appropriate theory. One can be a conventionalist and nevertheless agree that the first stage of adjudication involves a question of political theory.

we do not agree with the interpretation? There seems every possibility that interpretations of the existing law will be, on this acount, as variable as interpretations of *Hamlet*.

In his first book, *Taking Rights Seriously*, Dworkin distinguished between the 'enactment force' and the 'gravitational force' of a mistaken decision.[5] The idea seemed to be that, when a judge treated an earlier case (or a statute) as a 'mistake', he should not use the precedent as a basis for an argument of principle going beyond the scope of the rule established by the precedent, but he would nevertheless be bound to apply the rule so established to cases falling within its scope. This approach might be thought to offer Dworkin a way of responding to the charge that his theory renders law unacceptably indeterminate. In respecting the 'enactment force' even of mistaken decisions, Dworkin seems to respect established rules as much as any positivist: the difference from positivism lies in Dworkin's willingness to use arguments of 'gravitational force', beyond the scope of the explicit rules, when the precedent is not a mistake. This appears to introduce constraints of legal principle to an area of decision left purely discretionary by the positivist. On this view, therefore, Dworkin *increases* the determinacy of the law as against the positivist view.

The gravitational force/enactment force distinction, however, runs into two problems which will crop up again when we turn our attention to positivism. First and foremost is the difficulty of *discovering* a rule established in the precedent case which could enjoy such a thing as enactment force. Second is the problem raised by the apparent power of the courts to narrow, or otherwise modify, those rules which are expressly declared.

It is widely appreciated, even amongst non-lawyer students of jurisprudence, that courts do not generally offer express formulations of the rule upon which they base their decisions. Innovative cases, of the kind that become important precedents, generally turn on a complex of circumstances and considerations. Judgments generally review and weigh these considerations, but do not reduce them to the explicit form of a rule. The binding part of a decision is said to be its *ratio decidendi* or (in America) its 'holding'. But extracting the *ratio decidendi* is not a matter of pointing to an explicitly formulated rule established in the case: in most cases there will be no such explicit rule, and even if there is an explicitly formulated rule it is open to a later

---

[5] Dworkin, *Taking Rights Seriously*, 111; see also rev. edn. (London, 1978), 318.

court to say that the formulation is 'too wide', as not representing the
ratio. Theories about the process of ascertaining the *ratio decidendi*
have proliferated,[6] and the very existence of such disputes should serve
to demonstrate that no one can speak of the 'enactment force' of a
precedent as if this phrase referred to some familiar and identifiable
feature of case-law reasoning. Indeed, it may well be that the process
of extracting a rule from a case is indistinguishable from the use of the
case as the basis for an argument of principle.

Even if Dworkin could overcome the problem of identifying the
declared rule which possesses 'enactment force', however, a further
problem would remain. Dworkin's theory appears to permit judges to
modify established rules in order to bring them more closely into line
with the principles of the underpinning theory. Thus rules established
in mistaken decisions will not be strictly enforced, but may have new
and unenvisaged exceptions to them created. For instance, in
Dworkin's own example of *Riggs* v. *Palmer*,[7] the courts in effect created
a new exception to the established rules on testamentary succession
(the exception being that a murderer may not inherit under the will of
his victim). *Riggs* v. *Palmer* involved statutory rules, but it would be odd
to suggest that courts have greater power to alter statutes than they
have to alter rules of case-law. Indeed we shall see when we examine
Raz's views, in a moment, that in the area of case-law judges may
fundamentally reshape the rules as previously declared and are not
limited to the addition of excepting provisions. It seems then that
judges are not bound by declared rules in a way that would enable
Dworkin to sustain the enactment force/gravitational force distinction.
Such constraints as exist on the judicial power to tinker with the
declared rules must lie elsewhere. So far as Dworkin's theory goes, the
only place that such constraints could lie is within the deep
interpretative theory.

In his most recent book, Dworkin says nothing of the gravitational
enactment distinction.[8] He invokes instead a distinction between 'pure'
and 'inclusive' integrity.[9] Pure integrity is a matter of the moral
coherence exhibited by the substantive law. Inclusive integrity
incorporates a concern with what might be called institutional
considerations, such as the need to respect decisions of a democratic

---

[6] See the extensive bibliography in Laurence Goldstein (ed.), *Precedent in Law*
(Oxford, 1987).

[7] See Dworkin, *Taking Rights Seriously*, 23.

[8] Dworkin, *Law's Empire*.   [9] Ibid. 405–7.

legislature, or the need to stick by prior decisions of the courts. A concern with inclusive integrity will therefore lead to the toleration of rules that are mistakes from the point of view of pure integrity.

Like the earlier distinction, this distinction may be thought to confine the effects of the judge's interpretative speculations to those cases not covered by explicit rules. If, however, it was Dworkin's intention to treat the judges as strictly bound by such rules, he would need to reintroduce the gravitational/enactment distinction that we have already found grounds for rejecting. More probably, his present position is that a balance must be struck between pure and inclusive integrity, and the precise way in which the balance is struck will depend upon the underpinning interpretative theory that one adopts. Different theories will allow different degrees of subversion of the established rules to advance the cause of pure integrity. At this point, however, we must remind ourselves that the choice of interpretative theory not only depends upon individual moral judgement, but also appears virtually unconstrained by considerations of fit, since there seem to be no independent criteria of fit which must be satisfied. The capacity of the Dworkinian judge to subvert established rules is therefore very extensive indeed.

It is, of course, not only the absence of real constraints of fit that seems to render the Dworkinian mode of adjudication excessively lacking in determinacy. A more obvious feature of Dworkin's theory is its intensely 'Protestant' character, as Gerry Postema has aptly styled it.[10] Each individual must, in Dworkin's view, decide for himself what the law requires of him; and, in doing so, must rely upon his own moral judgement. The correctness of a legal interpretation that satisfies the constraints of fit (such as they are) is dependent upon the truth of the moral judgement that informs that interpretation. It follows from this that an individual judge (or, indeed, an individual citizen) may offer a highly idiosyncratic interpretation of the existing law, with which none of her colleagues agree; yet it is possible that she may be right, and everyone else may be wrong.

This seems a very direct assault upon the idea that law arises to produce convergence on a shared set of rules. For, given the vaporous nature of the constraints of fit, the only thing that prevents the judges from exhibiting extreme diversity in their legal opinions is the fact that they are likely to share broadly similar moral perspectives. No doubt

---

[10] G. Postema, ' "Protestant" Interpretation and Social Practices', *Law and Philosophy*, 6 (1987), 283–319.

T. O'Hagan is correct when he says that 'Most constructivists, like Dworkin, have an optimistic view that citizens of advanced democracies, both lay and professional, make up a community whose most general moral-political standards are more or less shared,'[11] but such a stabilizing convergence of moral opinion would be purely contingent from the standpoint of Dworkin's theory. In spite of his recent emphasis on the value of community,[12] Dworkin makes consensus no part of his theory of interpretation.[13] Community itself is treated as the susceptibility of social practices to a certain substantive interpretation in terms of equal concern and respect. It is therefore the *result* of interpretation, not the matrix, and the interpretative process itself remains stubbornly individualistic.

The failure of Dworkinian legal idealism to preserve an adequate degree of determinacy in law may incline us towards an austere version of legal positivism. What could be more determinate than a discrete and finite body of rules identified by strict source-based criteria? The tempting vision evaporates on closer inspection. On the one hand, the source-based rules that we *can* identify seem to lose their character as determinate guidelines the moment that we come to apply them. On the other hand, it seems difficult to treat case-law as a body of source-based rules in any suitably austere and determinate sense. To these matters we now turn.

POSITIVISM

In most contexts, an utterance is able to convey a more or less determinate meaning by virtue of a conjunction of semantics and pragmatics. Semantic rules determine the general range of meanings that the utterance might bear; the pragmatic context enables us to settle on this or that meaning as appropriate.[14] In one sense, positive legal rules seem to lack an immediate pragmatic context, since they are intended to apply generally and prospectively. Moreover, anything that might be introduced as a relevant pragmatic context can be challenged

---

[11] T. O'Hagan, 'Gadamer, Hermeneutics and the Law', *Archiv für Rechts- und Sozialphilosophie*, (1990), 199.

[12] Dworkin, *Law's Empire*, 195–216.

[13] Consensus may play a part in the political convictions of the individual interpreter: see ibid. 249–50.

[14] I would not deny that semantic rules are themselves ultimately dependent upon the pragmatic context. The division between semantics and pragmatics may itself be dependent on context.

as irrelevant. If we are inclined to think of law as creating order in a moral Tower of Babel, we will resist the invocation of this or that moral opinion as a basis for interpreting the law. If we are inclined to the view that the published rules constrain the action of government in pursuit of its objectives, we will resist the idea that governmental objectives provide the pragmatic context for the interpretation of published rules. In this way we can be forced back into one of two positions:

1. the empty pretence that semantic rules alone can provide a determinate interpretation; *or*
2. the insistence that specifically legal knowledge has been exhausted when the range of semantically possible interpretations has been stated, thereby leaving the choice of interpretation to extra-legal discretionary judgement.[15]

Some legal theorists have advocated a mode of rule interpretation that is oriented by the *purpose* of the rule. But (quite apart from the danger that this collapses important distinctions between legal judgment and bureaucratic policy implementation) purposes are hard to ascertain: as we will see in due course, many rules serve purposes that are obscure and debatable, or serve several different and partially incompatible purposes at once.[16]

It is very difficult to regard case-law as a body of source-based rules. Judges do not generally formulate explicit rules, and, when they do so, their formulations can be treated by later courts as too wide. The later courts will then create an exception to the rule, not envisaged in its original formulation.

The best attempt to explain this process of 'distinguishing' cases in terms of a source-based conception of law is that offered by Joseph Raz.[17] Raz adopts what he calls a 'strong' view of distinguishing which regards the process of distinguishing as a form of rule-alteration. The precedent court is regarded as laying down a source-based rule, but the later court has power to modify that rule, subject to two constraints:

---

[15] See e.g. Hans Kelsen, *The Pure Theory of Law* (Berkeley, Calif., 1967), 355.

[16] For an instance where a purposive mode of interpretation undercuts the positivism of a theory, see N. E. Simmonds, 'Rights, Socialism and Liberalism', *Legal Studies*, 5 (1985), 6–8.

[17] Joseph Raz, *The Authority of Law* (Oxford, 1979), 186–8.

1. the modified rule must be the rule laid down in the precedent restricted by the addition of a further condition for its application;
2. the modified rule must be such as to justify the decision made in the precedent.

This analysis, of course, assumes that we can extract some rule from the precedent in the first place, but we will overlook that difficulty; the analysis at least has the merit of showing how a judicial power to *modify* rules is compatible with the judges being *bound* by such rules.

Even so, the analysis is a failure. For the first of Raz's two conditions collapses on close examination, leaving only the second condition in place; and the second condition on its own is insufficient to preserve the notion of case-law as a body of source-based rules.

In *Felthouse* v. *Bindley*[18] an uncle wrote to his nephew offering to buy a horse for a certain price, and saying that if he did not hear from his nephew he would assume that the sale was agreed. The nephew was arranging an auction of his horses and, on receiving his uncle's letter, he instructed the auctioneer to withdraw the horse from the auction. The auctioneer failed to do so, and sold the horse to a third party. The uncle then sued the auctioneer for conversion of his (the uncle's) property. He argued that a contract of sale had been concluded and the title to the horse had, accordingly, passed to him before the auctioneer sold it. The reasoning in the judgments at first instance and on appeal is somewhat ambivalent, and on one interpretation the case is wholly concerned with the failure of the contract to comply with the Statute of Frauds, which required a memorandum of agreement in writing. Let us, however, adopt the conventional view of the case by interpreting it as holding that a contract cannot be concluded by mere silence. To fit in with Raz's view that cases produce explicit rules, we can imagine the judge expressly laying down the following rule: 'A contract is a bilateral relationship, binding on both parties, which will come into existence only when an offer has been accepted, and the acceptance communicated to the offeror.' This turns our case into a hypothetical *Felthouse* v. *Bindley*, rather than a real *Felthouse* v. *Bindley*, but it does not alter the substance of the issue.[19]

Now suppose that a later case arises, which we will call *Belthouse* v.

---

[18] (1862) II CB (NS) 869; 7 LT 835.
[19] My use of hypothetical, rather than real, cases is necessitated by the artificiality of Raz's assumption that precedents establish explicit rules.

Findley. In *Belthouse* v. *Findley*, Belthouse wrote offering to buy Findley's horse for a sum of £1,000 and saying that, if he heard nothing from Findley, he would take it that the sale was agreed. Findley did nothing, and some time later he sought to deliver the horse to Belthouse and to claim the £1,000. Belthouse refused to pay on the grounds that Findley never communicated his acceptance. It is likely that a court deciding *Belthouse* v. *Findley* might say something like this:

'*Felthouse* v. *Bindley* is a case where the offeror sought to *impose* liability on another by stipulating that silence would be treated as consent. But in the present case the offeror seeks to *escape* liability by pointing to the absence of a communicated acceptance. That he cannot do. In general the offeror has a right to be free of liability until acceptance is communicated. But in this case he has waived that right, and is liable for breach.'

It is difficult to formulate the ruling in *Belthouse* v. *Findley* in a manner compatible with Raz's first constraint, if that constraint has any real content. How can we present *Belthouse* v. *Findley* as simply adding a further condition for the application of the (hypothetical) *Felthouse* v. *Bindley* ruling? The two rulings move in completely different intellectual frameworks. Our hypothetical *Felthouse* v. *Bindley* ruling assumes a world where contracts bind either both parties or neither party, and spring in and out of existence only as the bilateral bond is created or discharged. Such a way of looking at things might seem quite satisfactory until *Belthouse* v. *Findley* comes up for decision. But, in the light of reflection on the facts of the latter case, we may conclude that it is sometimes right to hold that one party should be able to enforce the contract while the other should not. This requires us to break with the language of contracts either having come into existence or not having done so, and with the idea that the electric circuitry of offer and acceptance determines the existence or non-existence of the contract. For some purposes (if he is suing Belthouse) Findley is regarded as having validly accepted; for other purposes (if Belthouse sues him) he is not.

Raz's first constraint either permits this type of fundamental recasting of a rule or it does not. If it does not, it fails to fit familiar features of case-law reasoning. If it *does* permit such fundamental recasting it seems to impose no constraints beyond that imposed by the second requirement, namely that the rule as formulated in the instant case should be capable of justifying the decision in the precedent case. If, however, this second constraint is the only real one, the picture of case-law as a body of source-based rules has already been abandoned. As a matter of logic, the case might be subsumed equally well under an infinite number of different rules. There are few such rules that we would regard as acceptable *justifications* for the decision, but this restriction imports a moral element inconsistent with a view of case-law as a body of source-based rules: which rules count as acceptable justifications depends on whether they seize on likenesses and differences that we consider to provide adequate grounds for differential treatment. If the only restriction on propositions of case-law is that they should provide an acceptable justification for the individual decisions, the content of case-law will depend not on source-based rules but on moral judgement.

BLUNTNESS

Both positivism and idealism seem unacceptable, and unacceptable for the same reason: each theory offers a vision of law which is too demanding. The positivism which concerns me in this paper is not the minimal claim that an unjust law may nevertheless be law, but a theory which presents law as a finite body of posited rules providing a basis for social order in a world of moral uncertainty and dissent. This theory expects too much of law because it ignores the necessary dependence of law on a sustaining social environment characterized in part by moral diversity and in part by moral convergence. Law can never create order out of chaos because, detached from such a sustaining environment, its posited rules would lack determinate meaning, and the moral concerns which give its practices a point would lack widespread support.

The extent of one's legal rights and duties cannot be determined simply by consulting a discrete and self-contained set of rules. The rules must always be interpreted in the context of the relations and expectations that they serve to regulate. In this way law and its sustaining environment of social relations exist symbiotically, each tending to stabilize and give determinacy to the other.[20] An exclusive focus on posited rules all too easily leads to a collapse back into individual moral judgements. Thus, as we saw in our examination of Raz's discussion of 'distinguishing', the attempt to treat case-law in positivist terms rapidly suggests to us the false conclusion that

[20] See N. E. Simmonds, 'Between Positivism and Idealism', *Cambridge Law Journal*, 50 (1991), 308.

doctrinal reasoning is indistinguishable from the task of moral justification.

Idealism fails for more familiar reasons. The free-ranging Protestantism of Dworkin's theory threatens the ability of law to stabilize and provide some degree of certainty. But the law's concern to stabilize also ensures that the law will not be an expression of any moral theory which combines a high degree of abstraction with internal coherence. Rather, it will be an attempt to maximize and entrench those elements of moral convergence that already exist.

The difficulty of discovering any single moral vision within the law is exhibited by a feature of legal doctrines that I shall call their 'bluntness'. Rules and doctrines are blunt when, and to the extent that, they do not precisely embody any moral principle. Blunt laws are obliquely related to the values that they serve, and they may be so related to several distinct and perhaps incompatible values. In other cases, the failure of the blunt law to trace moral requirements more precisely is to be explained by the requirements of easy administrability.

The point is best explained by an example, and the example must of necessity be somewhat complex.[21]

In the law of contract, a promise is enforceable only if it is 'supported by consideration'. The doctrine of consideration cannot be accurately summarized in a sentence, but expressed crudely it requires that the promisee should have done or promised something in return for, and as the price stipulated for, the other party's promise. Thus, a contract may be the exchange of a promise for an act (where the promisor has stipulated the act as the price of the promise, and the act is therefore the consideration for the promise), or an exchange of promises (where each promise is the price stipulated by the giver of the other promise).

A problem arises when P seeks to enforce D's promise and argues that the consideration given for the promise was the promise to perform, or the performance, of a pre-existing duty. Duties can be distinguished according to whether they are owed by a general rule of law (public duties), owed to the promisor personally, or owed to a third party. Since we must also distinguish between the performance of the pre-existing duty, and the *promise* to perform the pre-existing duty, we have six situations to consider:

---

[21] Since I hope to make the example intelligible to non-lawyers, lawyers should prepare themselves for a brief return to the nursery. The explanation must be fairly brief, so it will also have to be fairly dogmatic.

1. performance of a pre-existing public duty;
2. promise to perform a pre-existing public duty;
3. performance of a pre-existing duty owed to the promisor;
4. promise to perform a pre-existing duty owed to the promisor;
5. performance of a pre-existing duty owed to a third party;
6. promise to perform a pre-existing duty owed to a third party.

The existing law in England seems to be that cases 5 and 6 are good consideration, but the other four cases are not.[22] In other words, the law distinguishes between the cases on the basis of the type of pre-existing duty, and treats the three-party case of a duty owed to a third party (5 and 6) differently from the two-party case (3 and 4) and the public duty case (1 and 2). At the same time, the law does not distinguish between the promise to perform a pre-existing duty and its actual performance.

We must now ask whether the existing law embodies any particular moral principle. What we will discover is that it does not accurately reflect *any* moral principle, but is obliquely related to several. The present rules are blunt, partly for reasons of easy administration and partly in order to occupy an area of convergence between *different* moral principles.

Let us assume first of all that the general doctrine of consideration (requiring that a promise should be in return for a reciprocal promise or act, which was stipulated as the 'price') is itself an embodiment of some moral principle. This is in fact a large assumption,[23] but on its basis let us ask whether the existing rules on pre-existing duties are a direct consequence of the general doctrine of consideration. In each of our six cases we must ask whether in promising to perform, or in performing, a pre-existing duty, P has given something of value in return for D's promise. We will take the cases one by one, but not in numerical order.

In case 2, P *may* have given something of value, in promising to perform his pre-existing public duty, if D stands to benefit from P's

---

[22] Some uncertainty is, however, created by the recent case of *Williams* v. *Roffey* [1990] 1 All ER 512. See below n. 31.

[23] But see P. S. Atiyah's observation that 'the doctrine is embedded deep in moral values and to get rid of it altogether might prove surprisingly difficult . . . Although no doubt there is a wide belief that to perform a promise is a moral obligation, there are conflicting moral attitudes about the unfairness of expecting to get something for nothing.' P. S. Atiyah, *An Introduction to the Law of Contract*, 4th edn. (Oxford, 1989), 159.

performance of that duty. This is because D would often have no claim for compensation for loss suffered as a result of P's failure to perform his public duty. By promising D that he will perform his duty, P has conferred on D a potential contractual cause of action with a claim in damages for resulting loss: this is valuable as a form of insurance.

Now, one often hears it said that the argument just offered is circular. Contracts only create a potential cause of action if they are binding; but they are only binding if supported by consideration; one therefore cannot argue that the consideration is the potential cause of action.

The allegation of circularity is fallacious. It is not *contracts* that are binding when supported by consideration, but *promises*. We must therefore break the transaction down into separate promises. Suppose that D promised P £100 per month in return for P's promise to perform his public duty (let us say, a duty to warn all potato farmers, including D, of infestations of colorado beetle). If we set on one side all arguments from public policy (on which see below), D should be able to enforce P's promise, because D has clearly given good consideration for it (the promise of money). D therefore has a potential cause of action. P's promise therefore conferred on D a potential cause of action. There is no circularity here.[24]

It is of course true that many cases of types 1 and 2 would involve considerations of public policy. We might say that those who have public duties should not profit from the duties; that the transactions smack of extortion; that beneficiaries of public duties would be divided into two classes of those who have paid and those who have not; etc. But we must distinguish between arguments of public policy and arguments drawn from the doctrine of consideration. We are presently asking whether the existing rules are a consequence of the doctrine of consideration, not whether they might be justified by extrinsic factors such as arguments of public policy. Indeed it will be my ultimate object to argue that the existing rules are partially but imperfectly supported by such extrinsic factors.

The argument that creation of a potential cause of action is good consideration applies equally well to case 6. But it does not apply to

[24] If the reader continues to feel troubled by a suspicion of circularity, he or she may be thinking of a form of circularity that is said to haunt the common law of contract generally (but which poses no *special* problem for pre-existing duty cases). See Richard Bronaugh, 'A Secret Paradox of the Common Law', *Law and Philosophy*, 2 (1983), 193–232.

case 4, since in that case D already possesses a potential cause of action against P.

The 'cause of action' argument will not apply to cases 1, 3, and 5, since in actually performing the pre-existing duty (as opposed to *promising* its performance) P gives D no new potential cause of action. But, by performing his pre-existing duty, P may nevertheless have given D something of value: he has given up his option of non-performance. Until P has actually performed he might choose *not* to perform. The result will be that he may be liable to pay damages to D (in case 3) or to the third-party beneficiary of the pre-existing duty (in case 5). But P may be able to make a profit from non-performance (by, for example, selling goods elsewhere) such that he can pay the damages and still make a net gain. The option of non-performance is therefore valuable, and is surrendered by actual performance. Actual performance should therefore count as good consideration in cases 3 and 5. Perhaps it should not do so in case 1 because of the difficulty of treating non-performance of a public duty as an 'option' (although that argument might amount to the introduction of 'extrinsic' factors of public policy); we can perhaps afford to leave this point open. The result of *strictly* applying the doctrine of consideration can be represented by the scheme in Table 1.

We have so far excluded all extrinsic considerations, such as arguments of public policy, and have looked only at the direct implications of the basic idea of consideration. Now let us note that such extrinsic considerations are likely to bear most conspicuously in cases of public duty, and duties owed to the promisor:

1. In public duty cases, there will often (though not invariably) be public policy arguments against enforcing contractual arrangements under which people secure payment for the performance of their public duty.
2. In cases involving a pre-existing duty owed to the promisor, there is likely to be an element of duress. Duress *may* be present in other cases, but it is especially likely in cases where the parties already have a contractual relationship with each other. If I extract from you a promise of more money in return for my performance of a contractual duty that I already owe to you, my extraction of the promise may have been made possible by the way I have induced your reliance on me. Thus, if sailors contract to work a ship home and then, when the ship is in danger on the high seas, demand extra

TABLE 1. *Strict application of doctrine of consideration*

	Actual performance	Promise of performance
Public duty	Not good consideration. Confers no cause of action; probably (?) does not surrender an 'option' of non-performance.	Good consideration. Confers potential cause of action.
Duty owed to promisor	Good consideration. Surrenders option of non-performance.	Not good consideration. Confers no new cause of action, and does not surrender option of non-performance.
Duty owed to 3rd party	Good consideration. Surrenders option of non-performance.	Good consideration. Confers potential cause of action.

money for performance of the obligation, the promise of extra money has been extracted by duress.[25] But duress will not always be present. Thus there was no duress in a case where the ship was lying safely in harbour in Kronstadt when the master promised the crew extra money for the performance of the existing duty: the master could have waited until another crew could be found in Kronstadt had his existing crew jumped ship, and the crew had in any case made no demand.[26]

In Table 2 these extrinsic factors are added to our scheme.

I pointed out earlier that the existing law does not distinguish between the promise of performance and the actual performance in this context. But the law does distinguish between the case of a duty owed to a third party, on the one hand, and the cases of public duty or duty owed to the promisor, on the other. In the case of a public duty,[27]

---

[25] See *Harris* v. *Watson* (1791) Peake 102. (The case was decided on public policy grounds.)

[26] *Stilk* v. *Myrick* (1809) 2 Camp. 317.

[27] *Glasbrook Brothers* v. *Glamorgan County Council* [1925] AC 270.

TABLE 2. *Application of doctrine of consideration modified by extrinsic factors*

	Actual performance	Promise of performance	Extrinsic factors
Public duty	Not good consideration	Good consideration	May be public policy objections to enforcement
Duty to promisor	Good consideration	Not good consideration	May be an element of duress present
Duty to 3rd party	Good consideration	Good consideration	—

or a duty owed to the promisor,[28] neither the performance nor the promise of performance will be good consideration. In the case of a duty owed to a third party, however, either the promise to perform or the actual performance will be good consideration.[29]

The existing law is not, therefore, the result of strictly working out the implications of a basic principle requiring a 'price' paid for every promise. Nor does the existing law perfectly reflect any other principle or moral value. The existing rules have two virtues:

1. They are relatively easy to administer, since they require attention only to the character of the pre-existing duty and do not require investigation of public policy considerations or questions of duress.
2. They *very roughly* approximate to the results that might be reached by applying more discriminating principles of public policy, duress, and consideration.

The category of case which is treated favourably by the existing law is the type involving a duty owed to a third party (cases 5 and 6). Such favourable treatment is consistent with a strict application of the doctrine of consideration, and the cases will not *generally* raise problems of duress or public policy. The other categories of case are

---

[28] *Stilk* v. *Myrick*, n. 26 above. But see now *Williams* v. *Roffey* [1990] 1 All ER 512.
[29] *Scotson* v. *Pegg* (1861) 6 H & N 295; 30 LJ Ex. 225.

patchily supported by the doctrine of consideration (in that there is consideration in cases of actual performance, but not of the promise to perform; or vice versa) and will frequently raise extrinsic problems of public policy and duress. Table 3 makes this clear by including the conventional legal rules in our scheme.

TABLE 3. *Application of doctrine of consideration modified by conventional legal rules*

	Actual performance	Promise of performance	Extrinsic factors	Existing law
Public duty	Not good consideration	Good consideration	Public policy?	Not good consideration
Duty to promisor	Good consideration	Not good consideration	Duress?	Not good consideration
Duty to 3rd party	Good consideration	Good consideration	—	Good consideration

It seems to me that legal rules very often stand in this blunt and oblique relationship to the values that they serve. Indeed it is often unclear precisely which values the rules *do* serve, for they may frequently be suggestive of distinct moral visions which may even be incompatible. For example, an emphasis on the importance and extensiveness of *duress* in contractual relationships might sit very well with a proposed *abandonment* of the doctrine of consideration. On the other hand, a belief in enforcing promises which have been paid for might find congenial company in a very restrictive view of duress, which would confine it (as a vitiating factor) to threats of physical damage. The existing rules on pre-existing duties are, like many other legal rules, partly a crude summation of complex arguments and partly a crude compromise between, and fudging over of, distinct moral positions.

In this respect, the law resembles much of our common-sense morality. We may, for example, feel much more confident about the judgement that a certain promise should not be enforced than we do about *why* it should not be enforced. Consider, for example, the following set of facts:

1. Ten sailors contract with the master of a ship to sail the ship to London. Half-way to London, the ship hits a storm. While the ship

is in distress, the sailors demand more money from the master. He promises to double their pay. On reaching London, the master refuses to pay more than the original agreed wage. The sailors sue.

Now we may feel quite strongly that this promise should not be enforced. But why? At least three different views are possible:

(*a*) the promise should not be enforced because the sailors are doing no more than they have already agreed to do;

(*b*) the promise should not be enforced because the ship is in distress, and the master has no effective choice but to give way to the sailors' demands;

(*c*) the promise should not be enforced because the master has no effective choice *and* he was placed in this situation by relying on the sailors' original contractual undertaking.

Each of these explanations for non-enforcement in our hypothetical case will have differing implications for other cases, e.g.:

2. When the ship is lying in harbour, midway through its voyage, the master promises the crew more money for completing their contracts. The ship is in no danger, and, if the existing crew jumped ship, the master could easily find another crew in the port.

3. While enjoying a swim in the sea, a holiday-maker is swept far off shore by strong currents. He is exhausted and in danger of drowning. A passing boat sees him and its owner offers to effect a rescue if the holiday-maker will promise to pay £2,000.

The point is obvious. In case 2 the sailors are doing no more than they originally agreed to do, but the master has made the promise quite freely. In case 3 the holiday-maker has no choice but to promise, but he was not placed in the position of having no choice by previous reliance on the boat owner's undertakings. The solution you favour to cases 2 and 3 will depend upon your reasons for favouring non-enforcement in case 1. Most people will feel a good deal of confidence about case 1, but opinions will differ, and uncertainty will increase, with cases 2 and 3.

The law will generally reflect our judgement in many of the clear cases about which we feel much confidence. But it is less likely to implement with great consistency any particular set of *principles* which would serve to explain these cases. Where firm rules *are* established, they are likely to be chosen for ease of application and will turn on easily established circumstances (such as whether the pre-existing duty is owed to the promisor or to a third party, for example). When the law has been unable to establish such rules, the failure is cloaked by general phrases which commit the doctrine to no particular moral vision. An enlightening example is provided by the law of duress in contract. Originally the law adopted a clear but narrow rule: only threats of unlawful violence would count as duress so as to vitiate an agreement entered into under such threats. Perhaps the strict rule was never really adhered to: in any event, it came to break down, and other varieties of threat were admitted to the category of duress. The extreme difficulty of establishing any coherent theory of duress, however, leads the courts to shelter behind an empty formula. By insisting that the threat must have overborne or vitiated the promisor's will, the courts give themselves a free hand to respond to their moral intuitions case by case, without actually committing themselves to any particular moral theory.[30]

Much of the law is like a thin crust of rules lying over a swamp of reasons. Certain fixed points of firm ground are dotted about the swamp, in the form of moral intuitions which would be widely shared. But when one tries to build outwards from these islands of firm ground, one is building over a swamp. Rules generalized beyond the firm ground lack support. Because they lack support, there is a constant temptation to break through the rules.[31] At first this may take the form of creating new exceptions to the rules, so as to bring them more closely into line with intelligible moral principles. But all too rapidly this process can so fracture the rules that one simply collapses into the swamp. Special vocabularies can be used to conceal the fact of collapse ('reasonable', 'undue', 'overborne', etc.) but they tend only to make the job of rebuilding firm rules more difficult. Many leading cases are a battle between the crust of rules and the swamp, and the stability of the crust varies from one area of law to another, and from one jurisdiction to another.[32]

---

[30] For an introduction to the problem, see Atiyah, *Introduction to Law of Contract*, 284–92.

[31] The case of *Williams* v. *Roffey*, n. 22 above, is an instance. The case concerned the performance of a pre-existing duty owed to the promisor (i.e. it was a case of type 3). The Court of Appeal was unclear as to whether they viewed the case as a departure from *Stilk* v. *Myrick* (n. 26 above) or an application of the principle in that case. Their actual decision is probably best regarded as an abandonment of the strict rule in *Stilk* v. *Myrick* in favour of a looser approach, more willing to examine questions of practical benefit, and of duress.

[32] The crust is a good deal more substantial in England than in America. See

BLUNTNESS AS A PROBLEM FOR DWORKINIAN IDEALISM

The bluntness of many legal rules, their oblique, imperfect, and ambivalent embodiment of moral principles, is a problem for Dworkin's theory of law. According to Dworkin, the judge must construct a moral or political theory which can be said to underpin the extant rules and doctrines. The Dworkinian judge must discover in the law a degree of moral coherence that provides an integrated system of principles offering guidance in the decision of novel cases and in the interpretation of established rules.

The blunt character of much of the law, however, must make us sceptical about the possibility of discovering any such sweeping and abstract set of moral principles implicit in the existing rules. The rules seek to reflect relatively fixed points in our moral intuitions, but frequently depart from the requirements of *any* coherent moral theory. The law seeks rules which will gain support from the convergence of distinct moral theories on particular issues, and which will be relatively easy to administer. Beyond the scope of such rules, it may seek to preserve its ambivalence between different moral theories by using vague formulae as a framework for more or less *ad hoc* decisions. The prospects of discovering an abstract and coherent moral theory in the law may look remote.

In reality, of course, the Dworkinian judge does not *extract* a moral theory *from* the legal doctrine. Rather, he or she reads such a theory *into* the doctrine. Whereas some may see the text as a source of insight to which we open ourselves, Dworkin regards the text as a source of 'constraint' on one's own moral judgement or aesthetic imagination. As we have seen, the constraint is a pretty nebulous one, requiring as it does no *particular degree* of fit. It may be that the very ambivalence and bluntness of the law will assist the Dworkinian judge in reading into it this or that set of moral principles: here and there it will seem to support most moral positions that have any intrinsic plausibility, and where the support runs out the law can be treated as a 'mistake'.

So the fact that the law does not closely fit *any* moral theory could actually assist the Dworkinian judge in the task of discovering his or her preferred theory in the law. Bluntness may play yet another role, still further increasing the ample leeway already enjoyed by the Dworkinian judge. For suppose that a Dworkinian judge accepts the

P. S. Atiyah and R. S. Summers, *Form and Substance in Anglo-American Law* (Oxford, 1987).

need for bluntness in the law, to the extent that rules must be easily administrable.[33] Such a judge has added to her armoury an additional way of explaining discrepancies of 'fit' between her overall interpretation of the law and its detailed 'text' of statutes and cases.

Suppose, for example, that the Dworkinian judge is faced by a case that does not fit her overall interpretative theory. She can deal with the case in one of two ways:

1. she can treat the case as a 'mistake';
2. she can say that the case deviates from the requirements of her theory only in a respect required by the easy administrability of the theory.

Bluntness in the law has a paradoxical effect. On the one hand it makes the Dworkinian theory seem improbable: more the product of a political vision than of sympathetic attention to actual legal arguments. Yet at the same time, if we *are* persuaded by Dworkin's theory, the existence of bluntness in the law increases still further the free-floating character of our legal interpretations.

BRICOLAGE

Dworkin's theory of interpretation has a hierarchical structure: one chooses that interpretation which, while satisfying the constraints of fit, makes the text into the *best* text of its kind that it can be.[34] To interpret a literary text one must draw on one's aesthetic judgement; to interpret a legal text one must draw on one's judgement about justice. In each case one draws on values which are in some sense dominant over the 'text'. The hierarchy continues: thus Dworkin tells us that our intuitions about justice must be interpreted by reference to deeper views about the self, or morality generally.[35] An infinite regress is generated by this argument.[36]

---

[33] Note that there may be a general problem here for Dworkinian judges who espouse non-consequentialist moral theories: how are they to accommodate such considerations of efficiency? See Dworkin, *A Matter of Principle*, ch. 3.

[34] Dworkin, *Law's Empire, passim.*   [35] Ibid. 425.

[36] See Simmonds, 'Imperial Visions and Mundane Practices' (n. 4 above), 465. It has been suggested to me that the infinite regress is not a vicious one: for it is not necessary that each stage in the regress should be *interpreted*, only that it should be *interpretable*. This response is a familiar one: see e.g. David Brink, *Moral Realism and the Foundations of Ethics* (Cambridge, 1989), 291–5. But my objection to Dworkin does not depend upon the claim that an infinite series of steps can never be performed: if that *was* the objection

Whatever the merits or demerits of this as a general theory of interpretation, it fails to capture the character of much legal thought. Legal reasoning is not generally a matter of abstracting to a higher plane of values and generality in order to interpret the conventional rules and doctrines. Something *like* this happens when the crust of rules is beginning to fracture and become peppered with exceptions: but even here, lawyers will try to avoid moving to a level of generality greater than the needs of the moment require. Lawyers are usually moving about on the plane of established rules and doctrines, trying to avoid raising issues that lie deeper. A conflict appears, for example, between two distinct doctrines: the duty to mitigate damage, and the right to treat a contract as subsisting even in the face of repudiation by the other party.[37] The court responds by deciding that the latter might take precedence, but it keeps its options open by suggesting that this will only be so when the party exercising the right has a legitimate interest in doing so. The court does *not* seek to offer a sweeping general theory about the duty to mitigate, or about repudiation, or about anything else. Lawyers traditionally see all such general theories and quests for abstraction as misconceived and hazardous.[38]

Lévi-Strauss's description of the bricoleur seems to me to fit the characteristics of the common law very well:

The 'bricoleur' is adept at performing a large number of diverse tasks; but, unlike the engineer, he does not subordinate each of them to the availability of raw materials and tools conceived and procured for the purpose of the project. His universe of instruments is closed and the rules of his game are always to make do with 'whatever is at hand', that is to say with a set of tools and materials which is always finite and is also heterogeneous because what it contains bears no relation to the current project, but is the contingent result of all the occasions there have been to renew or enrich the stock or to maintain it with the remains of previous constructions or destructions.[39]

One can of course argue that all intellectual activities, science and engineering included, are really instances of bricolage. But this

it *might* be appropriate to reply that each step must be performable but need not actually be performed. Rather, my objection was that the infinite regress leads into an argumentative vacuum, indeed into a situation where the text being interpreted cannot be distinguished from the values being invoked in adjudicating between interpretations. See Simmonds, 'Imperial Visions', 477.

[37] See *White and Carter (Councils) Ltd.* v. *McGregor* [1962] AC 413.

[38] See e.g. the wise words of JAVOLENUS: 'Every definition in civil law is dangerous; for it is rare for the possibility not to exist of its being overthrown.' D. 50. 17. 202.

[39] Claude Lévi-Strauss, *The Savage Mind* (London, 1966), 17.

observation serves as a salutary reminder of our permanent dependence on an inherited (though alterable) stock of ideas only because and in so far as it *relies* on the contrast between the bricoleur and the engineer.[40]

The bricoleur resembles the common law judge, and differs from the Dworkinian judge, in so far as he does not develop an abstract *conception* of the problem he faces and then seek to shape the tools that will solve it: he simply takes whatever is to hand to patch up the immediate problem. Another comparison, beloved of English lawyers since Blackstone,[41] is with the repair and refurbishment of an ancient building. The Dworkinian approach would be to form a view about what problems need to be solved and what solutions would 'fit' the character of the building. Such solutions would aim to 'fit' but might nevertheless require action to be taken in areas beyond the scope of the immediate problem (the leaking pipe, the lack of heating in the bedrooms). The common law/bricolage approach would be to take whatever is available to patch up the immediate problem, while avoiding any premature judgement on what further and related problems may arise (chewing gum for the pipe and an electric fire for the bedroom: but no general replacement of old pipes, and no installation of central heating). Which approach one favours depends on the confidence one has in individual foresight and rationality. In this respect the bricoleur is less of a 'Protestant' than is Dworkin.

In a famous passage, S. F. C. Milsom has described the history of the common law as consisting in the ceaseless abuse of its own elementary ideas.[42] Judges are more concerned to see their decisions directly subsumed under some well-established and *explicit* doctrine than they are to develop general principles which may be thought to be *implicit*. They are more concerned with the secure doctrinal justification of the present decision than with the long-run rational reconstruction of the law. They are less likely to develop some general theory of reliance in the law of obligations than to push and twist the familiar doctrines of waiver or estoppel, or to shift the analysis of a problem from contract to tort, in a way that will serve their immediate purpose. The doctrines which are available at any one time are (to quote Lévi-Strauss once again) 'the contingent result of all the occasions there have been to renew or enrich the stock or to maintain it with the

---

[40] Jacques Derrida, *Writing and Difference*, tr. Alan Bass (Chicago, 1978), 285.
[41] See Blackstone, *Commentaries*, iii. 17.
[42] S. F. C. Milsom, *Historical Foundations of the Common Law* (London, 1981), 6.

remains of previous constructions or destructions': the pushings and twistings of the past determine what will be possible in the future.

If we think of law as a system of rules and principles aimed at the implementation of some social vision, we will be disgusted by its vulgar and chaotic reality. But perhaps our error lies in thinking of law as an instrument aimed at improvement: improvement may indeed call for straight roads, but crooked roads can still possess an ingenuity of their own.[43] There is much to be said for a view of law as in itself a collective good, sustained by the continuous efforts of (amongst others) lawyers and judges.[44]

Recent discussions of the rule of law have tended to focus on law as a constraint on *government*.[45] This encourages an emphasis on the idea of law as a body of precepts, and discourages the idea of law as depending on the activities and understandings of *people*. If, however, we turn our attention away from an exclusive focus on the activities of government, we will see that law plays its most important part in helping to stabilize the expectations that individuals have about the conduct of others (and not just their expectations about the conduct of government). It is not the (sole or principal) object of law to give fair warning of the use of force by government; law's primary object is in the encouragement of stable expectations generally.[46]

Rules and institutions, practices and understandings, that form no part of the law nevertheless contribute in essential ways to the formation and maintenance of stable and reliable expectations. The law is only one contributing factor. Indeed, the law itself could not function adequately if it did not stand upon the foundation of such informal practices and conventional understandings. Legal rules and doctrines are interpreted partly in the light of the expectations that

---

[43] 'Improvement makes straight roads; but the crooked roads without improvement are roads of Genius.' William Blake, *The Marriage of Heaven and Hell*.

[44] See, for an enlightening discussion, J. Griffiths, 'Is Law Important?', *New York University Law Review*, 54 (1979), 339.

[45] See e.g. Andrew Altman, *Critical Legal Studies: A Liberal Critique* (Princeton, 1990), 23–4. Altman explains the 'liberal model of the rule of law' in terms of two principles: 'fair notice', which requires organs of the state to give fair notice of when and how the state may intervene in the lives of citizens; and 'legal accountability', which 'requires that any deployment of power by the organs of the state be authorised by a pre-existing system of authoritative legal norms'. The same view is found in Dworkin's 'fair warning' version of conventionalism. See Dworkin, *Law's Empire*, ch. 4; and see N. E. Simmonds, 'Why Conventionalism Does Not Collapse into Pragmatism', *Cambridge Law Journal*, 49 (1990), 63. A similar set of assumptions may underlie Raz's argument that the rule of law is a 'negative' virtue. See J. Raz, *The Authority of Law* (Oxford, 1979), ch. 11.

[46] See Simmonds, 'Why Conventionalism Does Not Collapse' (n. 45 above).

characterize the activities regulated by the rules. They gain some stability also from the conventions and understandings of the profession, understandings which stabilize social practices through the media of legal advice and professional drafting. In this way, law and the society in which it applies are mutually supportive, each stabilizing and lending determinacy to the other. The law provides a framework of concepts in terms of which social relations may authoritatively be understood, and in this way law fixes the meaning of those relations. Yet, at the same time, the bald precepts of contract and tort law would lack any determinate meaning if they were not constantly interpreted in the light of the understandings and expectations that shape social relations. The law cannot be *reduced* to a set of precepts precisely because its meaning and content is so bound up with the practices that it regulates. Still less can it be reduced to the theoretical product of individual moral judgement playing over the constraining or not so constraining features of cases and statutes.

From time to time I have had the experience of dreaming up a (to me) ingenious legal argument and trying it out on a practitioner. I expect the practitioner to be amazed and impressed by the brilliant way in which I have subverted and overturned the conventional understanding of this or that legal doctrine. Instead, he pauses for a moment, and then says 'Oh, I don't think that *that* can be right!'

I used to take this as evidence of widespread imbecility on the part of practitioners. I now take it to be a valuable insight into the nature of our law. The practitioners were clear that my argument *must* be wrong, precisely *because* it overturned settled understandings. In the face of firmly established expectations of this kind, arguments of abstract principle are bound to be ineffective. Good lawyers are not generally quirky, original people who find it easy to approach matters from an unconventional perspective.[47] They are people who get a firm grip on the conventional view of things. At the same time, they do not stick to principles rigidly, but are prepared to qualify them when the principles lead to unexpected conclusions. Good lawyers tend to identify

---

[47] 'At least in the Western European legal tradition of private law successful creative work consists in a combination between intelligent plagiarism and systematisation of what is lifted from others. This is so partly because of the ramifications of the concept of authority; what the writer says appears more persuasive if it is the same as what others have said. Partly the explanation lies in the close connection between private law and certain moral ideas which have remained relatively static over long periods.' A. W. B. Simpson, *Legal Theory and Legal History* (London, 1987), 178.

conventional understandings with good judgement, and in doing so they may not be far from the truth (see n. 48 below).

SOME BRIEF, AND FRAGMENTARY, CONCLUSIONS AND SPECULATIONS

1. Positivism is right to emphasize the role of law in providing a basis for order in a world of moral disagreement. But it is wrong if it suggests that one's legal rights and duties can be determined by consulting a discrete body of rules. Law cannot create order in a vacuum: it can only exist against the background of practices and informal rules, expectations and understandings that already possess *some* stability apart from law. Read in isolation from such a context, legal precepts would lack any sufficiently determinate meaning. Within such a context, the legal doctrines and the social practices can each contribute to the determinacy of the other.

2. Community is not the *result* of interpretation (as Dworkin seems to imagine) but its matrix. It is within a world where certain understandings are settled that meanings can be conferred: it is not agreement in criteria that is required, so much as agreement across a range of settled instances.[48] Community of this kind requires shared practices and understandings, but no particular set of egalitarian values.

3. If the interpretation and application of law is to be more than an empty frame within which judges apply their personal moral theories (or strive, in bureaucratic fashion, to advance governmental purposes), it must draw upon the practices, expectations, and understandings that characterize existing social relations. The attempt to employ law as an instrument for the radical restructuring of social relations is likely to convert judges into bureaucrats.

4. Law does not *legitimate* social relations from the perspective of some sweeping theory of justice. Law assists in the stabilization of social relations, and tends to reproduce those features of social relations which this or that set of political commitments might regard as unjust and oppressive. Law can reproduce hierarchy and oppression yet still be valuable and important.

---

[48] 'What one acquires here is not a technique; one learns correct judgments. There are also rules, but they do not form a system, and only experienced people can apply them right.' Ludwig Wittgenstein, *Philosophical Investigations*, tr. G. E. M. Anscombe (Oxford, 1953), 227.

5. Is my view of law too heavily shaped by *private* law? Yes, probably. But the idea that there must be some single account of law that reflects its essential nature strikes me as itself a piece of legal idealism, assuming as it does that law must embody some single point, value, or moral principle. Law is complex, multifaceted, and very important: but it is not the earthly manifestation of some single moral vision. Public law *does* to some extent lack the context of informal social relations that, as I have suggested, gives law a determinate content. But, in the context of public law, judges seem faced with a choice. Do they turn themselves into bureaucrats who implement governmental purposes? Or do they seek to develop some theory which mediates relations between the state and the citizen? Since the latter type of theory would have to be a deliberate product of their own moral invention, it seems to me to reinforce my analysis: outside of the realm of sustaining social relations, the law lacks an adequate interpretative context.

2

Making Sense out of Nonsense

DAVID HOWARTH

At the heart of jurisprudence lies the theory of adjudication. It concerns itself with questions about how judges decide cases and how they ought to decide cases.

Traditionally, two schools of thought competed for the allegiance of scholars. One school maintained that the law should be thought of as a gapless system of rules, in which the task of the judge in a disputed case was to discover what the law already said. The other school contended that the law was not gapless, and that the task of the judge in a disputed case was to fill the gap with whatever rule seemed best.

For most practical purposes, this traditional dispute between the conceptualists and the realists is over. Both sides have lost. The conceptualists have had to admit that there is more to deciding a case than just reading statutes and old cases—the judge is more than a machine, and the law is not a computer program. But for their part, the realists have found it impossible plausibly to describe the way judges decide cases without referring to rules, principles, and the desire for consistency.

Conceptualism could not ignore the fact that concepts are tools of human invention, and are not self-defining and self-executing. Realism found that understanding the judges involved understanding the law.

But as soon as a new consensus seemed to be forming out of the defeat of both the old dogmas, the old dispute has broken out in a new form. In the new dispute, no one denies that law is an interpretive activity, or that judges do not feel free to ignore past decisions, or that judges are liable to make mistakes. The dispute is rather a normative one. It is about whether judges should abandon the attempt to justify their decisions in terms of precedent and statutory interpretation and instead should allow legal argument to become free-wheeling ideological debate.[1]

Put very crudely, two factions have formed over these issues. One follows Ronald Dworkin, the other follows the line of the Critical Legal Studies movement. The central issue is whether the law, that is pre-existing legal materials such as statutes and past cases, is so incoherent that when judges set out to make sense of it, they are simply wasting their time, and everyone else's.

The Critical Legal Studies position is that the law is so full of contradictory values and so obviously the outcome of political conflict that judges can never make fully coherent sense out of it. They may try hard to remove inconsistencies, and to gloss over conflicts of value but, like jelly held in the fingers, the contradictions eventually ooze out somewhere.

The Dworkinian position denies that there are any contradictions in the law that cannot be unambiguously resolved by reference to local political tradition. What for the Critical Legal Studies school is contradiction between two legal ideas is for the Dworkinian merely two principles 'in competition', both of which are honoured in the political tradition, but one of which is usually clearly more important than the other for the case at hand. The Dworkinian claim is that the judge can sufficiently often find a solution to a case and justify it, in a way that 'fits' into the existing law better than any other solution, that the judge is always justified in assuming that the law is capable of making sense in any particular case. The opponents of Dworkin assert that the values that he says are in 'competition' are in reality so fundamentally opposed to one another that the decision in any particular case will frequently undermine so much of the pre-existing law that the whole process of legal argument has to be called into question.

For the participants in this debate, the key to success is to provide accounts of existing legal doctrine that demonstrate either that it does or that it does not make sense. Supporters of the Critical Legal Studies position claim to have found fundamental contradictions in various parts of Anglo-American law, including the basic topics of tort, contract, and property.[2] Dworkin himself counters by claiming that his

---

[1] R. Unger, *The Critical Legal Studies Movement* (Cambridge, Mass., 1984), 2–3, 16, 20–2, 43.

[2] See M. Kelman, *A Guide to Critical Legal Studies* (Cambridge, Mass., 1987), 18–25, 76–9, 103–7 (contract); 37–8, 109 (tort); 38–40 (property); 258–60 (omnipresence of contradiction). See also: Duncan Kennedy, 'The Structure of Blackstone's Commentaries', *Buffalo Law Review*, 28 (1979), 205; id., 'Form and Substance in Private Law

'smoother and more attractive' interpretations are just as good as any 'flawed and contradictory account',[3] and that the burden of proof is on his opponents to show that the flawed and contradictory account is 'the only [account] available'.[4]

The purpose of this essay is to suggest a way in which this new dispute might be brought to an end in the same way in which the old dispute was brought to an end, namely by showing that both sides are wrong. It will then go on to consider some of the consequences of its argument against both camps for the future of the theory of adjudication.

THE GARFINKEL EXPERIMENT

The American social psychologist Harold Garfinkel once carried out the following experiment.[5] Ten undergraduates were solicited by telling them that research was being done in the Department of Psychiatry to explore alternative means of psychotherapy 'as a way of giving persons advice about their personal problems'. Each subject was seen individually by an experimenter who was falsely represented as a student counsellor in training. The subject was asked first to discuss the background to some serious problem on which he would like advice, and then to address to the 'counsellor' a series of questions each of which would permit a 'yes' or 'no' answer. The experimenter–counsellor heard the questions and gave his answers from an adjoining room, via an intercommunication system. After describing his problem and furnishing some background to it, the subject asked his first question. After a standard pause, the experimenter announced his answer, 'yes' or 'no'. According to the instructions, the subject then removed a wall-plug connecting him with the counsellor so that 'the counsellor will not hear your remarks' and tape-recorded his comments on the exchange. When these were completed, the subject plugged the microphone in and asked his next question. After he received the answer, he again recorded his comments, and thus

---

Adjudication', *Harvard Law Review*, 89 (1982), 1685; id., 'Distributive and Paternalist Motives in Contract and Tort Law . . .', *Maryland Law Review*, 41 563; C. Dalton, 'An Essay in the Deconstruction of Contract Law', *Yale Law Journal*, 94 (1985), 997; M. Kelman, 'Trashing', *Stanford Law Review*, 36 (1984), 293; For a more level-headed version of the CLS position, see C. Sampford, *The Disorder of Law* (Oxford, 1989).

[3] R. Dworkin, *Law's Empire* (London, 1986), 274.   [4] Ibid.

[5] H. Garfinkel, *Studies in Ethnomethodology* (Cambridge, 1984), 79 ff.

proceeded through at least ten questions and answers. The subject had been told, 'Most people want to ask at least ten questions.' The sequence of answers, evenly divided between yeses and noes, was predecided with a table of random numbers.

Garfinkel then reports the conversations between two of the subjects and the counsellor, together with the subjects' tape-recorded remarks, and states conclusions based on the responses of all ten subjects.

There are several remarkable features of the subjects' responses. First of all, and most significantly, they all made strenuous efforts to make sense of the 'advice' that they were being given. When answers were seen as 'incomplete', subjects simply supplied the rest of the answer, explaining that it was the method of giving advice that caused the deficiency, not the adviser. When subjects found that an answer was inappropriate, they devised elaborate explanations for the answer in terms they found more appropriate, and thereafter they treated their own explanation as if it had been given by the adviser. If the answer was incongruous or contradictory, the subjects would explain away the incongruity or contradiction. For example, subjects decided that the adviser had learned more about the problem in between the first answer and the second answer, or that the adviser was still unsure about what exactly was being asked because the question had not been well phrased.

Garfinkel also noted several themes in the ways that his subjects resolved contradictions or reduced uncertainty. For example, intentions and motives were often attributed to the 'adviser' without any evidence. They also drew heavily upon values that they themselves held (for example, religious tolerance or the value of university degrees for certain types of career), and on existing social institutions and pieces of conventional wisdom.

Garfinkel concludes that subjects were very much concerned with searching for and finding patterns in the answers. No one even entertained the idea that random answers were being given. Even those subjects who suspected that all was not as it seemed assumed that they were being deliberately deceived, itself a sort of pattern. And when told the details of how the experiment had worked, many subjects assumed that the whole exercise was really an attempt at therapy by deceit and criticized it on that basis.

Garfinkel's experiment is not just of significance to psychologists. It suggests a point of importance for all the human sciences. People, it seems, are influenced by a will to sense just as much as they are influenced by a will to power or a will to maximize utility. Garfinkel's experiment shows that people have an extraordinary capacity for making sense out of nonsense.

GARFINKEL AND LAW

The Garfinkel experiment can stand as a sort of parable about legal interpretation. Judges are in a position somewhat similar to that of Garfinkel's subjects. The problems they have to resolve are their cases. They receive advice, or what they take to be advice, not from a taciturn adviser, but in the even more inert form of statutes and reports of old cases.

Judges react to the advice they receive in a way that one of Garfinkel's subjects might well recognize. The conventional way to interpret statutes, for example, is to look for the intention of the legislature, an intention that is supposed to be non-contradictory and to aim at some particular, though usually undisclosed, purpose. Garfinkel's subjects similarly attributed non-contradictory intentions to their adviser. And just as Garfinkel's subjects placed the advice they were given in the context of well-known social institutions and pieces of conventional wisdom, so judges may interpret statutes on the basis of a number of conventional presumptions—for example that the statutes do not operate retroactively, or that they do not contradict the government's international obligations.

There are also parallels between Garfinkel's subjects' methods of rationalization and the techniques judges use for dealing with case-law. For example, the subjects' technique of saying that the adviser had changed an answer because he previously had not quite understood the question is very similar to the judicial technique of distinguishing a case on the grounds that it was not quite on the same point as the present one and therefore not intended to decide it. And the idea that the adviser had changed an answer because he had 'learned more' is close to the explanation of a change in the common law on the ground that the common law has to be flexible and to keep up with the times.

Of course, the parallel is not exact. The judge knows, for example, that the decision he or she makes will itself turn up as a piece of advice for some future judge, and so the judge has an insight into the way in which the advice he or she receives was itself probably constructed, an insight that the Garfinkel subject did not have. On the other hand, if the judge realizes that his or her own judgments suffer from guesswork and arbitrariness, the conclusion to be drawn may be that other judges must find themselves similarly affected. Moreover, the judge receives no insight at all, merely from being a judge, into the way statutes are put together, and in this regard the Garfinkel experiment is a fairly exact analogy.

The debate between the Dworkinian and the Critics may now be presented thus: the Critics say that, for all the sense that the legal materials appear to make, the judge may as well be in a Garfinkel experiment. Any sense that the materials seem to have is liable to have been created entirely by the judge, just as Garfinkel's subjects created 'advice' from their own values and presuppositions. The Dworkinians, on the other hand, say that law is not a Garfinkel experiment, and that judges construct their interpretations out of materials that for the most part already make sense.

At first sight the debate, presented in this way, is a walkover for the Critics. The Critics can say that the Dworkinians are in no better position than the judges when it comes to assessing whether or not the law is coherent. Just as the judges can be accused of submitting to their own will to sense, to making sense out of nonsense, so also the Dworkinians can be dismissed as self-deluding Panglossians. The Critics' claim that the law could be a Garfinkel experiment seems undeniable.

But the Dworkinian resources are not exhausted so quickly. A Dworkinian could say that just because the law could be a Garfinkel experiment does not mean that it is such an experiment. The original experiment worked, the Dworkinian would continue, precisely because giving out random answers to requests for psychiatric advice is a rare event. Such advice is expected not to be random, which is why the subjects continued to try to make sense of it. If, as a matter of experience, psychiatric advice was found to be random, or to be so incoherent that it might as well be random, subjects would no longer bother to make sense of it. Similarly in the law, the fact that judges continue to try to make sense of the law indicates not that the law is random, but that it is not random.

This reply, however, does not quite succeed. In the first place, it does not work for statutes. Changes in government, and changes of policy by governments, not to mention governments with inconsistent policies, are likely to lead to parliament producing statutes whose underlying assumptions about social ills and their cures vary widely. Although efforts are made by those who draft statutes to make sure that potential conflicts with existing law are explicitly provided for, there is no strong reason to believe that this process is always successful, or indeed that politicians always want statutes to resolve such conflicts. Nor is it an answer to point to the theory of implied repeal (which says that subsequent statutes prevail over earlier ones) since the crucial issue is usually not what to do about a conflict between statutes but whether the later statute should be interpreted so that such a conflict comes into existence.

Secondly, the Dworkinian's reply assumes that the process of judicial decision over the years works to eliminate case-law that might originally have been produced either randomly or otherwise capriciously. The assumption is that against the background of coherent doctrine, capricious decisions would look so obviously out of place that they would quickly be eliminated. This assumption is, however, not justified. Common law courts, especially in England, are peculiarly committed to the doctrine that *communis error facit ius*.[6] Examples abound of courts refusing to expunge from the law a rule that patently offended against justice, common sense, and the rest of the law, a refusal made purely on the ground that the rule had been pronounced by several judges on previous occasions. One example is the long and brutal career of the common employment doctrine, the principle, drawn from the anomalous and misunderstood case of *Priestly* v. *Fowler*,[7] that employees were debarred from suing their employers for injuries suffered at work if the injuries were caused by a fellow employee. Another example is the survival of the so-called rule in *Pinnel's Case*, which says that an agreement to pay off part of a debt with a lesser sum is not enforceable by the debtor.[8]

Furthermore, as Dworkin himself points out,[9] legal coherence is usually judged in relation not to the law as a whole but to a particular subdivision of the law (for example sales, employment contracts, directors' duties). In these subdivisions, random or capricious decisions may easily survive for a very long time, simply because they are never considered in conjunction with the rest of the law. Once

---

[6] For an extended discussion of *communis error facit ius*, giving many examples of its application, see C. K. Allen, *Law in the Making*, 7th edn. (Oxford, 1964), 321–46.

[7] (1837) 3 M. & W. 1. See Allen, *Law in the Making*, 329 ff.

[8] (1602) 5 Co. Rep. 117a. See Allen, *Law in the Making*, 337 ff. See further *Williams* v. *Roffey Bros.* [1990] 1 All ER 512 for an interesting method of avoiding the effect of *Pinnel's Case* and its nineteenth century champion *Foakes* v. *Beer* (1884) 9 App. Cas. 605—they are just ignored.

[9] Dworkin, *Law's Empire*, 250–4, 402–6.

established in its niche, such a decision will be very difficult to dislodge, and may even eventually extend its influence to other fields of law. *Priestly* v. *Fowler* is itself a good example of such a decision, for it influenced the whole of tort law by giving authority to the pernicious notion that tort plaintiffs may be denied recovery on the ground that they have 'impliedly' accepted the risk of injury.

The pure Dworkinian position, therefore, seems unsustainable as a straightforward matter of fact. There is no particular reason why, in general, the law should be coherent or incoherent. It may well be either.

But the Dworkinian is not beaten yet. Although there might be no empirical grounds for assuming that the law is on the whole coherent, there are, the Dworkinian might now argue, normative grounds for giving coherence the benefit of the doubt.

A DUTY TO MAKE SENSE?

The point the Dworkinian might attempt to establish is that even though one cannot tell whether the law really is coherent or not, one ought to presume that it is coherent, and therefore one should be prepared to take the risk that one might be making sense out of nonsense.

The argument for such a duty to make sense out of the law that we shall consider here is drawn from the work of Dworkin himself. Dworkin asserts that a coherent society is inherently better than an incoherent one, and then invokes a moral duty to interpret the society in which one lives in the best possible light.[10] Hence, one should presume that one's own society is coherent, and one should make this coherence the basis of the way one makes sense of that society's law.

Note that Dworkin admits that one could 'make sense' out of the law by attributing to it an ineradicable degree of incoherence, which would itself satisfy the will to sense. What he says is that one should not make sense of the law in this way, but instead make sense of it by presuming that law is coherent, on the ground that coherence is better than incoherence.

Dworkin's justification for saying that coherence is better than incoherence is that coherence is gained from and contributes to a feeling of common purpose, of 'community', and that 'community',

---

[10] Dworkin, *Law's Empire*, 52–3, 176 ff.

especially community built on common principles (and on a commitment to interpret those principles coherently) is an unalloyed social and political good, even to the extent that it justifies the use of violence and other forms of coercion by political institutions.[11] Dworkin's argument has two parts. The first says that we have an obligation to interpret our society in a way that makes it the best it can be. The second says that since coherence is better than incoherence, the obligation to interpret our society in the way that makes it the best it can be includes an obligation to treat it as prima facie coherent.

Both parts of the argument are open to attack. In the first place, why is coherence necessarily better than incoherence? It might be true that individuals search for coherence in their own lives, and it may be that for individuals, searching for coherence is either desirable or inevitable, but it does not follow that societies ought to be coherent. What is true of an individual is not necessarily true of a group.[12]

Indeed, one can make a case that coherence ought not to be pursued at the level of whole societies. Aiming for coherence in society as a whole suggests that one wants a society without conflict and disagreement. In practice, this means aiming for a society characterized by uniformity and rigidity.[13] Incoherence at the societal level, on the other hand, can be the result of variety and of creative conflict, and though it may not be an end that can be pursued for its own sake,[14] its presence is a sign of health.[15]

Dworkinians may attempt to escape from this criticism by saying that they are aiming for a society in which people agree to disagree, in which there is a principle, about which everyone agrees, that there

---

[11] Ibid. 206–15.

[12] See, for the classic demonstration of the difficulties inherent in the notion of collective choice, K. Arrow, *Social Choice and Individual Values* (London and New Haven, Conn., 1951, 1963).

[13] See T. Parsons, *The Social System*, 2nd edn. (New York, 1964), ch. 2, esp. pp. 36–45, for an attempt to counter the argument in the text by assuming that the drive for coherence ('integration') is as inevitable for societies as it is for individuals. Parsons did not support his claim with much relevant evidence apart from a schematic presentation of 'Principal Types of Social Structure' (ibid. 180–200).

[14] For further discussion of goods that cannot be pursued directly, but which are nevertheless goods, see J. Elster, *Sour Grapes: Studies in the Subversion of Rationality* (Cambridge, 1985; first pub. 1983), 43–88, esp. 44–52 and 91–100; 'The Obsessional Search for Meaning' (pp. 101–8) is also interesting for complaining about what amounts to making sense out of nonsense in sociology. See further id., *Solomonic Judgements: Studies in the Limitations of Rationality* (Cambridge, 1989), 11, 17, 25–6, 121–2 ('hyperrationality').

[15] See also Václav Havel, 'Letter to Dr Gustáv Husák', in J. Vladislav (ed.), *Living in Truth* (London, 1987).

should be free debate and the free pursuit of interest. But this is not aiming for a coherent society but rather surrendering, as no doubt one should, to incoherence, to a society that is not characterized by common purpose but by conflicting interest.

Secondly, the obligation to interpret our society in the best possible light arises, according to Dworkin, from the fact that we live in a 'community', or more particularly, in a 'community of principle'. But, as Dworkin says,[16] the question of whether we do indeed live in a 'community of principle', as opposed to living, for example, in an oppressive and unprincipled society, is a matter of interpretation. As a matter of interpretation, however, it must itself fall foul of the Garfinkel problem. How do we know whether our conclusion that we live in a community of principle derives from the material laid before us or from our own predisposition to believe that we do? The answer is that we cannot know.[17]

So far, therefore, the presentation of the debate between the Critics and the Dworkinians in terms of an analogy with the Garfinkel experiment indicates difficulties for the Dworkinians. There are, however, more points that the Dworkinian might make, but they will be considered after we have discussed the position of the Critics.

GARFINKEL AND THE CRITICS

Even after some consideration, the Garfinkel experiment seems to be good news for the Critics. Garfinkel's result, that sense can be constructed out of nonsense, supports the Critics' claim that the surface appearance of the law as rational and coherent may be deeply misleading. People who expect, and hope for, coherence from the law will no doubt find it there, but that is no guarantee that the law is indeed coherent. Even the fact that large numbers of people have for a very long time assumed that the law was fundamentally coherent is no evidence, if Garfinkel's result is taken seriously, that it is.

Nevertheless, the Garfinkel experiment is not such good news for the Critics as it first appears, for it helps to bring into sharp focus some

---

[16] Dworkin, *Law's Empire*, 208–9.

[17] None of this, however, should bring much comfort to the CLS school. If we have no good reason to interpret our own society in the best possible light, there is equally no good reason to interpret it in the worst possible light. And if incoherence is not necessarily a good thing in a society, it is unclear how an interpretation that concludes that our own society is incoherent is in any way the negative assessment that Critical Legal scholars appear to want it to be—indeed it sounds more like praise.

of the difficulties of the Critics' own position. We should start by distinguishing between two sorts of Critics: the Garfinkel experiment presents the two different sorts of Critic with different challenges.

The first sort of Critic claims that the law contains within itself certain fundamental contradictions that reflect conflicts in society at large. Each contradiction can be traced to a particular social conflict. Thus, for example, the contradictions in contract law between doctrines that hold parties strictly to their bargains and doctrines that help parties in inferior bargaining positions can be traced to the basic social conflict between debtors and creditors, between the poor and the rich. The incoherence of the law, in the view of the first sort of critic, is not the result of random accidents or mistakes, but is the inevitable consequence of predictable social conflicts. Legal decision-making may still be fairly predictable if judges strongly favour one particular side of a given conflict, but the desire of judges to be thought neutral in social conflicts militates against their making many clear commitments.

The second sort of Critic is less sociological in outlook. The incoherence of the law results, on this view, from the fact that legal problems often require answers that presuppose particular solutions to notoriously difficult philosophical problems. For example, criminal law cases about intention and voluntariness may require answers to questions about free will and determinism.[18] In consequence, although the law may achieve some degree of predictability in practice, it can only do so by suppressing the underlying philosophical difficulties.

To the first sort of Critic, the Garfinkel result poses the question of whether the Critic's own explanations of the law, as the outcome of predictable social conflicts, are not themselves the product of the Critic's ability to construct sense out of nonsense. Explanations of conduct such as those that rely on the struggle of capital against labour, the conflict of one ethnic group against another, or the oppression of women by men seem always to be capable of sufficient manipulation that they can meet the theoretical requirements of those who already believe in them.

The challenge, therefore, for Critics of the first sort is to construct tests of their views that will convince observers who are not already committed to the same view. This is not as easy as it sounds. Neutral outsiders are not easy to find. Some people will be hostile to the Critic

[18] Kelman, *Guide to Critical Legal Studies*, 12–14, 86–113.

and, by applying Garfinkel's result in reverse, will probably be able to make nonsense out of the explanation even if it makes sense. Others, perhaps the rest, although not actively hostile, will find themselves committed to whatever conclusions they came to when they first considered the matter. First impressions can set up presumptions that are difficult to dispel.[19]

Garfinkel's result, therefore, should produce in the first sort of Critic an increased level of uncertainty about his or her preferred explanation. Ordinary intellectual honesty (the deliberate search for counter-examples, the willingness to consider other explanations, conscious discounting of known biases) may provide some comfort. But the underlying difficulty remains that the threat of the Garfinkel result is directed at the very activity of understanding itself—for it suggests that to the extent that understanding consists of seeing how something fits into a pattern, it may be largely a matter of will and imagination. This is a major difficulty because to be conscious of the strength of one's own powers of imagination is not easy. People who lack imagination will be unable to imagine what it is like to have a strong imagination, whereas people with a strong imagination will be able to imagine people with even stronger powers than themselves. Thus, the person with weak imaginative powers will judge himself or herself to be imaginative, but the person with a strong imagination may well judge himself or herself to be unimaginative.

The second sort of Critic, who believes that coherence in the law is only achieved by the suppression of difficult philosophical questions, is in a better position to withstand the challenge of the Garfinkel result. There is already a strong Garfinkelian flavour about the views of the second sort of Critic. The challenge of the Garfinkel result to this sort of Critic is rather to the belief that incoherence in the law flows from

---

[19] One of Garfinkel's findings is that people see patterns extraordinarily quickly (*Studies in Ethnomethodology*, 91) and that they use the first pattern that occurs to them to interpret all the subsequent data, even though they might have come to completely different conclusions if they had suspended judgement for longer. The same conclusion is drawn by another researcher, Charles Perrow, in his book on accidents. Perrow convincingly explains a number of major accidents, including collisions at sea and accidents at nuclear power stations, in terms of an initial misperception in the light of which people disastrously reinterpret all subsequent information. This is not to say that prejudices cannot be revised in the light of experience, for it is obvious that they can be, but it is to say that revision will be less frequent than one might expect, and even the revisions themselves are subject to the same problem, that the first revision that makes tolerable sense will be seized upon and the rest of the evidence reinterpreted to fit. See C. Perrow, *Normal Accidents* (New York, 1984), esp. 45–6, 215–18, 351–2.

the inability of lawyers, or anyone else, to resolve difficult philosophical questions. The Garfinkel experiment indicates that there is no need for the questions to be difficult philosophical questions. Ordinary everyday questions suffice perfectly well. There is no need, therefore, for the second sort of Critic to engage in elaborate exercises of tracing connections between the problems of case-law and the problems of philosophy.

But the very ubiquity of the Garfinkel difficulty undermines the second sort of Critic in another way. The point of the Critical approach is to give the impression that there is something sinister going on in the law, that in some way lies are being told and power is being maintained by fraud. But the Garfinkel difficulty is so far-reaching that it is unreasonable to single out lawyers and judges as particularly bad offenders against standards of honesty and openness.

COPING WITH UNCERTAINTY

At this point, it is worth taking stock of exactly what the Garfinkel experiment shows. It does not show that rationality is impossible or that there is no such thing as coherence. All it shows is that it is very difficult to tell whether such coherence as is claimed, for example for the law, is the result of creative activity by the interpreter or is the outcome of the underlying consistency. It has to be recognized that no methodological trick can hope to reduce this basic uncertainty below its minimum Garfinkelian level. Consequently, any attempt at a theory of adjudication will contain claims that other interpreters may legitimately doubt, on the grounds that the claims result from hostility or friendliness towards the material, or that they involve the suppression of relevant evidence, or, most of all, that they under- or overestimate the degree of randomness in judicial decision. The risk that there may not be a general theory of adjudication, of whatever degree of complexity, is a risk that any interpreter of judicial behaviour must be prepared to take. The question is how to cope with this ineradicable uncertainty.

The obvious point is that for some people the degree of uncertainty they are now asked to accept may simply be too great. They may say that since one can probably get through life without developing a theory of adjudication, the best course is to say that the question of how judges decide cases is too complicated and too full of uncertainty to bother with, and that one should dedicate one's energies to some other question.

The option of dropping out of the debate about adjudication is one that is open to many people, perhaps to most people. But it should be understood to whom it is not open.

First, it is not open to judges to drop out of constructing theories of adjudication, at least in legal systems which recognize the importance of previous judicial decisions as guides for the future. A judge who does not care how previous decisions were reached cannot possibly understand those decisions. Moreover, it would be irresponsible for a judge not to care how his or her own decisions might be interpreted by judges in future cases.

Secondly, dropping out of the debate about adjudication is not open to anyone who is interested in changing the law by legislation, even less to anyone interested in constitutional change, for it would be perverse to support a new law or a new constitution without caring about how judges would decide cases based on it. Those, for example, who claim that a new statute or constitution is undesirable because of the way in which it would be applied have an obvious interest in how judges decide cases, as do those who claim that the law would not be interpreted in the way its opponents claim.

Thus, dropping out of the debate about the theory of adjudication is not open to any who interest themselves in ordinary political life, and the irreducible uncertainty introduced by the Garfinkel experiment is just something that such people have to live with. Their problem, therefore, is not whether one should engage in theorizing about adjudication, but what sort of theorizing one should attempt.

Of course, taking part in ordinary politics is not something that everyone wants to do. Many people find attractive one of the various forms of political quietism. One can reject ordinary politics in favour of religious contemplation, or in favour of a purely domestic existence, or in favour of revolutionary politics (of the customary armchair variety).

The important question of whether, as a matter of personal commitment, one should reject political quietism is beyond the scope of the present essay, but we can at least be clear about what is involved in such a rejection. Activity leads to risk.

DWORKIN AGAIN

At this point the Dworkinian might object that if we treat the Garfinkel result only as establishing that there is an irreducible level of uncertainty in interpretation, we must retract our criticism of Dworkin's position, for Dworkin has never claimed absolute certainty for himself or for anyone else. This is indeed the case, but the point remains that the Dworkinian still has to let go of the claim that the law is coherent enough to justify a working presumption that the law will make sense in every case. To the extent that this claim was based on an observation that judges and scholars generally appear to succeed in making sense of the law, it is a claim that should, in the light of the Garfinkel experiment, be treated with very great suspicion. And to the extent that it is based on an argument that we all have a duty, grounded in the common good, to treat the necessarily uncertain conclusions of judges and scholars as authoritative, it should be rejected, since it amounts to saying that we should lie about our degree of confidence in the coherence of the law. In the place of the Dworkinian claim, we can put only the modest empirical claims that common law judges appear to be under great pressure to justify their decisions by means of making sense of the law, and that judges may well be able to make their lives more comfortable by internalizing this pressure, by turning it into a duty to make sense of the law, even though the result of acting in accordance with such a duty might be that they occasionally, or even frequently, over-rationalize the law and make sense out of nonsense.

One reply is to say that all is well if the judges are acting in good faith,[20] that is, if their interpretations, though over-rational, are honest attempts at making the legal material seem the best it can be. But all this amounts to is saying that we should not tell the judges about the Garfinkel experiment; for as soon as we do, their efforts will no longer be in good faith unless they openly acknowledge the possibility that they are making sense out of nonsense. Perhaps this is exactly what judges should do.[21] But it is not what they do now, which is what Dworkin sets out to justify.

[20] Dworkin, *Law's Empire*, 52.

[21] Cf. Sampford, *Disorder of Law*, 275, where the author proposes that judges should set out initially to make nonsense of the law, by making it always appear that there are a number of competing political theories lurking in the background of all legal disputes, and that they then should openly announce their decision as a choice among the political positions, giving reasons if they can. Undoubtedly such a procedure would be an improvement on the present practice of denying that there could ever be such

Another possible reply in favour of the Dworkinian position arises out of the interpretation of the Garfinkel experiment as establishing that making sense is a risky business: that the net costs of making sense out of nonsense are too low to bother about at all. What does it matter if a few interpretations of the law are no more than imaginative leaps of the judicial mind?

The answer is that there are quite serious costs attached to making sense out of nonsense in the law. The first cost is that we give a false, and inflated, impression of the wisdom of judges. We imply that they are architects of some great cathedral of law, when in fact they may be throwing bricks in the dark. Secondly, by ignoring the possibility of randomness in previous decisions, we eventually force ourselves to elevate *ad hoc* distinctions into the status of principles, and thus to boost principles which, on any reasonable view of the subject, ought not to be boosted at all. And thirdly, to the extent that we believe that we are 'seeing' sense in the material to be interpreted, rather than acknowledging that we may be creating sense out of nonsense, we are deceiving ourselves.

Dworkin's own position seems to be rather more radical. He implies that, even if the underlying material really is nonsensical, the fact that it has been interpreted so that it makes sense should be greeted not as a mistake but as a great achievement, just as an oil painting is better than splodges on a palette.[22] Legal interpretation, he says, must be constructive interpretation, the imposition of pattern on the legal material so that it looks as good as it can do.

But if judges admit, to themselves as much as to everyone else, that their activities may amount to a sort of Rorschach test in reverse, in which the judges try to convince us that ink blobs can be seen as 'attractive' pictures,[23] one begins to wonder why we should do as they say. What kind of authority is it that rests on an ability to fool other people into believing that nonsense is sense? It is this final question to which we now turn. We will look at the problem from two points of view, that of the judges and that of the citizenry.

---

fundamental conflicts, but it goes too far to presume that fundamental conflicts affect every case. Making nonsense out of sense is no more praiseworthy than making sense out of nonsense.

[22] See Dworkin, *Law's Empire*, 228.
[23] Ibid.

LEGITIMACY AND CERTAINTY I: JUDGES

Why are common law judges under pressure to make sense of the law in order to justify their decisions? One possibility is that judges believe that consistent decisions are more likely to be obeyed than inconsistent ones. Clearly, people are mostly motivated to obey judicial decisions by fear of the consequences of not doing so. But it is at least plausible that people may also be motivated to obey a judicial decision if they think that it is fair, which in turn might include the idea that decisions are fair if they are based on consistency.

But research into the question of whether consistency influences lay people's attitudes to law shows that, although litigants do care about consistency, they are likely to care about it much less than they care about other aspects of procedural justice.[24] When, as often happens, litigants have no basis for comparing their case with others, they may ignore consistency completely.[25]

It might be the case that judges mistakenly believe that lay people care about consistency more than they really do. But it is more plausible that the idea that consistency tends to produce obedience plays only a small part in the judicial tendency towards consistency.

Another explanation for judges' caring about consistency might be that judges, as lawyers, through their work and through the law reports, do have a broad basis for comparing one case with another, and therefore that they have more opportunity to care about doctrinal coherence than the lay public.[26] But the gap in this argument is that

[24] E. A. Lind and T. Tyler, *The Social Psychology of Procedural Justice* (New York and London, 1988), 108; T. Tyler, 'What Is Procedural Justice? Criteria Used by Citizens to Assess the Fairness of Legal Procedures', *Law and Society Review*, 103: 22 (1988), 121-3.

[25] Tyler, 'What Is Procedural Justice?', 130-1.

[26] The fact that such coherence is, for obvious Garfinkelian reasons, difficult to establish or to refute, is therefore more of a problem for lawyers than for anyone else. One other study from the procedural justice literature has an interestingly Garfinkelian result. Of 192 undergraduate students at an American university who took part in an experiment in which they were asked to complete a simple task and were then paid for it, some were paid more than others. Some were told that the difference had to do with their competence in completing the task; others were told that, although some students were better at the task than others, the differences in pay were merely random. This study is generally known for its result that the students who received higher payments were less likely to be concerned about procedural fairness than those who were paid less, but that the two groups were in agreement as to which procedure was fair and which was not. The result means that the salience of fair procedure increases as scarcity increases,

just because lawyers have the opportunity to make more comparisons of one case with another does not explain why they appear to have taken that opportunity. What has to be explained is how lawyers came to invest so much in case to case consistency, and consequently in doctrinal coherence. Why did they not instead decide to exalt straightforward political expediency or some substantive political or religious ideology? This is a question, of course, that cannot be answered in anything shorter than a very long book.[27] But one might mention three processes that may have been important.

First, consistency with previous decisions provides a version of justice that depends on knowledge of the previous cases, knowledge that is open only to a few professionals. It therefore provides those professionals with an argument for non-interference in their affairs by outsiders, especially interference by the executive branch of government. Thus, in the Case of the Prohibitions of the King in 1607,[28] Chief Justice Coke reports himself as having told King James I, who was claiming to be entitled personally to give judgment in lawsuits, that:

[T]rue it was that God had endowed his Majesty with excellent science and great endowments of nature, but his Majesty was not learned in the laws of his realm of England, and causes which concern the life, or inheritance, or goods, or fortunes of his subjects are not to be decided by natural reason, but by the artificial reason and judgement of law, which law is an act which requires long study and experience before that a man can attain to the cognisance of it.

but that what people take to be fair procedure is not determined by how much the procedure gives them. See J. Greenberg, 'Reactions to Procedural Justice in Payment Distributions: Do the Means Justify the Ends?', *Journal of Applied Psychology*, 55: 72 (1986). The result gives some comfort to the Rawls approach to the theory of justice (since 'fairness' is not merely an ideological construct that differs in content depending on whether one is rich or poor), but it also adds a caution to Rawls that people may not care so much about fairness if they are well off. The interesting point about the study for present purposes, however, is not its relevance to Rawls, but its relevance to Garfinkel; for it is significant that the procedure that was universally condemned as unfair was the procedure that paid people randomly. Despite the obvious theoretical attractions of the lottery as a way of distributing benefits and burdens, it seems clear that randomness is disliked. Some people, perhaps most people, prefer distributions that can be associated with a detailed justification, even one that they have no means of checking, to a random distribution, just as many people appear to prefer to impose a pattern on events than to acknowledge that there is no pattern. For a slightly different formulation of the same idea (in terms of 'hyper-rationality', i.e. trying to think through that which is not worth thinking through) see Elster, *Solomonic Judgements* (n. 14 above).

[27] For a rather brief attempt, see Sampford, *Disorder of Law*, 151–5. For a rather more extended, but diffuse, discussion of similar questions, see M. Weber, *Economy and Society*, tr. G. Roth and C. Wittich (Berkeley, Calif., 1978), 641–900.

[28] 6 Coke's Reports 280–2.

Secondly, in periods of ideological conflict, lawyers may want to keep the ordinary business of the law going without being forced to make a choice between one side or the other. The doctrine of consistency may help them to avoid committing themselves, because it allows them to present themselves as concerned only with the past, not with the present or future. Indeed, a divided political élite might itself encourage such an attitude, in the same way as it might encourage the notion of a politically neutral civil service.

Thirdly, after the triumph of the doctrine of parliamentary sovereignty, democratic politicians might demand of lawyers and judges that they do as little as possible that might appear to encroach on parliament's sphere of operation, and in return lawyers and judges might find it politic to appear to be doing as little as possible to change the law. An apparent obsession with consistency with past cases, and with doctrinal coherence, might serve both sides well.

The will of judges to consistency, therefore, is justified to the extent that one believes that a constitutional settlement is satisfactory in which judges buy their independence at the price of impotence.

LEGITIMACY AND CERTAINTY 2: CITIZENS

To what extent should we who are not judges base our decisions about whether to comply with judicial orders on the extent to which the judges make sense of the law?

Answers to the question of whether there is a general obligation to obey the law usually assume that many of the practical reasons why people do in fact obey the law are morally insufficient. Fear of punishment or hope of immediate reward are therefore counted not as ethical arguments but as matters of prudence. There are, however, many other arguments for obeying the law. Here I will consider only the arguments that are relevant to the question of why judges should be obeyed, rather than why the law in general should be obeyed. The form of the argument therefore is to assume the legitimacy of the state and to worry about how judicial authority partakes of that legitimacy.

This form of argument brings the nature of judicial authority sharply into focus. Even if one accepts that the state as a whole deserves obedience, which itself may be controversial, the position of the judge is not automatically similar. The problem often comes from the nature of the argument put forward for the legitimacy of the state as a whole, for that argument may not extend to judges. To take the most obvious example, and the one nearest to our own circumstances, if one argues along the lines that a state deserves obedience if and only if it is democratic, how can judges participate in the same authority if they are not themselves elected?

One of the main tasks of jurisprudence has been to put forward reasons to bridge the gap between the legitimacy of a democratic state and the authority of non-elected judges. The obvious argument, in Britain, is to say that the judges hold delegated authority from the democratically elected parliament, since anything they do that the representative body dislikes can be reversed by it. Judicial authority, therefore, is merely derivative and, since it is subject to reversal, even retroactive reversal[29] no more than provisional. One has a duty to obey the judges only as long as parliament does not intervene. The common law, for example, is only provisional law. It is tolerated by parliament for the time being, and only in that sense is it authorized by parliament.

The objection to this delegation theory is that it relies on a very implausible interpretation of the practical powers of parliament. It may still, just, be true that parliament is in theory entitled to make any law that it likes on any subject. But does this mean that in reality parliament could change the whole of the common law? It would take more than an act of parliament to change the habits of mind and the taken-for-granted categories and ideas of British lawyers.[30]

In addition, parliament is unlikely to find the time to bother with reversing every single decision that it does not like. It may be true that parliament is capable of very swift action, indeed, on some views, destructively swift action, to reverse judicial decisions that threaten to frustrate important government policies.[31] But for the ordinary common law case there is very little chance of the government finding parliamentary time to reverse a rule that it does not like. One might argue that if parliament does not care enough to find time to reverse a judicial decision, it should be counted as acquiescing in the decision. But, equally, if there is a decision which, in all probability, parliament

---

[29] e.g. the War Damages Act 1965, which retroactively overruled *Burmah Oil* v. *Lord Advocate* [1965] AC 75.

[30] For just how difficult, see G. Williams, 'The Lords and Impossible Attempts, or *Quis Custodiet Ipsos Custodies*', *Cambridge Law Journal*, 45 (1986), 33. The House of Lords' subsequent capitulation to the act of parliament in question, the Criminal Attempts Act 1981, resulted more from Professor Williams's extremely effective attack than from the Act itself.

[31] In 1972, for example, a decision of the Northern Irish courts to declare illegal a great number of internments without trial was reversed by Act of parliament on the same day.

would disapprove of if it found the time to vote on it, how can that decision count as being democratically supported?

Finally, there is an inherent difficulty in trying to legislate case by case. If a court announces a decision that parliament objects to, parliament has two options. It may attempt to undermine the rule which, according to the court, was the basis of its decision, or it may describe the facts of the case and announce that in future the other side should win. If parliament chooses the first option, it risks undermining other rules of law that it does not object to, since parliament cannot be expected to be able perfectly to predict the course of future judicial decision. At this point, it has to legislate again, with further unpredictable effects. The only alternative to this potentially chaotic process is to attempt a codification of the law, but, of course, one cannot in practice issue a new code every time there is a decision that one objects to.

But if parliament chooses the second option, namely to issue a statute that looks like a case, the risk is that the courts will treat the new statute exactly as if it were a case, which means that the statute will be open to the various forms of distinguishing and narrowing.[32]

The failure of the delegation theory lies at the heart of the motivation of theories, such as that of Dworkin, which try to justify judicial authority by reference to judicial fidelity to law. Judges are not supposed to exercise directly the mandate of the democratic legislature, but instead judges are entitled to obedience as long as they develop the law in a rational and coherent manner. Where democracy is lacking, rationality makes up the shortfall.

---

[32] In fact, the delegation view should have been discredited from the very start by the lesson of those twin legal disasters of the 1790s, the attempt of the French National Assembly to act as a court of appeal on points of law, and the Prussian *Allgemeines Landrecht*. In the former case, the French Constitution of 1791 provided for courts to refer to a committee of the legislature any points of uncertainty. It was not the object of this provision to allow the legislature to decide individual cases, for that was thought to violate the principle of the separation of powers, but nevertheless it was intended to give the legislature power to maintain its supremacy over the law. The result was a mess. More and more cases were referred to the legislature, and certainty in the law started to disappear. In the 1795 constitution, the legislature's power to intervene was abolished. In the latter case, the Prussian *Allgemeines Landrecht* of 1794 attempted to remove any need for judicial interpretation by trying to anticipate every imaginable dispute. The result was a code of 19,000 paragraphs. It was unimaginably complex and virtually impossible to amend to keep up with changing conditions because of the difficulty of tracing through the effects of any particular change. See A. von Mehren and J. Gordley, *The Civil Law System* (Boston, 1977), 60, 220–3.

But it is precisely these theories that are most vulnerable to the implications of the Garfinkel experiment. We have already seen how the fundamental assumption lying behind such theories, that the state is deserving of loyalty because of its democratic or communal character, is itself undermined by the argument that what is responsible for such an interpretation of the character of the state may be the will to sense of interpreters combined with their favourable predisposition towards the existing polity. Now we see that even if that objection can be overcome, the idea that the law is deserving of respect because it is coherent (or is largely coherent, or can be made coherent without undermining itself) is something that is extremely questionable. It is not the law that makes sense, but people who make sense of the law.[33] Why should one obey people simply because they can make coherent sense out of the law when there are people who can, in good faith, make coherent sense out of the completely random responses of Garfinkel's student counsellor? The ability to bring order out of chaos may bring comfort, but is comfort enough to justify obedience?

In the case of Britain, there is another point to make. If judges have authority because of their ability to make sense of the law, regardless of whether the underlying legal material is nonsense, why should not others who have the same ability have the same authority? If the ability to make sense of the law justifies authority, then all who can make sense of it should have the same authority.

But the wider point remains. Why should the ability to make sense out of the law justify the exercise of authority at all? One argument is that making sense out of the law reduces uncertainty about the law and thus reduces anxiety. But since no judge ever attempts to make sense of the whole of the law in every case, the potential for future uncertainty and lack of clarity are not necessarily reduced by attempts to make part of the law consistent. And the techniques of distinguishing cases mean that, unlike the position in other disciplines, extra information does not necessarily lead to greater certainty. Indeed, given the possibility of random or mistaken or mischievous decisions, more information, in the shape of more cases, can lead to greater uncertainty. And even if the process of making sense of the law, whether or not the law makes sense to anyone except the judge in the present case, does increase certainty about how judges might act in future cases, how does this provide a reason for the parties in the

---

[33] Dworkin makes a similar point—see *Law's Empire*, 52.

present case to obey the judge's order? Their obedience or disobedience does not in any way affect the level of uncertainty that future litigants may have in what the court will say. Future judges will be guided by what the present judge said about the present case, not by whether the parties to the present case eventually did as they were told. Any reason the parties have to obey relates therefore not to whether the law makes sense, but to their respect for order regardless of sense.[34] As for future litigants, it is true that they will be more likely to be able to comply with the law if it is not self-contradictory, but this is not the same as a reason to obey judicial orders in the first place. One may choose to ignore a judicial pronouncement completely even though it makes perfect sense.

Thus, if judges want to claim rational support for their authority (which may well in reality rest on habit and tradition), they will have to look elsewhere than their ability to make sense of the law.

These points do not exhaust the resources of the approach that seeks to justify judicial authority by reference to the legitimacy of the state, but they do suggest that the method based on the content of judicial reasoning is unlikely to succeed. A better approach might be to stress what judges can do, rather than what they say, and to stress also the way they can act, that is their procedural virtues. On the one hand such an approach would stress the separation of powers and the idea of constitutional checks and balances, and on the other it would stress the notions of procedural justice. A full exposition of such an argument lies beyond the scope of this essay, whose nature is mainly critical rather than constructive, but it should be noted that such an approach best suits a political position that assesses the legitimacy of the state in terms of its ability to deliver certain goods, for example its ability to maintain certain forms of personal liberty, rather than in terms of whether it uses democracy, or some other form of government, to deliver those goods. It may be that democracy is a useful way of ensuring that liberty is maintained; it may even be a necessary condition of maintaining liberty; but democracy, on this view, is a means, not an end in itself.

---

[34] See Sampford, *Disorder of Law*, 152–3 for a similar point. Sampford's main point, however, is that since he doubts, perhaps excessively, whether coherence in fact leads to order, he thinks that there is no need to look for coherence even if one wants order. This is slightly different from the point made in the text, which is that coherence provides no reason for an individual to obey the law even if coherence does lead to order for other people. It is respect for order that counts, not respect for coherence.

CONCLUSION: WHAT DIRECTION FOR THE THEORY OF ADJUDICATION?

The question that provoked the discussion in the preceding sections was 'what kind of theory of adjudication should we attempt?' The answer that seems to come from the discussion is that we should stop worrying so much about whether our theory of adjudication justifies judicial authority.

Obviously, any empirical investigation of judicial decision-making should not be inhibited by whether its conclusions are consistent with judicial authority. But normative theorizing about the same question—how should judges decide cases?—should also be prepared to countenance a change in the relationship between questions of adjudication and questions of the legitimacy of judicial authority. Instead of assuming that the legitimacy of judicial action must arise out of the way judges decide cases, we should take as our starting-point merely that the way judges ought to decide cases should be constrained by the nature of their authority.

For example, if we come to the conclusion that the point of having a judicial branch of government, unelected and operating case by case, is to maintain individual liberty against the tyranny of the majority (a plausible though far from complete view), we might then go on to say that judges should not decide cases in ways that undermine individual liberty—for instance they should not decide cases on the basis of which outcome would be most popular or which outcome would maximize utility. But if we conclude that the point of the judicial branch is merely to enforce the will of the majority of voters in cases in which it is too inconvenient to ask parliament (or a referendum) to decide, then judges should indeed ask themselves which outcome is the one that most people would vote for.

We should also change our (or at least Dworkin's) notion of what the relationship should be between existing judicial practice and judicial authority. Instead of assuming that the way judges now decide cases defines what it is to be a judge, and therefore that any successful theory of legitimacy must explain the legitimacy of whatever it is that judges do, we should instead ask whether any theory of legitimacy that might explain existing practice is a good theory, and if we think it is not, we should say how judicial practice should change in order to fit a better theory of adjudication.

Thus, if we find that judges spend most of their time dodging difficult questions and evading hard decisions, we should not conclude that judicial authority ought to rest on the passive virtues of restraint and non-interference in political controversy. Instead, we should ask whether judicial authority can be justified solely on the grounds that judges do not usually have the final word—to which the answer is probably no—and then ask instead what sort of judicial behaviour would fit a satisfactory theory of judicial authority, were we ever to construct one.

3

Theories of Justice, Traditions of Virtue

ONORA O'NEILL

SOME HISTORICAL PUZZLES

Justice was once one of the virtues—a cardinal virtue. European traditions saw the concerns of justice and of (other) virtues as closely linked until at least the eighteenth century, hence both before and through the period of the Enlightenment and the writings of what are taken to be the ancestor texts for modern liberalism.

Yet contemporary liberals and their critics view matters quite differently. Today justice and the virtues are more often seen not merely as distinct but as inimical, even as the central figures of incompatible orientations to life, politics, and practice. Theorists of justice now often claim to be neutral about conceptions of the good, or agnostic about the Good for Man. If they have any view about the virtues, it is that these are concerns of a private sphere, which they value as an arena for pursuit not of virtue but of preference. The friends of the virtues now often depict virtues as specific to and emblematic of particular traditions and ways of life, and claim that abstract universal principles of justice are hostile to lives of virtue.

These changes prompt a number of questions. What is the source of divergence? When and why did it begin? Is it inevitable? One answer might be that the divergence is inevitable, because social life in circumstances of modernity cannot be guided solely by traditions of virtue, whether embodied in individual character or in social relations, but has rather to rely on a legal order and on impersonal, public institutions, whose normative regulation must appeal to standards of justice. However, this answer misses the point. No doubt the life of a modern society cannot rest *solely* on the virtues of its members or of its traditions: but that shows neither that the virtues of its members are incompatible with justice, nor that a just society can do without those virtues. Both the Natural Law thinkers and the Moral Sense theorists of the early modern period take it that, while justice can no longer be seen merely as one virtue among others, still it must be complemented by an account of the virtues. The thought that justice and (other) virtues are in fundamental conflict is quite recent.

CURRENT THEORIES OF JUSTICE

Most contemporary theories of justice present some form of liberalism—ranging from anarcho-capitalism to market socialism. For the last twenty years or so, disputes among the numerous advocates of justice have mainly been about the weight that liberty and equality should respectively have in an adequate account of justice. Despite the length and the frequent ferocity of this dispute, the protagonists on both sides are in many ways similar. Recent theories of justice of both types are mostly classified rather vaguely as Kantian, although nearly all of them rely on conceptions of agency and rationality that are closer to Utilitarianism and to empiricism than to Kant's account of either. Typically these theories are premised on a certain conception of the rational individual, who is taken to pursue given preferences by efficient means, and offer arguments to establish what such beings either will or would consent to. They are therefore basically versions of, or mixtures between, actual consent theories and hypothetical consent theories. Typically (although not necessarily) contemporary theories of justice use these starting-points to establish some account of human rights, and construe justice in the first instance from the recipient's perspective of the right-holder. Obligations of justice are introduced as corollaries of whatever rights have been vindicated.

Two distinct ranges of philosophical criticism of contemporary theories of justice are prominent. One range of criticisms attacks the premises: these are said to be abstract or too abstract. They assume falsely that human beings are abstract individuals. The other range of criticisms takes the conclusions to task. These typically consist of universal principles which are said to define the claims of justice. Here the criticisms take two incompatible forms. The more popular criticism, offered by those friends of the virtues who favour rules of the right, contextual sort, is that universal rules and principles are ethically offensive, because they overlook the particularities of human situations, disregard or deny differences between cases, and prescribe rigorously uniform action. The more discerning and deeper criticism, offered by those friends of the virtues who want no truck with rules of any sort, is that they are mythical, because there is nothing behind or beyond acts by which agents can guide and others can judge what they do.

CURRENT PICTURES OF VIRTUES

Most contemporary accounts of the virtues claim the converse merits: they insist that virtues are embedded in the particularities of lives and ways of life. The friends of the virtues are variously Wittgensteinians, neo-Aristotelians, neo-Hegelians, moral realists, and 'other voice' feminists. That they have rather varied views of sundry virtues is to be expected, since they have varied starting-points and don't expect to reach universal principles. Many of them unite in celebrating concern for particular cases, and responsiveness to their specific character. All of them stress the role of judgement and discrimination in lives and traditions of virtue. For the most part (a select band of moral realists are exceptions) contemporary friends of the virtues are relativists, and most often historicists, who see virtues as embodied in traditions and ways of life.

Where these diverse writers are at one is in hostility both to abstract models of man and to universal principles—hence to 'Kantian' ethics. Many of them have little but hostile remarks to make about theories of justice; and especially about human rights. Justice is criticized as rigidly rule-bound; rights are doubly criticized because they are both rigidly rule-bound and the hallmark of an egoistic and conflict-ridden ethical outlook.[1]

ABSTRACTION AND IDEALIZATION

These supposed contrasts and incompatibilities are, I believe, illusory. Commitment to universal principles of justice and attention to the particularities of lives and situations are compatible, and there are good reasons to combine them. It follows that early modern writers may not have been deeply confused when they tried to integrate an

---

[1] Early hostilities to rights-based ethics can be found in the work of Bentham, Burke, and Marx, some of whose writings on the subject have been brought together usefully in Jeremy Waldron, 'Nonsense on Stilts', in *Bentham, Burke and Marx on the Rights of Man* (London, 1987). The renewed hostility of the last 20 years is best known in the work of communitarians, especially that of Alasdair MacIntyre, Charles Taylor, and Michael Sandel. Parallel hostilities and parallel arguments can be found in work on 'other-voice' feminism inspired by Carol Gilligan, *In a Different Voice: Psychological Theory and Women's Dependence* (Cambridge, Mass., 1982).

account of justice that would be appropriate in modernizing polities, in which state and society were increasingly differentiated, with an account of the virtues. However, before that task can reasonably be resumed, the antagonisms between the advocates of justice and the friends of the virtues must be shown illusory.

A useful way of doing this is to look critically at some of the supposed dichotomies used by partisans of both positions when they contrast commitment to abstract principles of justice and to context-sensitive lives and traditions of virtue. This scrutiny will focus particularly on the contrasts between abstract and idealized starting-points, and between universal and uniform ethical requirements.

A long-rehearsed complaint against the basis of theories of justice is that they abstract. The views that they take of human beings are abstract fictions such as the 'possessive individual' or 'rational economic man' or the latest recruit, the 'deontological self'.[2] All of these grand figures are variants of the abstract individual who figures in classic Hegelian and Marxist criticism of Kant and of Political Economy.

Here I believe an important distinction has already been slurred. Abstraction in itself is something both innocuous and unavoidable. We abstract whenever we make claims or decisions or follow policies or react to persons on a basis that is indifferent as to the satisfaction or non-satisfaction of some predicate in a given case. A shopkeeper abstracts from the colour of hair of a customer if she would charge the same whatever colour his hair was. Abstraction in this traditional, technical, and boring sense is quite unavoidable, and is not avoided by relativists or by friends of the virtues. Even those friends of the virtues who most prize attentiveness to differences between situations and the specificity of traditions will acknowledge this. Those who think that justice differs in Athens and in Sparta will still think that the principles of Athenian or of Spartan justice will have to apply to a variety of cases, from whose differences Athenians or Spartans must abstract. Taken strictly, abstraction is a corollary of the indeterminacy of language and not avoidable.

However, there is a quite different matter, which is far from innocent, and which is often misleadingly termed abstraction. This is the case where a claim or decision or practice is based not on

---

[2] This ugly phrase is used to refer to the idealized conceptions of the self assumed by liberal theorists of justice, in particular by Rawls. It was introduced in Michael Sandel, *Liberalism and the Limits of Justice* (Cambridge, 1982).

abstracting from the satisfaction or non-satisfaction of a certain predicate in the cases to be dealt with, but on the satisfaction of specific 'ideal' predicates. Social and political theories which introduce fictions such as rational economic man or ideal moral spectators do not merely abstract. Their theorizing is predicated on idealization: taken strictly it cannot apply to real-life cases that do not measure up to the assumed ideal.

Idealization is a highly restricting move in theory-building, which may have theoretical purpose and pay-off in certain contexts. However, we should be clear what its costs are. Since a theory that makes idealizing assumptions may not apply to non-ideal cases, its relevance to such cases must be shown rather than assumed. Often the benefit of idealizing assumptions can be vindicated—'frictionless motion' clearly is an idealized predicate not satisfied by mundane movements, but the models that use this predicate give good predictions. However, idealizing models of man are not so readily vindicated as relevant to the activity of non-ideal human beings.[3]

From these considerations only a modest conclusion can be drawn: while it would be a reasonable—if perhaps rebuttable—criticism of a social or political or ethical theory that it was premissed on idealizing assumptions, whose relevance to non-ideal actual cases is not demonstrated, it would not be a reasonable criticism that it was abstract. Nobody avoids abstraction taken strictly: neither the friends of the virtues or of traditions, nor those who insist on respect for difference or on attentiveness to the other or to other voices succeed in this.

UNIVERSALITY AND UNIFORMITY

A second distinction that is constantly blurred in debates about justice and the virtues is that between universality and uniformity. This conflation usually forms part of criticisms not of the starting-points, but of the conclusions of theories of justice.

A principle or rule is universal when it applies to all cases in a certain domain. For example, it may apply to all human beings, or to all

[3] Some writers are more careful to vindicate any reliance on idealizations than are others. For example, John Rawls frames his use of the idealizing conception of the Original Position within the non-idealizing conception of Reflective Equilibrium, and locates the latter within the actual debates of historically determinate communities. However, the argument strategy raises difficulties about defending his conception of justice to those who are not already liberals.

nationals of a certain state, or to all taxpayers of some jurisdiction. Universality in this sense is linked to abstraction: we must abstract from at least some predicates in order to formulate any universal principle, of however narrow a scope. Universality is a matter of holding for all cases within a certain scope, and is not a matter of content. Questions of scope are always important, and nobody can present a full and convincing account of justice or of the virtues without addressing the question of how scope should be fixed. However, here the question of scope can be bracketed rather than addressed.

For present purposes it is enough to point out how universality and uniformity differ. A principle demands uniform treatment for all cases within its scope if it demands just the same treatment. Many universal principles patently do not require uniform treatment. For example, principles such as 'Nobody may be punished without due process of law' or 'Taxation ought to be proportioned to ability to pay' are universal in form, but do not prescribe uniform treatment. They demand only that some very specific aspect of treatment be made the same. Even where it seems that a universal principle imposes uniform treatment—for example 'Everyone will pay the same poll-tax'—here too there is no true uniformity: all that is required is that an aspect of what people do be the same. To the extent that principles under-determine what is done by those who follow them, they not merely may but must leave wide scope for non-uniform treatment.

Why has the confusion between universality and uniformity been so common in recent writing in political philosophy and ethics? A likely reason is that many critics of liberalism have thought that those who advocate universal principles of action must be advocating universal algorithms, which are to determine precise and uniform answers for all cases falling under them. However, most practical principles are constraints rather than algorithms—that is to say, they prescibe action within a certain range, or proscribe action within a certain range—but they do not, and strictly they cannot, prescribe uniformity.[4] The advocates of principles and rules in ethics and political philosophy

---

[4] Algorithms fully determine solutions only within formal systems. Uses of algorithms—e.g. in adding, in playing noughts and crosses—underdetermine the particular way in which a move is made. Rules and principles always underdetermine their application: a point which goes back to the *Critique of Pure Reason*, A133–4/B172–3; this seems not to inhibit those who suspect that Kantian ethics consists of rigidly uniform requirements.

assume that these all underdetermine action, and that processes of deliberation and interpretation are unavoidable whenever a rule or principle is acted on. Whether they are discussing principles of justice, social norms, or enacted law, theorists of justice assume that interpretation will lead to differentiated action in differing cases. The tasks of political debate, of legal interpretation, and of the hermeneutics of everyday life can never be avoided by appeals to principles, laws, or rules. Principles guide action without fully determining it, simply by providing standards which may rule in or rule out certain lines of action, without pointing to a unique or even to a narrowly defined course of action. With this we are entirely familiar in daily practice, and it is odd that people imagine that principles should do more. Principles will not make our decisions for us—as perhaps both Sartre and Wittgenstein in certain moments apparently imagined the advocates of principles believed. It does not follow that principles are pointless, but only that they cannot do everything. Principles may determine action in part, even if nobody can derive decisions from principles alone.

The willingness with which theorists of justice acknowledge that rules are not algorithms, and that interpretation is indispensable, does not, however, answer all the criticisms made against them on this count. Certain writers have argued that it is illusory to distinguish between rules and applications of rules. What we have is simply a series of acts or interpretations, and there is no rule standing behind them by which they can be judged better or worse. Rule-following is an illusory activity. This point has, of course, Wittgensteinian origins and affinities, but its deployment in writing on ethics and political philosophy has on the whole not been undertaken by Wittgensteinians— unsurprisingly perhaps, given that many Wittgensteinians who write on ethics are rather taken by rules, provided their scope is limited to particular forms and traditions of life, and that few Wittgensteinians have wanted to say much at all about political philosophy. The central concern of those who think rules illusory is that those who succumb to the temptation to describe actions as rule-following fail to explain the status or even to show the existence of the supposed rules or principles followed. Rules cannot usually be plausibly thought of as present to agents' consciousness; yet if they are not present in this way, what is to show that certain acts or judgements are better or worse interpretations of any specific rule? It seems as if the picture of rule-following projects an illusory backing to explain action—and reaches only illusions of explanation and provides only illusory guidance. The mere fact that we can describe somebody's activity, or that it is goal-directed, does not show that they are following a rule.[5]

However, the fact that acts and aspects of action are not always understood as enacting rules does not prevent them being assessed by reference to rules. The more obvious cases of rule-governedness are those of legal and institutional action, where rules are evidently independently ascertainable, so that actions and interpretations can be judged as measuring up to or failing to measure up to the rules. However, the point is far more general: the embodied norms of traditions and practices give ample scope for thinking of rules as being observed or flouted, for distinguishing agents who conform to the spirit and those who conform only to the letter, for guiding children and others into unfamiliar reaches of life. This is acknowledged by all socially and historically aware friends of the virtues, in particular by communitarians, who direct their polemic not against rules as such, but against the rules of justice which they take to prescribe relentless uniformity. The criticism that rules are illusory shadows of action depends crucially on forgetting that they are socially, linguistically, and institutionally embodied and recognized.

CONCEPTIONS OF PRACTICAL REASON

So far I have undertaken a negative and defensive task. I have suggested that, while we have reason to be quite suspicious of principles that prescribe uniformity or that are predicated on idealized conceptions of human agency or rationality, we have little reason to be suspicious of universal principles, if questions of scope can be settled, and none to be afraid of abstract principles. However, if we think of rules as incorporating only defensible forms of universality and abstraction, we must also accept that rules will always underdetermine practical reasoning.

However, the same intellectual currents that have led to the conflation of abstraction with idealization and of universality with uniformity allow for other possibilities. These possibilities emerge

---

[5] The literature on rule-following is once again too extensive to list; most of it focuses on questions of understanding rather than ethics. For discussions of its relevance in ethics see particularly John McDowell, 'Virtue and Reason', *Monist*, 62 (1979), 331–50, reworked as 'Non-Cognitivism and Rule-Following', in Steven Holtzmann and Christopher Leach (eds.), *Wittgenstein: To Follow a Rule* (London, 1981), 141–62; in which see also Simon Blackburn, 'Rule-Following and Moral Realism', pp. 163–87.

more clearly if we look at the range of idealizing assumptions about reason, action, and freedom that have been characteristic of a lot of work in social and political studies and philosophy. Here I shall provide only a caricature, which mainly highlights contested views of reason or rationality.

If we assume that rational agents have a set of transitively ordered and connected preferences, and pursue these with well-informed instrumental rationality, then we are—give or take beefing up the metric assumptions—within spitting distance of a range of maximizing models and their theorems. These will allow for determinate 'optimal' solutions and offer theoretically exciting centre-pieces for behaviourist and more broadly empiricist approaches in the social sciences for investigations of models of rational choice, and for the ethical debates affiliated with both of these. Such idealizations are tempting because they introduce premises with which one can get to interesting and important places.

Everybody is familiar with a range of criticisms of these models of rational agency. However, a long-standing difficulty has been to discern any comparably powerful yet non-idealizing account of rationality and agency. A critique of instrumental rationality that merely denounces normative arbitrariness is neither impressive nor helpful. Many contemporary friends of the virtues have met this problem by dismissing instrumental rationality as inadequate. In its place they recommend a historicist or other relativist account of human agency or rationality. (Presumably they do not intend to dispense with instrumental reasoning—although some enthusiastic critiques of instrumental rationality give that impression.) On these accounts, to be a rational agent is to internalize the socially established norms of rationality—more generally of reasonableness—of a given time and place.

Broadly speaking, this approach to reconstruing questions of rationality has two deficiencies. The first, much attended to by those who hope to establish universal principles of justice (such as human rights), is that it will not apply transculturally, because it presupposes the standards of some actual community or tradition. Since it divides the world into insiders and outsiders, it seems to these and to many other critics ethically deficient. A second line of criticism, which may be more powerful because it is internal critique, is that every actual tradition is in fact filled with disputes about the interpretation of its principles, so that even a conception of reason that seeks to anchor itself in established social practice and convention must, contrary to ostensible claims, be indeterminate and abstract, and indeed will rely on universal principles, albeit of restricted scope. In this respect there is less structural difference between communitarianism and liberalism, and more generally between virtue ethics and theories of justice, than most recent friends of the virtues have seemed willing to acknowledge. Those friends of the virtues who pay the price of relativism do not escape from abstraction, from indeterminacy, or from principles.

A few contemporary friends of the virtues are willing, and perhaps rather more are tacitly inclined, to take a third view of agency and reason. They reaffirm versions either of classical or of Christian perfectionism, and assert that an objective account of the good or the right is possible (that is, not just one that will satisfy the standards of internal realists). On this view, practical reasoning is defined by its object: to reason is to strive to realize the objectively good. The well-known difficulty of such views is that they need a strong metaphysical argument that will underpin either an intuitionist moral epistemology or a definitive conception of the human *telos*, which generations of their proponents have not delivered.[6]

What can be done if instrumental accounts of rationality are both weak and arbitrary, historicist accounts both erratic and arbitrary, and perfectionist accounts impressively strong but not established—hence also arbitrary? Is any other account of practical reason possible? I believe there is another family of possibilities, which I will label constructivist. I take the label from Kant—though not from the Kant favoured by his critics, who (despite his explicit disclaimers) is often depicted as torn between a metaphysics that would fit with perfectionism and an individualist account of action that could sustain only instrumental rationality.[7]

In speaking of a constructivist conception of rationality—of reason—I have in mind the account that we may reach if we ask a question of roughly the following sort: what principles, if any, must we

[6] For some recent work on moral realism, see the articles by McDowell cited in n. 5 as well as Peter Railton, 'Moral Realism', *The Philosophical Review*, 95 (1986), 163–207; David O. Brink, *Moral Realism and the Foundations of Ethics* (Cambridge, 1989).

[7] For discussions of the textual basis and other considerations behind a constructivist reading of Kant's account of reason, see Onora O'Neill, *Constructions of Reason: Explorations of Kant's Practical Philosophy* (Cambridge, 1989), esp. chs. 1 and 2; ead., 'Enlightenment as Autonomy: Kant's Vindication of Reason', in Peter Hulme and Ludmila Jordanova (eds.), *The Enlightenment and its Shadows* (London, 1990); and ead., 'Vindicating Reason', in Paul Guyer (ed.), *A Companion to Kant* (Cambridge, 1992).

accord a quite general authority in the conduct of life and thought? The question reflects Kant's explicit repudiation of Platonist conceptions of reason: we cannot establish the teleological conception of reason of classical and Christian perfectionism unless we can establish the metaphysics of transcendental realism. However, the question also invites an answer that goes beyond both instrumental and historicist conceptions of rationality.

If a principle is to have quite unrestricted authority, it would have to be one that *at least* could be followed by all, whether or not they shared a tradition or actual norms—that is, it would have to be universaliz*able*. This minimal principle is a stripped-down version of the principle that Kant calls the Categorical Imperative—and on occasions the Supreme Principle of Practical Reason. Although Kant presents this stripped-down version as the basis for theoretical as well as for practical reason, hence as relevant for the conduct of thought as well as of action, for present hurried purposes I shall take the narrower domain and with it brush up against some long-standing polemics against Kant, which are ancestors to current criticisms of liberal principles and theories.

There are at least two deep problems here. The first is to understand why universalizability should count as the basis of practical reason. The second is to show whether a requirement that the underlying principles of thought or action be universalizable has any significant normative or other implications. Answers to both questions are helped by articulating the modal claims. A requirement of universalizability itself is only a requirement that principles which can be willed for all be treated as fundamental—and more significantly that those that cannot be rejected. The underlying requirement that must be accepted by all—the 'supreme principle of practical reason'— is only that of rejecting principles that cannot be willed for all. The authority of this principle rests simply on the thought that discourse and action that is not informed by it must be inaccessible, hence not even a candidate for being judged rational.

In understanding what implications this minimal conception of practical reason has, it is important to remember that universalizable principles must not only be formulable as principles for all (where scope must be fixed by other considerations), but must be willable as principles of action for all. If this point is missed, then the objection holds that virtually all principles of action are universalizable, since they can be formulated as universal principles. But the requirement that principles be willable for all is not empty formalism. To see that, it is necessary to bear in mind that instrumental rationality is not rejected, but put in its place—*aufgehoben*—in a constructivist account of practical reason, and that this place is central to an account of willing. Willing is neither a matter of wishing nor of mere thinking: rational agents must will both some means to anything they will and the foreseeable results of whatever they will. Hence they can will as universal only principles where the foreseeable results of universal conformity would not undermine necessary means for their enactment by all. Universalizable principles that meet these constraints might neither be universally accepted, nor universally liked or preferred. Universalizability does not covertly revert to actual or to hypothetical consent theories, because it is formulated without reference to a preference-based theory of action. It requires only that the deep principles of our lives and institutions be capable of being willed as universal laws.

The second classical objection to universalizability is that, even if it can be read in ways that do not make it in principle trivial, still it cannot be used to draw significant ethical distinctions. After all, the limited conception of practical reason just proposed enjoins only the rejection of non-universalizable principles, on the grounds that these are not even competent for general authority in guiding thought or action. A constructivist account of reason is only a rather weak second-order constraint on our adoption of principles for dealing with life and thought. Hence this approach must answer to the classical criticisms aimed at Kant. In particular it must rebut contemporary versions of the complaint that the Categorical Imperative is empty formalism. The arguments offered above may be enough to show that universalizability is a requirement of rationality, and that there may be ethical or political principles that can be universalized without prescribing uniformity. But they do not show us that or how universalizability can identify significant moral constraints. Nor, more concretely, does the argument show whether or how this approach can underpin a position that connects principles of justice and of virtue. So I shall offer the merest sketch to suggest why there may actually be arguments from a constructivist account of practical reason—that is, from universalizability—to certain principles of obligation, and that these include principles both of virtue and of justice.

FROM PRACTICAL REASON TO JUSTICE

Arguments *from* the demand to make universalizable principles fundamental to an account of justice lie in the heartland of Kantian and also of contemporary liberal debate—although in the latter case the Kantian origins are muffled by an empiricist theory of action. The contemporary forms of these arguments run into difficulties, mainly, I believe, *because* they rely not on Kantian—that is constructivist—conceptions of practical reason, but on the instrumental conceptions of rationality that fit with preference-based accounts of agency. For then the demand that principles be such that all could adopt them has to be reformulated as the demand that principles be such that all would (given their actual preferences) endorse them or that they be such that all would (given corrected, ideal preferences) endorse them. Down the first route lie Lockean theories, down the second Hobbesian theories and most contemporary liberalism—the traditions that rest political legitimacy respectively on actual and on hypothetical (that is, idealized) consent.

A more restrained approach, that neither hinges practical rationality to preferences nor relies on a merely instrumental conception of rationality, can do no more than reject those principles which could not be willed for all. It can demand only that principles which agents cannot will as principles for all be rejected. It is plausible to think that this line of thought would treat the rejection of at least victimization and deceit as fundamental principles of justice. For those who deceive must predicate their action on trust, hence cannot will that deceit by a universally adopted principle, since that would undermine the very trust which is an indispensable means to their own planned deception. Those who victimize seek to undermine (some) others' capabilities for action, yet must predicate their action on a world in which at least their own capabilities for action are exempt from undermining. Principles of deceit and of victimization cannot be willed for all in a world of finite and mutually vulnerable agents. Anybody who is committed to universalizable principles must then refuse to make either deception or victimization fundamental to their lives, to policies or to institutions. (This does not rule out the possibility that elements of deceit and victimization are unavoidable in any adequate institutionalization of non-deceit and non-victimization.)

Of course, these are very indeterminate principles—although notably less so than the principles of liberty and equality that have recently been the preferred building blocks for theories of justice. No doubt there could be many distinct sorts of action and institution that met the constraints of rejecting fundamental principles of victimization and deceit; these principles of obligation certainly do not prescribe uniformity of action regardless of differing circumstances. Nevertheless these are more powerful constraints than may initially appear. For they identify as unjust types of institutions or policy or action whose most fundamental principles are those of victimizing (for example slavery, torture, other forms of oppression) or deception (such as fraud, manipulation, Orwellian Newspeaks).

The tendency of these principles can be indicated by hand-waving gestures in the direction of a wider range of their possible institutional embodiments for the actual social conditions of contemporary, developed societies. First, it seems to me, that rejection of victimization or deceit cannot be achieved in a world that either fails to achieve order or unites too much power. Both anarchy and domination institutionalize conditions for deception; hence anybody who rejects these must shun both lack of order and the emergence of Leviathan. At a global level this argument points away both from anarchy, from world government, and from too-sovereign states, and towards a plurality of political units linked by co-ordinating institutions, such as modes of federation and confederation or regional co-operation. Secondly, and for the same reason, it is an argument that points towards a division of powers both in matters political and in matters economic. Hence it points towards the separation of state and society, so towards limiting state power and fostering the sphere of civil society. Likewise it points towards the separation of state and economy, hence away from central planning and towards markets, but equally away from unfettered market power and towards regulated markets. Finally it is an argument that within individual states points away from tyranny and concentration of power and towards the rule of law, forms of *Rechtsstaat* and the independence of the press. It certainly points towards human rights of various sorts, and it may even suggest ways more fruitful than the cold war debates between advocates of liberty and of equality have proved for working out which human rights can be vindicated and how they might be institutionalized. I take it also that it points towards institutions to limit poverty, since poverty always institutionalizes vulnerability and hence victimizability, but leaves it undetermined—but not undeterminable!— whether at a given juncture poverty is most effectively limited by *laissez-faire*, by insurance systems, by welfare state structures, or by Basic Income structures.

These same principles of justice can inform individual characters and lives and social traditions, as well as the public institutions of society. Neither the characters of just men and women nor long traditions of fairness can guarantee justice in a modern society: but it does not follow that their distinctive virtue is redundant, let alone ruled out, in just societies.

OBLIGATIONS AND RIGHTS

This sketch of principles of justice and of just institutions has yet to show why one might think of the rejection of deception and of victimization as fundamental specifically to justice. This can be readily shown by considering the relationship between rights, which have become the central concern of most recent work on justice, and obligations which have been viewed as correlative to rights.

Most contemporary accounts of justice begin with an account of claim rights (often both liberty and welfare rights; sometimes liberty rights in splendid isolation) and then infer the corresponding obligations. By so doing they neglect, indeed obscure, the possibility of obligations lacking corresponding rights. Yet there is no intrinsic reason, once we have noted that principles need not fully determine action, why all principles of obligation should determine *for whom* the obligations should be performed. There may well be some obligations which are not merely universal, in the sense that they can be held by all agents, but in the sense that they can be performed for all others. Such obligations will evidently have to be negative, and may be matched by corresponding universal rights. But there is no reason why there should not be other principles of obligation which are universal in the sense that they are held by all, but are not universal in the sense that they are owed to all. Any obligations that make positive demands on the obligation-holder will be of this sort. For example, any action that fulfils an obligation to help those in need has to be selective even if everybody has an obligation to help the needy.

This, it seems to me, is an enormously strong reason for reversing the perspective taken in most current accounts of justice, and taking obligations rather than rights as fundamental. If we start with obligations where action on some principle is owed by all to all, we can still talk about a universal right to claim it, and we gain the possibility of talking about principles of action which (though they may hold for all) cannot be claimed by all. The definition of correlative rights—that is, the allocation of obligation-bearers to rights-claimants—provides a marker for those principles that are specifically principles of justice, since such allocation is a precondition for obligations to be claimable, waivable, or enforceable by conventional legal procedures. By contrast, obligations whose enactment cannot be claimed by any, since they are owed neither to all nor to some specified recipient (as in the case of special obligations), will have to be embodied less in social relations and legal structures and more in the character of agents, and in the ethos of traditions and institutions. Individual agents, the officials of institutions, and the bearers of traditions will have to determine not merely the content but the allocation of action, since no recipients are defined by the principle. Hence the domain of such principles—often traditionally spoken of as principles of imperfect obligation—corresponds to much of what has traditionally been thought of as the domain of the virtues, and in particular of the social virtues, and specifically of character and tradition.[8]

Nor should this be surprising, given that until rather recently justice and the virtues were thought to represent complementary rather than mutually exclusive orientations to life and action. One condition for this view of the matter was that nearly all older accounts of justice began from the perspective of action, agency, and obligation rather than from the narrower perspective of recipience, claimant, and rights. It is not surprising that accounts of justice that treat rights as primary overlook imperfect obligations, which lack corollary rights—and not surprising that they then are accused of promoting an adversarial and rancorous ethical vision. If nothing has been gained by giving the perspective of rights theoretical primacy, and much has been lost, we have good reasons to reverse the perspective once again. This is not, of course, to deny that we may often want to give the perspective of rights political primacy in particular settings. However, it may be no damage to the Human Rights movement, but rather a considerable strengthening, if it were not to take the perspective of rights as primary for theoretical purposes.

---

[8] For the many different distinctions that have been drawn between perfect and imperfect obligations see T. D. Campbell, 'Perfect and Imperfect Obligations', *The Modern Schoolman*, 102 (1975), 185–294. For some of the ways in which these distinctions bear on a shift from rights-based to obligations-based approaches to justice and to virtues, see O'Neill, *Constructions of Reason*, esp. chs. 10 and 11.

FROM PRACTICAL REASON TO VIRTUE

There remains the task of moving from a constructivist account of practical reason towards an account of principles of virtue. Some examples must suffice. One might be the rejection of principled unconcern for others. A being who depends on others in multiple ways cannot consistently take it that others' assistance is universally dispensable. The Thrasymachean view that the stronger do not need the weak, nor the rich the poor, is an illusion, usually fostered by redefining what counts as dependence. For finite beings to will universal unconcern is to will a world in which indispensable means even to their own projects would not be forthcoming, hence is intrinsically irrational. Another example might be indifference to the development of human potential. Beings whose own projects depend on complex social arrangements and interactions cannot consistently will a world in which the capabilities that such arrangements and interaction require are not developed. This commitment does not, of course, show which forms of potential—economic, cultural, human—should be developed by whom or in whom or at what cost. It only argues that there is ethical failure in lives lived on the basis of rejecting all commitment to the development of human capabilities.

These remarks offer only hand-waving gestures towards an account of the embodiment of virtue in actual characters, lives, or traditions. However, it is at least clear that nobody's concern for others and for the development of human potential can be expressed in enactment of concern or action to develop human potential that is allocated to all others. Hence there can be no universal rights to be helped or to have all one's (no doubt partly incompatible) potential capabilities developed. The obligations of virtue are imperfect, that is incomplete, in this quite precise sense. However, the conclusion that the social virtues (helpfulness, care, concern, beneficence) are 'only' imperfect obligations does not mean that the poor or needy are without rights or entitlements, so that they can look only to selective and sporadic charity to meet their needs. As suggested in the previous section, the limitation of poverty is a matter of justice: because poverty institutionalizes vulnerability and hence victimizability, any commitment to universalizability requires commitment to systematic and socially enforced means of eliminating dire poverty. However, these institutions will never—as the friends of the virtues rightly point out—eliminate all contexts where people need particular help from particular others. Although the locus for the social virtues cannot be relations that hold universally between any two agents, they can nevertheless be embodied as traits of character both in agents and in the various special relationships and traditions that are characteristic of a particular society, including those that define its specific forms of familial, educational, working, professional, cultural, and civic life.

SOME CONCLUSIONS

This essay has offered two linked sketches. The first, and the more detailed, highlighted some doubts about conventional maps of the possibilities for coherent reflection on politics and ethics, which line up the advocates of justice and the friends of the virtues in the uniforms of opposing ideological camps, and demand that we join one camp or the other. I have argued that the confrontation is contrived, and can be avoided, and have suggested that we have reason to avoid it.

The second sketch outlined a way of developing an alternative, constructivist approach to practical reasoning, which may enable us to appreciate and restore the ancient alliance between justice and the virtues, without demanding that we also either establish or fantasize the ancient certainties of realist metaphysics or of perfectionist ethics.

4

Modern Retributivism

NIGEL WALKER[1]

Time was when retributivists were straightforward believers in the moral duty to punish. If they differed from each other it was over the nature of this duty, as we shall see. What has been called 'modern retributivism'[2] is something else: a disillusioned reaction from utilitarianism.[3] The disillusionment has been created partly by penologists who have questioned the efficacy of attempts to deter or reform, partly by moralists who have argued that such attempts are unethical even if effective. I shall argue that the penologists' evidence has been the subject of exaggerated interpretations; that the moralists' objections rest either on failures to make necessary distinctions or on outright fallacies; and that modern retributivism has not solved the problems of classical retributivism.

Consider first general deterrence. Discouragement in this case is the effect of rhetoric rather than close reasoning. General deterrence has been discredited partly by its grim association with the death penalty, partly because the evidence was said to show that 'it never works'. So far as capital punishment was concerned all that the evidence suggested was that it deterred no more people from homicide than did the prospect of long incarceration.[4] For potentially homicidal people who are in deterrible states of mind prolonged imprisonment appears to be a *sufficient* deterrent. Both they and those whose states of mind are undeterrible may well fear death more; but those who are deterrible are deterred by the sufficient deterrent. Being run over by a

---

[1] I want to record my gratitude to Joel J. Kupperman, of the University of Connecticut, and to Ian White, of St John's College, Cambridge, for their comments on an early draft of this essay.
[2] e.g. by Andrew Ashworth in *Sentencing and Penal Reform* (London, 1983).
[3] I shall use 'utilitarianism', in preference to 'consequentialism' and 'instrumentalism', to refer to the justification of penalties and other measures by their reductive effect on the frequency of breaches of the criminal law.
[4] See e.g. N. Walker, *Punishment, Danger and Stigma* (Oxford, 1980), 66–7.

motor cycle is less to be feared than being run over by a lorry; but pedestrians are deterred by both.

This point does not satisfy the out-and-out sceptic who claims that the effect of both kinds of penalty—indeed any kind—is nil. (A former Director of the Howard League once wrote in *The Times* that 'deterrents never work'.) This extreme position is not easy to maintain in face of the evidence. Although there is not room here for a review of the vast research literature, it can be said briefly that

1. There are many sorts of conduct from which most people do not normally need to be deterred, being restrained by the effects of upbringing, training, peer opinion, or common-sense prudence. But many do.
2. Some offences are committed in undeterrible states of mind. But there are few types of offence of which it can be said that all perpetrators are in such states of mind. Even compulsive thieves, arsonists, and sex offenders tend to choose time, place, and *modus operandi* so as to minimize the risk of identification.
3. On potential offenders in deterrible states of mind it is the subjective probability of being identified and convicted which has the most powerful effect. But the subjective probability that the result of conviction will be imprisonment, and the expected length of the prison sentence, add to this effect.[5]
4. By some potential offenders the stigma of conviction is feared more than the likely penalty, especially when this is a non-custodial penalty. But (*a*) many potential offenders have already been stigmatized as such, and fear no further stigma; (*b*) many belong to subcultures in which even the stigma of imprisonment is negligible.[6]
5. 'Displacement' can be mistaken for deterrence. Offenders may simply choose more propitious places or times of day. But this mistake is more likely to vitiate local statistics for short periods than national statistics covering long periods. In any case displacement seems more likely to result from local increases in the *risk* of detection than national increases in the severity of penalties.

These points undermine what might be called the strong hypothesis of general deterrence: that the nature and severity of expected

[5] See the review of the econometric evidence in D. E. Lewis, 'The General Deterrent Effect of Longer Sentences', *British Journal of Criminology*, 26: 1 (1986), 47 ff.
[6] See e.g. J. Martin and D. Webster, *The Social Consequences of Conviction* (London, 1971).

penalties is the *major* disincentive for everyone who contemplates lawbreaking. What they do not contradict is the weak hypothesis: that some degree of expectation of incurring some sorts of penalty deters some people in some circumstances. More exactly, that in a populous and not very moral society[7] the number of people who can be deterred from lawbreaking by a lively expectation[8] of penalties such as imprisonment and fining is more than negligible. The onus of disproving this still lies on the sceptics, who have done nothing to discharge it. Nor is it easy to envisage an empirical study that could discharge it. The undeterred are visible, the deterred are not.

THE MORAL OBJECTION

Less influential among sentencers, but more popular with philosophers, is the Kantian objection that to penalize someone with the sole aim of deterring others is to use him as a means when we should be treating him as an end. Using someone as a means was not necessarily wrong. Soldiers are used to win wars, many of them without their consent, in a way that Kant did not condemn. But where penalties were concerned he held that they ought to treat the offender as an end, whatever useful by-products they might have.

'Treating him as an end' meant more than merely 'having regard to his interests'. It could even mean 'making an end of him' (Kant saw no objection to capital punishment), which is in his interests only if the next world is nicer. In any case, having regard to an offender's interests smacks of utilitarianism, which Kant abhorred. What he— and most Kantians—mean by 'treating as an end' is 'punishing' in the retributive sense. Offenders should be dealt with in a way which recognizes that they are autonomous beings or, more precisely, beings that are capable of acting autonomously. To act autonomously is to accept the force of moral principles and behave accordingly. Modern Kantians such as Duff acknowledge that there are exceptions to the assumption that all human beings are autonomous: very young children, for instance, and people suffering from severe mental disorders.[9] (Duff

---

[7] The hypothesis might not be true of small, very moral communities. The island of Foula was crime-free for many decades.

[8] The strength of the expectation (technically 'the subjective probability') must exceed a threshold, and this must vary with the individual's personality (he may be over- or under-anxious), his confidence in his competence (which may be high or low), and the situation (which may be propitious or the reverse).

[9] See R. A. Duff, *Trials and Punishments* (Cambridge, 1988).

also acknowledges the existence of 'unrepentantly immoral criminals' and 'principled rebels'—an awkward category which he mentions but then ignores.)

We need not be too concerned about the nature of autonomy or who is capable of it; and the possible reasons for regarding punishment as obligatory will be discussed later. For the moment what is important is to see that behind the rhetorically persuasive antithesis between 'using as a means' and 'treating as an end' is nothing more than an assertion: namely, that the aim of penal measures should be retributive punishment. Kant did not object to the utilitarian by-products of such measures: only to regarding those by-products as their justification.

Often, however, a slightly different objection is mixed with Kant's: the objection to measures which may benefit others but which certainly *harm* the offender himself. (Kant's objection does not depend on harm.) This usually assumes that sentences are either completely harmless (probation perhaps being an example) or inflict harm which is serious and permanent, as capital punishment undoubtedly does. Yet in between these extremes is a wide range of penalties. Some inflict no more than irksome inconveniences: for instance wheel-clamping. Others involve deprivations, fines being an example (modern fining systems are designed so that they should not lead to hardship, even if in practice they sometimes do). Imprisonment causes deprivations and sometimes hardships, but it is a minority of prisoners who suffer mental or physical harm of a permanent or even lasting sort.[10] What this objection amounts to is that some sorts of deterrent should never be used, and some others should be used selectively and with precautions.

CORRECTING INDIVIDUALS

So much for general deterrence. What about the 'correction' of the individual? 'Correction' is a well-chosen American term, denoting both 'reform' and 'individual deterrence', and thus begging no question as to which, if either, takes place. In practice the measures which sentencers normally impose are more likely to deter than improve character. Probation may be an exception; but even this is regarded by many young offenders as an irksome imposition, so that it may be a weak deterrent. It may, on the other hand, achieve something

[10] See N. Walker, 'The Unwanted Effects of Long-Term Imprisonment', in A. E. Bottoms and R. Light (eds.), *Problems of Long-Term Imprisonment* (Aldershot).

which is neither deterrence nor reform: the probationer may simply be introduced to ways of living which are more attractive than a life of petty crime.

Whatever 'correction' means when it takes place, how often does it take place? Again the literature of research is huge; but the answer sems to be not very often: whatever form the corrective takes, the offender is sooner or later returned to the milieu from which he came, and subjected to the same influences as before. It is only after very long prison sentences that complete 'resettlement' is likely to be achieved. Our best evidence—and even it has shortcomings—consists of follow-ups of reconvictions over periods of five or six years.[11] So far as adult males are concerned, if they have already been convicted more than once the measure chosen by the sentencer—fine, imprisonment, probation, or suspended sentence—makes little difference to the likelihood of their being reconvicted, which is as high as 90 per cent, if they have five or more previous convictions.[12] The most that can be said is that the least effective choices are 'nominal' measures— suspended sentences or discharges.

It is only when dealing with first convictions, with very young offenders, or with the mentally ill that sentencers' choices have much chance of affecting future behaviour. Some mentally ill offenders can be successfully treated. Some first offenders seem to respond to the unpleasant experience of a prison sentence. Some teenagers benefit from probation, although it is doubtful whether even this means that they are 'reformed characters'. More often they are steered into legitimate jobs or—failing jobs—activities. Now and again some charismatic handler will change a probationer's outlook; but charisma is not learnt on courses. When the young are allocated to different custodial regimes the results, in terms of reconviction at least, are not very different. Either traditional regimes deter as many as are reformed by enlightened regimes, or both function as equally effective or ineffective deterrents.

Better results might be achieved, it is said, if we could distinguish those who are more likely to respond to deterrents from those more likely to respond to reformative regimes, and allocate them accordingly.

[11] The usual shortcomings are that the offenders were not randomly allocated to different sorts of 'treatment'; that too many were able to reoffend without being reconvicted; and that they were not questioned about changes in their lifestyle which might have affected opportunities for reoffending.

[12] And the remaining 10% or so include those who have died, emigrated, enlisted, been disabled, or simply learnt how to avoid detection.

Experiments in the USA seem to suggest that YAVINS ('young, anxious, intelligent, verbal neurotics') belong to the latter category.[13] Even experts, however, do not seem very adept at making the necessary distinctions; nor can those who allocate ensure that offenders consistently receive the sort of treatment which is intended.

MORAL OBJECTIONS TO CORRECTION

If we could be sure that attempts to correct 'never work' there would be an obvious and irrefutable moral objection to the deprivations and inconveniences which they impose. Since the situation is not quite so clear-cut it is necessary to consider objections of the kind raised in C. S. Lewis's resounding condemnation of what he called 'The Humanitarian Theory of Punishment'.[14] He pleaded that offenders should be spared the indignity of being treated by 'men in white coats':[15]

> To be cured against one's will, and cured of states which we may not regard as disease is to be put on a level with those who have not yet reached the age of reason, or those who never will; to be classed with infants, imbeciles, and domestic animals. But to be punished, however severely, because we have deserved it, because we 'ought to have known better', is to be treated as a human being made in God's image.

He also disapproved of individual deterrence, although he was not as explicit about his reasons.

What he was asserting was the moral superiority of retribution, again without explicit reasoning. Reform he saw as degrading, and acceptable only in the case of infants, imbeciles,[16] and animals. It may, he pointed out, be used to suppress religion or other desirable ways of thought, or for 'unlimited' interference with our lives. This is slippery-slope reasoning, with a vision of the Lubianka at the foot of the slope. Retribution's slope is quite as slippery and sinister. Nor does he consider the possibility of guard-rails. It is true that penal agents can

---

[13] See J. Q. Wilson, ' "What Works?" Revisited: New Findings on Criminal Rehabilitation', *The Public Interest*, 61 (1980), 3 ff.

[14] In *Res Judicatae: The Journal of the Victorian Students' Society, Victoria* (Australia) (1953). It was a pity that he used 'humanitarian' as he did, because it begs questions as to the real nature of humanitarianism. See N. Walker, *Why Punish?* (Oxford, 1991).

[15] He visualized psychologists as dressed thus, working in 'Viennese laboratories'. He knew very little about psychotherapy, and in particular seemed unaware that it cannot work without the patient's consent.

[16] He may have meant to include the mentally ill: his rhetoric was never precise.

duck under guard-rails; but in our sort of society they are usually too afraid of penalties and stigma to do so.

Shorn of all his rhetoric, however, his argument was essentially the declaration of a right. Owners of personalities, like owners of faces, had the right not to have them improved. But it was a waivable right: adults could waive it, and agree to be treated (a little surprising, since he thought that such treatment was degrading). Lack of consent could be ignored in the case of a child, an imbecile, or conduct of 'enormous ill-desert'. In the case of children and imbeciles his reasoning must have been that they are not capable of sensible choices, so that adults are justified in making them on their behalf. In cases of 'enormous ill-desert' he must have reckoned that this forfeited the right to choose, although it is not clear how this is consistent with his preference for retributive punishment, especially if the 'ill-desert' is 'enormous': one would expect him to be even more insistent on the infliction of desert. However that may be, the implication is the same: that a sensible chooser would allow his personality to be improved. It follows that there is nothing inherently degrading after all in trying to improve personalities. This makes it hard to see why he was so insistent on the consent of adults whose conduct, though not of *enormous* ill-desert, is anti-social. Why must the desert be 'enormous', not just 'considerable' or even 'more than negligible'?

It is worth noting, by the way, that Lewis's position was more extreme than Kant's. He did not assume that all sane adults are capable of autonomy; but he would have been obliged, I think, to argue that without their consent no attempt should be made to make them capable of it.

INCAPACITATION

Utilitarians are on firm ground when it comes to incapacitating measures. So long as these are enforced they achieve their aims with a high degree of success. The success rate is highest for capital punishment, a little lower for incarceration (because of escapes and premature releases). Non-custodial precautions such as disqualification are effective when enforced, and although it is not easy to enforce disqualifications for activities such as driving or trading the frequency with which they are obeyed makes a more than negligible contribution to the reduction of accidents and frauds. Other kinds of disqualification are easier to enforce.

It is the moral objections that have to be taken seriously. They are hardly ever concerned with non-custodial precautions, and are concentrated on incarceration for long periods which exceed the normal duration thought necessary for retribution or deterrence ('precautionary detention').[17] The most common objection is that precautionary detention entails too many mistakes. Studies of cases in which offenders subject to it have been released[18] before this would normally have been thought safe have shown that many of them did no further serious harm to anyone. Where some kinds of offence are concerned this is probably true of the majority.[19] If so, precautionary detention involves more mistakes than would a policy of automatic release as soon as the prisoner has been detained for whatever period is normal for his offence.

I have called this 'the arithmetical fallacy' because it simply counts mistakes without making the all-important distinction. A mistaken release has very different consequences from a mistaken refusal of release. A policy which merely seeks to minimize mistakes ignores the difference between harm to innocent victims and the extension of incarceration for a prisoner who is not innocent.

Attempts have been made to avoid the arithmetical fallacy by arguing that a policy which involves any mistaken detention is unjustified. 'Incapacitation as a reason for penal interventions means that a person is punished not for what he has done but for what it is believed he may do in the future.'[20] More sleight of hand here, this time by a whole committee. It is assumed that a measure of incapacitation is a retributive punishment; and underlying that is another assumption—that a criminal court cannot or should not order anything that is not a retributive punishment. Seldom can two such important questions have been begged in so few words.

[17] I hope that I need not deal with the moral objections to capital punishment. Few if any utilitarians would try to justify it solely on the ground that it is very effective at incapacitating; and as we have seen it cannot be justified as a superior deterrent. The case for it is almost always made by retributivists and the case against it by humanitarians.

[18] e.g. by decisions of appellate courts.

[19] It is petty thieves and con men, indecent exposers and drunks who are most repetitive, and they are not the subjects of precautionary detention.

[20] The Working Group of the Swedish National Council for Crime Prevention, in *A New Penal System* (English Summary: Report No. 5; Stockholm, 1978).

PENALTIES AS SYMBOLS

Finally, utilitarians who have been daunted by rhetorical condemnations of general deterrence, individual correction, or precautionary detention have resorted to the 'symbolic' function of sentencing: its potential for conveying a message. (I call this 'penal McLuhanism': the measure is supposed to be the message.) Most interesting are those who regard this as the (or 'the main') justification for penalizing: we need only notice that there are some who make the more modest claim that it is a valuable by-product (Bosanquet and Feinberg are examples[21]). Durkheim was a nineteenth-century McLuhanist. Lord Denning revived the notion when he told the Royal Commission on Capital Punishment that it was 'the ultimate justification' of the death penalty.[22]

Symbolists differ about the content of the message. For Durkheim it was 'the only means of affirming . . . the unanimous aversion which the crime continues to inspire'.[23] For Denning it was much the same: 'the emphatic denunciation by the community of a crime'. For the Court of Appeal (Criminal Division) it was something more: 'Society, through the courts, must show its abhorrence of particular types of crime'; but 'The courts do not have to reflect public opinion . . . Perhaps the main duty of the courts is to lead public opinion.'[24]

In other words, sentences do more than express the public's aversion: they reinforce or increase it. Sadly, my experiments suggest that while people's moral disapproval of conduct can be increased by including it in the criminal code it is not increased by making sentences more severe.[25]

For Hyman Gross the message is simpler. Without penalties, he points out, the criminal law would be 'merely a guide and an exhortation to right conduct'. Adding penalties 'maintains the rules as a set of standards that compel allegiance in spite of violations'.[26] Whether they

---

[21] See B. Bosanquet, *Some Suggestions in Ethics* (London, 1918); J. Feinberg, *Doing and Deserving* (Princeton, NJ, 1970).

[22] See the *Minutes of Evidence Taken before the Royal Commission on Capital Punishment* (London, 1950), Ninth Day.

[23] See E. Durkheim, *The Division of Labour in Society* (1893), tr. G. Simpson (New York, 1933).

[24] In *R.* v. *Sargeant* (1974) 60 Cr. App. R. 74.

[25] See N. Walker and C. Marsh, 'Do Sentences Affect Public Disapproval?', *British Journal of Criminology*, 24: 1 (1984), 27 ff. (reprinted in N. Walker and M. Hough, *Public Attitudes to Sentencing* (Aldershot, 1988)).

[26] See Hyman Gross, *A Theory of Criminal Justice* (Oxford, 1979).

deter or not, penalties are visible demonstrations that the law is not broken with impunity. Without such a demonstration even law-abiding people would lose respect for the law. This is more plausible than the Court of Appeal's belief. But is it more realistic? When so many offences are widely known, by law-abiders as well as lawbreakers, to escape observation, prosecution, or conviction (or to be dealt with by suspended sentences or probation), the most that sentencing can be expected to convey is a highly conditional message: that if you are an unlucky or incompetent offender you run the risk of being penalized. The message could be strengthened, but only by a policy which Gross is certainly not advocating: that is, by ensuring that someone, guilty or innocent, is penalized for every crime that receives publicity. Whether any utilitarian need be committed to such a policy is discussed later in this essay.

Nor are symbolists always explicit about the intended recipients of their message. When it is expected to educate we can infer that it is aimed at potential offenders (or those who influence them). In some versions, however, it is possible that all that is being claimed is the satisfaction derived from expressing condemnation, or more precisely from hearing (of) the expression of condemnation: the sort of satisfaction which commination services used to provide for their congregations. If so, the intended audience may extend beyond potential offenders. Walter Moberley believed that both sentencers and the sentenced benefited from the message, the sentencer reinforcing his own values, the sentenced learning better values.[27] The former may well take place; the latter is more uncertain.

All these versions of the symbolic justification are consequentialist, however ill-defined or unimpressive the alleged consequences. There is at least one version, however, which makes virtually no consequential claims, and when we turn to the problems of retributivists, classical and modern, we shall see why some resort to it.

I have covered a lot of the utilitarian's territory at the run because I have been making a single point. They may have been too optimistic in their estimates of the efficacy of most of their techniques, but they were not trying to make something out of nothing, except possibly when they talked about symbolic functions. They provoked moral objections, but those which have so far been discussed (others will

---

[27] See Walter Moberley, *The Ethics of Punishment* (London, 1918).

crop up later) seem weak or downright fallacious. The retreat from the utilitarian justification of punishment has been too hasty.

THE RETRIBUTIVE JUSTIFICATION

Nevertheless it is not hard to see why 'just desertion' has proved attractive. Most Benthamite techniques seem to be of the hit-or-miss sort, offering no certainty of success in particular cases. What retributivism appears to offer is an aim that is achievable with virtual certainty in every case.

At first sight anyway. But Portia[28] and Hegel raise an awkward question. Is retribution achieved if more or less than the exact amount of flesh is forfeited? As Hegel put it, 'Injustice is done at once if there is one lash too many, or one dollar or one cent, one week in prison or one day too many or too few.'[29] Can we ever be sure that the suffering, hardship, or inconvenience actually imposed on the offender is commensurate with his or her culpability? It is hard enough to measure either, let alone construct a scale which lays the measures side by side.

Nowadays the task is made all the harder by the recognition of a third dimension, although it is usually ignored by philosophers of punishment. It was the utilitarian Bentham who pointed out that offenders' 'sensibility' to penalties (we would call it 'sensitivity') varies with their age, gender, and other circumstances.[30] Today even retributive sentencing is expected to take account, and does. Commensurability is a problem with three, not two, dimensions.

PROPORTIONALITY

Led by Hegel, or more precisely Rupert Cross's interpretation of Hegel,[31] modern retributivists have substituted 'proportionality' for commensurability. What the proportionalist envisages is two ladder-like scales whose rungs roughly correspond. On the penalty ladder each rung is meant to differ in severity from its neighbours. There is of course no way of being sure that the intervals between rungs are in all cases the same. A two-year custodial sentence exceeds

---

[28] True, her suit was a civil one, but the point was the same. It had been made by medieval writers.

[29] See Hegel, *Philosophy of Right* (1854), tr. T. M. Knox (Oxford, 1942).

[30] See J. Bentham, *Introduction to the Principles of Morals and of Legislation* (London, 1789).

[31] See R. Cross, *The English Sentencing System* (London, 1971).

an eighteen-month sentence by the same amount as the latter exceeds a one-year sentence; but the two-year sentence may be served in a pleasanter prison than shorter ones. A short sentence may not lose a man his job when a slightly longer one would. In this and other ways the measurement of the intervals on the scale depends on the offender's circumstances. 'Overlap' too is a problem, especially acute when a sentencer is hesitating between a custodial and a non-custodial sentence. The former is not always the more severe. Some offenders prefer a short time 'inside' to paying a heavy fine, and demonstrate this by defaulting. The rungs on the ladder are not merely loose: 'sensibility' means that some are interchangeable. There can be no penalty-ladder which holds good for a whole society: only one which holds good for an individual. Yet what proportionalists offer is the former.

The other scale is usually even cruder, although it could be improved if proportionalists took the trouble. Its rungs consist of offences distinguished by legal definitions: murder, rape, robbery, and so forth. This is crude because legal definitions do not distinguish degrees of harm: after all there are murders and murders. Better would be a ladder in which the rungs were precisely defined harms. And since retributivists are concerned with culpability they ought to be not harms done but harms intended or knowingly risked. Yet if culpability is what matters the rungs need to be elastic, so as to take into account mitigating and aggravating considerations such as provocation, extreme temptation, good intentions, unnecessary cruelty. No wonder proportionalists are vague in their descriptions of this ladder.

Now the proportionalist juxtaposes his two scales. If he hopes that they will tell him the appropriate penalty for a mercy killing by an aged wife, or a robbery by a mentally dull teenager, he will be disappointed. They may tell him that one should be punished more severely than another, but not by how much; and in some cases they will not even tell him which should be punished more severely. They will certainly help to induce sentencers to reason less idiosyncratically when choosing penalties, and so to be more consistent. But that is all.

The retributivist can retort with a debating point. His notion of proportionality may have its shortcomings, but the utilitarian can have no sense of proportionality at all: no principle that sets limits to severity or tells us why one sort of offence should be punished more severely than another. This is not quite true. Beccaria, the grandfather of utilitarian penology, made two points.[32] First, that if severity exceeds what is sufficient—for example to deter—the excess is an unjustified evil: a principle which Bentham called 'frugality'.[33] Secondly, if two crimes of unequal seriousness—assassination and poaching, for example—are punished with equal severity, this destroys people's ability to distinguish between them so far as seriousness is concerned. The second point may or may not be sound; my experiments at any rate do not support it.

The 'frugality principle' certainly sets limits to the severity of penalties, and if different degrees of severity are sufficient to minimize the frequency of different offences it could result in a table of offences and their penalties which would look like the proportionalist's table if one did not look too closely at it. In theory at least: in practice it would be virtually impossible for the frugal utilitarian to identify the 'sufficiency point' for the severity of any offence. If prison sentences are his deterrent he cannot be sure that, say, five-year sentences will deter *all* potential burglars, and that six-year sentences would not deter some more. (No doubt the gain diminishes as the curve rises; but at what point can further gains be regarded as negligible?) More important is the objection that a table based on 'sufficiency' would probably, when closely examined, assign levels of severity which the man in the street would regard as wildly inappropriate. It might, for example, have to specify greater severity for illegal parking than for theft.

Modern philosophers have tried but failed to do better than Beccaria and Bentham.[34] The only solution for the pure, uncompromising utilitarian is, I suggest, to recognize that he must be a politician as well as a philosopher. His criminal justice system must *work*; and it will do so only if it is acceptable to most members of the society for which he is catering. Since most will accept only the sort of proportionality which pays attention to the degree of harm and culpability, utilitarians must at least pay lip-service to it, if they want their systems to be more than pipe-dreams. To philosophers this may seem to break the rules of the game by slashing at the Gordian knot instead of unravelling it. Yet the utilitarian can justify it without inconsistency.

---

[32] See C. Beccaria, *Dei delitti e delle pene* (1764), tr. as *On Crimes and Punishments* by H. Paolucci (New York, 1963).

[33] See Bentham, *Introduction to the Principles of Morals and Legislation*.

[34] See e.g. C. L. Ten, *Crime, Guilt and Punishment* (Oxford, 1987).

WHAT DESERVES?

Mitigation and aggravation have not only undermined proportionality: they have made it difficult to answer the question 'Exactly what is it that deserves blame and punishment? A particular act (or omission) in a certain state of mind, or a personality which has shown itself capable of such conduct?' Until Fletcher published *Rethinking Criminal Law* the answer seemed obvious.[35] Most sentencers would say that they sentence for offences, not character. Yet they regard evidence of good character as relevant. Provocation mitigates. Previous convictions for similar offences aggravate. The staleness of an offence (that is, a considerable lapse of time since it was committed) mitigates, and in some jurisdictions is even a defence. All this—and other examples— makes more sense if it is character that is seen as the proper target of blame. The relevance of excuses and mitigations is that, if believed, they tell us that the offender's offence cannot be taken as evidence that 'he is like that', because the circumstances were unusual, or the offence so stale that he may now be 'a different person'. The relevance of aggravations such as previous similar offending is that they *can* be taken as evidence that 'he is like that'. Otherwise it is very difficult to show why previous offences for which a person has already been punished should be a reason for punishing him more severely when he commits another.[36]

Retributivism's central problem, however, lies deeper still. Consider the necessary conditions that must be fulfilled if a person is said to deserve punishment. We need not pay too much attention to primitive formulations which merely required that he has done harm. Modern retributivism adds 'or attempted it' (or even 'conspired at it'). It must of course have been done intentionally, or with the intention of doing some other harm, or at least recklessly (or in some cases negligently). It may not always be necessary that harm was intended or risked: if the conduct is forbidden by law (or some other code of rules) the breach may be regarded as deserving of a penalty even when in the circumstances no harm could possibly have resulted.

The second necessary condition is that the person must have known or have been capable of knowing that he was breaching the law (or a rule of a code). Ignorance of the law may be no excuse in most jurisdictions (there are exceptions); but to be incapable of knowing it

---

[35] See G. Fletcher, *Rethinking Criminal Law* (Boston, 1978).
[36] A point well argued by A. von Hirsch in *Past or Future Crimes* (Manchester, 1986).

is. We are amused or horrified by the medieval trials and executions of domestic animals which had killed or maimed people (although, for mainly utilitarian reasons,[37] we nowadays simply put them to death without the formality of trial) not because they did not intend what they did (they usually did), but because, like Adam and Eve before they ate the forbidden fruit, they were incapable of knowing right from wrong. In order to 'deserve' a person must know, or be at least capable of knowing, that he is breaching a rule which is not merely prudential but moral.

These necessary conditions, however, do not make it clear why the guilty party 'ought' to be punished, in the moral sense of 'ought'. Retributivists have offered quite a few answers.

Some are intuitionist: the duty to inflict desert is simply perceived by our moral sense.[38] The perception that tells us we ought not to kill people also tells us that we ought to kill those who do, or at least inflict some serious harm on them. Perceptions of this kind, however, seem to be less unanimous than sense-perceptions. There is more agreement about the sweetness of sugar than about the sweetness of revenge or of legitimate punishment, let alone their morality. As for duties, most people would say that they are learnt rather than perceived; and learnt, what is more, from people who can explain why they are duties. Intuitionists seem to deny us any right to an explanation.

Most retributivists concede us this right. Their explanations tend to be either superstitious or metaphorical. The superstitious kind need not detain us for long. In some cultures, more common in the past than in the present, a grave crime such as homicide or incest is seen as creating a sort of contamination that can be sanitized only by some transaction which gets rid of the offender (whether by death, by banishment, or by some nasty magic). Some forms of some religions see the offender's suffering as needed to carry out the will of a deity (which makes it legitimate to speculate about the deity's reasoning).[39] Some Christian theologians justify punishment on the ground that it may promote spiritual improvement.[40] This is not necessarily Benthamist utilitarianism: it is the offender's immortal soul they have

---

[37] Of course the reason is sometimes less rational. Few people want to have around them a domestic animal that has killed a member of the family.

[38] See M. Noore's discussion of intuitionism in 'The Moral Worth of Retribution', in F. Shoeman (ed.), *Responsibility, Character and the Emotions* (Cambridge, 1987).

[39] Islam is an example.

[40] See e.g. E. Moberley, *Suffering, Innocent and Guilty* (London, 1978).

in mind, not his temporal future. Yet spiritual improvement is highly improbable unless he accepts or can be brought to accept the justice of his suffering. If he cannot, his punishment must be either unjustifiable or justifiable by some other reasoning. This is the point at which theologians, like philosophers, tend to resort to metaphors.

METAPHORICAL EXPLANATIONS

Metaphors are treacherous friends, turning tail when one needs help most. (They are, after all, just a special kind of analogy, and so by definition not precisely what is meant.) Consider, for instance, the popular explanation that offenders 'owe a debt', usually 'to society' rather than the victim. (Even retributivists who want victims to be compensated may also believe that the offenders owe something to society.) The debt is not literal. If I try to borrow and am refused, I owe no debt; but if I attempt a crime unsuccessfully, I am said to owe something to society. Again, what a debtor owes is something that will benefit the creditor; but it is not easy to see what benefit an afflictive penalty will confer on society (unless of course it takes the form of a fine). Richard Burgh suggests that the benefit is the public declaration that the crime is condemned;[41] but this turns retribution into the weak sort of utility which was discussed in the section headed 'Penalties as Symbols'. Burgh admits, too, that there might be societies which feel so secure and certain of people's moral values that public condemnation is unnecessary; and however unlikely this seems, it is a thought-experiment which helps to undermine the metaphor of a debt.

Another metaphor talks of 'annulling' or 'cancelling' the offence; that is, it seems, restoring a status quo ante in which the crime had not been committed. Certainly in the case of theft or criminal damage it is usually possible for restitution to undo virtually all the harm, if one ignores fear and outrage; but nobody can be unmurdered, unraped, or unmugged. Nor, again, would this broken-backed analogy justify the punishment of inchoate crimes. As Bosanquet realized,[42] the most that punishment can be claimed to do on these lines is to *symbolize* cancellation, not achieve it.

Should metaphors be accepted as genuine currency in a transaction of this kind? Metaphorizing retributivists could plead that they are

---

[41] See R. Burgh, 'Guilt, Punishment and Desert' in F. Schoeman (ed.), *Responsibility, Character and the Emotions* (Cambridge, 1987).

[42] See B. Bosanquet, *Some Suggestions in Ethics* (London, 1918).

trying to describe something so special that its nature can be grasped only by intuition, but that a metaphor—or two, or three—can guide the interlocutor's intuition to the point at which he should be able to say, 'Now I see.' This would be more convincing, however, if they had done their best to guide us with literal statements before resorting to metaphors.

At least two inter-war philosophers did so. W. D. Ross suggested that when the state punishes it is keeping promises made in its criminal code.[43] The aim of the code is to protect citizens' rights; but the obligation to punish lies in the nature of a promise. J. D. Mabbott's suggestion was very similar.[44] If a disciplinary code prescribes penalties for infringements, this is a sufficient and compelling reason for imposing them on infringers. These explanations were non-superstitious and non-metaphorical. They allowed that the institution called 'punishment' may have been included in the criminal code (or in other disciplinary codes) for utilitarian reasons, yet accounted for the retributivist's feeling that there is an obligation to penalize.

Modern retributivists could have done worse than develop Mabbott's point. Post-war ethnomethodologists have demonstrated the extent to which people are rule-making and rule-following animals.[45] All sorts of social transactions, even speech, are rule-governed, and breaches of the rules arouse feelings which range from outrage to embarrassment. Formal codes of conduct such as the criminal law and disciplinary codes include rules which specify penalties for breaches of the substantive rules. If a substantive rule has been breached, a failure to apply the appropriate penalizing rule adds one more breach. This may well be the logical core of the feeling that penalizing is obligatory, and it is often reinforced by dislike of the offender because of what he has done. There are awkwardnesses to be overcome. In particular, many (but not all) penalizing rules are nowadays permissive rather than prescriptive: they do not specify what *must* be done to the transgressors, only what *may* be done. Even so, the sentencer (or other disciplinary authority) may regard himself as bound by other rules to choose one of the permitted penalties (for example by the guidelines of the Magistrates' Association or by the dicta of appellate courts).

[43] In an appendix to W. D. Ross, *The Right and the Good* (Oxford, 1930), which received little attention.

[44] J. D. Mabbott, 'Punishment', *Mind*, 48 (1939), 190 ff.

[45] e.g. H. Garfinkel, in *Studies in Ethnomethodology* (Englewood Cliffs, NJ, 1967), and, more systematically, R. Harré and P. Secord, in *The Explanation of Social Behaviour* (Oxford, 1972).

Yet post-war retributivists who have seen the need for non-superstitious, non-metaphorical explanation of desert have overlooked the need to preserve the element of obligation. Robert Nozick, for example, resorts to symbolism.[46] He takes great care to make clear that it is not merely of the consequentialist sort that holds out hope of improving crime-rates:

> The hope is that delivering the message will change the person so that he will realize he did wrong, then start doing things because they are right . . . Yet, if it does not do this, still, punishment does give the correct values some significant effect on his life . . . The nonteleological [sc. non-utilitarian] retributive view . . . sees punishment as effecting a connection between the wrongdoer and the correct values that he has flouted.

In other words, if the message has a good effect on the wrongdoer's behaviour so much the better, but that is not essential.

This gets rid of the metaphorical bathwater, but loses the vital baby: a reason why we should feel an obligation to inflict desert. Why *ought* a 'connection' to be effected between the wrongdoer and the correct values which he has flouted, if it does not matter whether this improves his behaviour?

Von Hirsch thinks he can save his message of 'censure' from this criticism. The state is under an obligation to respond in some way to criminal lawbreaking. This obligation need not be a retributive one: von Hirsch seems to regard it as utilitarian. But 'it should do so in a manner that testifies to the recognition that the conduct is wrong. To respond in a morally neutral fashion, to treat the conduct merely as a source of costs to the perpetrator, is objectionable because it fails to provide this recognition'. This sounds like a utilitarian argument for 'censure'; but he goes on: 'Even if we failed to discover evidence confirming that the criminal sanction reinforces people's desire to be law-abiding . . . the sanction should still express blame as an embodiment of moral judgments about criminal conduct.' This has narrowed the gap, but still fails to show us how to cross it. If the censorious message need have no utility, why is it morally necessary? It is not hard to find a *psychological* necessity. Our feelings about a crime may well make us want to convey such a message to the criminal or others, but that is not a moral necessity.

---

[46] See R. Nozick, *Philosophical Explanations* (Oxford, 1981).

THE NEGATIVE PRINCIPLE

Retributivists, however, claim that they have solved at least one problem which utilitarians cannot. The universally honoured principle that people should not be penalized for what they have not done, or for what they have done excusably (for example by accident) is one which utilitarians are said to be unable to justify without recourse to the notion of desert. Indeed utilitarianism is accused of being a doctrine which, if carried to its logical conclusion, would require the penalizing of the innocent or excusable whenever this seems likely to contribute to the efficacy of, say, general deterrence, or to reduce public alarm. One such scenario supposes a small community in which a horrifying crime has been committed. The criminal has not been identified, so that members of the community are in a state of fear, and believe that such crimes can be committed with impunity. A utilitarian police chief sees a way of 'framing' one not very valuable member of the community so that his conviction and execution will reassure the rest, and dispose of the belief that such crimes can be committed with impunity. He knows that his 'suspect' is innocent, but nobody else need know it. Why should he not proceed?

The only answer, say retributivists, is the principle which Herbert Hart has called 'retribution in distribution',[47] clearly founded on the notion of desert. Innocent or excusable people must not be penalized because they do not deserve it. If utilitarians honour this principle it must be because they acknowledge that desert has meaning.

The utilitarian can make a debating point. The infliction of deserved punishment on guilty people often inflicts as much or more 'punishment' on their nearest and dearest, so that the retributivist's insistence on the duty to punish infringes the distributive principle much oftener than the utilitarian would need to. The retributivist can of course reply that the sufferings of prisoners' dependants are not 'punishment', being unintended; the prisoner 'should have thought of his family' before committing his crime. The utilitarian might comment that these are consolations rather than justifications; that the distinction between inflicting harm with intention and doing so without intention but with the knowledge that it is an inevitable consequence is rather a fine one.

A 'tu quoque', however, is no more than a debating point. The

---

[47] In H. L. A. Hart, *Punishment and Responsibility* (Oxford, 1968).

utilitarian can do better. Hart himself suggested an answer. No doubt deterrence would be enhanced and one kind of fear reduced if someone, innocent or not, were to be penalized for every crime (or at least every publicized crime); but the result would be that everyone would live in fear of being chosen as that someone. The result would be a more apprehensive and unhappy society than one which honours the distributive principle. This would be true if all societies were of the 'open' kind, in which information about the policies of law enforcement agencies is leaked to the news media. Yet there have been, and still are, societies in which the control of trials and publicity has been such as to conceal law enforcement policies. Hart's argument would not apply to them.

The utilitarian may have a better answer, based on Rawls's notion of 'fairness';[48] imagine his 'rational, non-altruistic' man faced with a choice between life in one of two contrasting jurisdictions. Rawls's 'veil of ignorance' prevents him from knowing whether he will or will not be a lawbreaker (a not entirely artificial supposition; but that is by the way). All he knows is that in Jurisdiction A he will be punishable only if he has broken the law, whereas in Jurisdiction B he may be punished either because he has done so or because it is expedient to treat him as if he has. Hart's utilitarian would choose Jurisdiction A for altruistic reasons: it sounds like a happier society. Rawls's chooser, however, is not an altruist; he will prefer Jurisdiction A simply because, whether he turns out to be a lawbreaker or not, *his* chances of being penalized in it are smaller than they would be in Jurisdiction B. This calculation holds good whether these jurisdictions belong to 'open' societies or not. Only one rather unlikely possibility would make Jurisdiction B a better choice: that its policy of ignoring the negative principle is so effective that its subjects are much less likely to become the victims of crimes.

Hart was talking sound sociology when he called the negative principle 'retribution in distribution'. There is no doubt that it is honoured because it is believed to be based on desert. Yet it can be based on Rawlsian 'fairness', and respected by a utilitarian who refuses to use the notion of desert.

⁴⁸ See J. Rawls, *A Theory of Justice* (Oxford, 1972).

CONCLUSIONS

Utilitarians' claims need to be realistic. As general deterrents, penalties are less effective than they would like, but not totally ineffective. As correctives they are not easy to apply effectively because of the difficulty of identifying those who will respond to them, and the added problem of ensuring that the corrective is applied as it was meant to be; but again they are not totally ineffective. Precautionary detention achieves its purpose so long as it lasts, and non-custodial precautions are not totally ineffective. It is only symbolists' claims that can be dismissed as in all probability visionary. Moral objections to deterrents, correctives, and precautions are at best weak and at worst fallacious. Even the assertion that utilitarians must invoke notions such as proportionality and desert to explain why severity should be limited, or why the innocent should not be penalized, turn out to be false: there are non-retributive answers.

Modern retributivism, unlike its classical predecessor, is not so much a theory of punishment as a *pis aller*, born of two rather superficial parents: exaggerated interpretation of research and moralists' rhetorical attacks on utilitarianism. It is tempting to turn rhetoric on to modern retributivism, for example by emphasizing Nozick's approval of capital punishment; but that would be unfair and unnecessary. It is sufficient to list the crucial questions which it has failed to answer satisfactorily. What exactly is it that is deserving of blame and punishment—acts or dispositions? Exactly why is the infliction of desert without utility desirable? (Its answers to this question are less superstitious and less metaphorical than those of classical retributivism, but have lost sight of the element of duty.) If commensurability is beyond human expertise, is proportionality a satisfactory alternative? Is punishment which involves innocent dependants defensible?

Modern retributivists are apt to resort to compromises. They may try to endow desert with some sort of utility.[49] They may go further, conceding that there is no moral obligation to punish, and that the retributive principle merely limits the distribution and the quantum of punishment. There is no room in this essay for a description, let alone a discussion, of all the varieties of compromise that have been

---

[49] Including Andrew von Hirsch himself, the popularizer of 'just deserts'; see his *Past or Future Crimes* (Manchester, 1986).

offered.[50] One point, however, needs to be made. Compromises are of two kinds: political and intellectual. Utilitarians, as we have seen, would be foolish not to accept a political compromise where proportionality is concerned. Intellectual compromise, however, is another matter. It is necessary only when *both* parties' positions suffer from serious and irremediable weaknesses. If only one of the parties is in such a position, the other can sit tight. I have been arguing that it is only retributivists who need an intellectual compromise.

[50] My book *Why Punish?* (Oxford, 1991) devotes a chapter to the different sorts of compromise that have been suggested.

5

Preventing Impunity

HYMAN GROSS[1]

I

My purpose here is to suggest a new way of looking at what in general is going on when people are brought to book for their crimes. I hope that what I have to say will make clear what the important questions are, though I shall not attempt to pursue those questions here. In a nutshell, my suggestion is this.

We enforce the law simply because we cannot tolerate letting people get away with their crimes. Preventing impunity (by which I mean not *allowing* people to get away with their crimes) is the one and only good reason we have for enforcing the law as we do. It is not crime itself, but rather the possibility of being *allowed* to get away with it, that really matters when the very system of law enforcement itself is thought to need justification. The aim of making people pay for their crimes will not do the job, nor will the aim of reducing the number of crimes that will be committed in the future.

There are two main reasons why general impunity would be intolerable. First, the universal feelings of outrage and frustration it would produce could not be met by any argument seeking to justify it. Secondly, it clearly would make life in society as we know it impossible in ways that almost no one would be willing to accept.

It is law enforcement, rather than punishment, that I think needs justification, since punishment in any developed legal system of the modern world is simply the outcome of last resort in cases where anything else but punishment will undermine the credibility of the system of enforceable laws by allowing the perpetrator to get away with

[1] I am grateful to Ross Harrison, Peter Lipton, John Thompson, and Nigel Walker for their very helpful comments. Professor Walker has pointed out that the views I present here are in some respects different from the views expressed previously in *A Theory of Criminal Justice* (Oxford, 1979), and that in his essay in this volume he addresses those earlier views of mine.

his crime. It is usual to view law enforcement simply as a necessary prelude to punishment, with punishment taken to be the true business at hand when a crime has been committed. This seems to me to be profoundly misleading for two reasons. First, the entire process of law enforcement, and not simply its last stage, is meant to counteract impunity. Calling to account, not punishment, is what we require when a crime has been committed. Secondly, we very much welcome other ways of disposing of cases at the sentencing stage whenever it is possible to adopt an alternative to punishment that is consistent with not allowing the perpetrator to get away with his crime.

A preliminary word about impunity is in order. Clearly, bringing the perpetrator of a crime to justice, while sufficient, is not what is necessary to prevent impunity. Our efforts to enforce the law often fail, and many who commit crimes that we know about escape detection or apprehension or conviction. There are many crimes that remain unknown, and so many opportunities for law enforcement that do not even come to light. Even though people may have got away with their crimes, none of these cases are instances of impunity as long as we have not *allowed* the perpetrator to get away with his crime. There also are times when we do allow someone who has committed a crime to escape liability for some good reason. Giving evidence to convict others is perhaps the best-known example, but there are many others. In such a case we do not have an instance of impunity, but rather a case in which a dispensation has been granted for some good reason in the course of carrying on the general programme of law enforcement. So long as we seek to enforce the law as best we can on those occasions when there is no good reason not to, we have not failed to prevent impunity.

A word about justification is also in order. Like war, or like killing another person, criminal punishment (and therefore law enforcement) needs justification because it is so awful. Because lives are wrecked we need to be quite certain that the terrible things we do are necessary and that we may reasonably expect them to accomplish whatever it is that makes them necessary. This very high standard of justification means that whatever reasons we have to justify what we do must be taken to be uncontroversial. Whatever the merits of the argument may be, it is not good enough that the argument is, all things considered, better than any argument on the other side. The reasons given must constitute a case so strong that there appears to be no plausible argument on the other side. To meet this high standard and keep the practice uncontroversial we often find it necessary to impose stringent conditions on those who engage in the practice.

Within the criminal law itself, there is a strong hint of this. Proof beyond a reasonable doubt that satisfies every one of a dozen jurors has been the traditional standard to justify imposing serious criminal liability. By contrast, a preponderance of the evidence is normally sufficient to justify imposing civil liability. Because criminal liability is such an awful business we must be quite certain when we impose it. If it is wrong to impose criminal liability when only a preponderance of the evidence points to guilt and there is room for reasonable doubt, it must also be wrong to have a system for imposing it that rests on less than certain foundations. Terrifying institutional practices, such as law enforcement or war, can themselves be tolerated only when the need for them is made apparent beyond a reasonable doubt.

II

I have said that neither reducing the number of crimes in the future nor making people pay for their crimes will do the job of a general justifying aim. Neither aim enjoys the uncontroversial status that is required, and this fact is both reflected in our practice and borne out by arguments that are presented against the pursuit of these goals.

Crime reduction is thought to depend on making everyone think twice by having constant examples of what happens to those who commit crimes. Or it is thought to depend on making those who commit crimes less likely to reoffend as a result of their experience of what happens to them, or as a result of some other beneficial experience they have while in the grip of the law. Or it is thought there will be less crime simply because those who are likely to commit crimes are being kept in a place where they can do no harm to the rest of us.

In order for any of these aims to justify the practice of law enforcement, they must first of all be reflected in its actual practice, and not merely in the very economical and rather unreal idea of a practice which philosophical theorists contrive for purposes of justification. In fact the actual practice of law enforcement hardly reflects any of these aims, though judges, politicians, and almost everyone else often talk as though it does. Publicizing punishment in ways that were calculated to warn and frighten others would certainly be regarded as atavistic. What are the aims in dealing with those who are kept in custody is a thoroughly confused matter except for the immediate aim of preventing trouble in the institution. And while it is true that certain offenders are believed to be more dangerous than others and are for that reason kept inside for a longer time, that fact is not reflected in the body of criminal law that prescribes sentences. There is no attempt to match seriousness of the offence with dangerousness of the offender, or to impose criminal liability on a person who might certainly be thought to be criminally dangerous though there is not yet any evidence of his having committed a crime.

Other matters make it clear that such deterrent or incapacitative aims are far from uncontroversial. Most serious crimes are committed by people who clearly could not be expected to be under the influence of the remote warnings and threats that general law enforcement provides. For the minority of serious crimes that are planned by people who might engage in such reflection and deliberation, the reasonable conclusion would be that in general there is an excellent chance of their getting away with a crime since only a very small percentage of those who commit a serious crime are detected, apprehended, and convicted. There is also the moral controversy surrounding the use of those members of the community who have committed a crime as examples for the rest, which clearly marks such an aim as controversial. The criminalizing effects of prison experience on large numbers of the prison population is a regular feature of law enforcement that further marks the aim of crime prevention as not uncontroversial. Finally, the legal machinery that has been designed for incapacitating those who are believed to be dangerous falls outside the system of law enforcement and under the principles of civil commitment that afford protection against the acts of those who cannot be relied on to control themselves and are therefore a danger to themselves or others.

The animating insight that makes deterrence seem a plausible aim is the fact that we could certainly expect a great deal more crime if we had no system of enforceable laws in operation. This, however, is not because there would then be no threats and warnings, but because total freedom combined with constant imminent danger would inevitably make crime a major part of daily life. Concern about dangerousness also has its kernel of truth. Without law enforcement and with criminal harm a normal part of daily life the world would be a far more dangerous place.

Making the perpetrator pay for his crime is similarly inadequate as a general justifying aim because it too cannot purport to be uncontroversial. Our sentencing practice regularly admits and even seeks out good reasons for imposing a sentence that is less than what is deserved for the criminal conduct that took place. Many different sorts of reasons are accepted, some based on compassionate grounds, some based on co-operation with the authorities, some based on the perpetrator's personal history, and some based on some policy consideration of the moment. It is not deemed objectionable when sentences are reduced for a good reason that has nothing to do with the crime, even when it is perfectly clear that as a consequence the perpetrator is not being required to make proper payment for his crime. For this reason making the perpetrator pay cannot be said to be the unassailable aim that is required for justification. Conversely, mere compensation for injuries suffered is generally thought to be inadequate payment for any serious crime. The retributive aim of making the perpetrator pay for his crime is not fulfilled by adding suffering to compensation since the added ingredient must represent the vengefulness or vindictiveness that even retributivists in our time generally eschew. We are left, then, with a justificatory theory that is at best prey to difficulties.

Another form of retributivism has recently been in fashion. Some current discussion of punishment for crime attempts to make sense of it by highlighting the supposed unfair advantage that crime produces. Breaking the law itself is supposed to be a matter that calls for redress in the interest of fairness. When we punish a crime, we remedy the unfairness that is suffered by all the law-abiding members of the community who honour their undertakings to abide by the law and who in exercising this restraint have been put in a position of relative disadvantage by those who broke the law.

The concern about impunity that prompts this approach is plain enough. It is not at all clear, however, that in general those who abide by the law suffer any disadvantage because others break the law. If some were *allowed* to break the law, that could certainly be seen as conferring an unfair advantage on them, but that is not what is being complained of here. And in any case, it can hardly be accepted that penalties with life-shattering effect are necessary simply to remedy such unfairness, though that is what the criminal law prescribes for serious crimes. Clearly those who hold this view are not providing the uncontroversial theory that is needed.

Still, retribution does suggest that justice is somehow done when those who commit crimes are brought to book and made to pay. Even if it is hopelessly difficult to explain, it is very widely felt that there is justice in punishing crime, and it would not be unreasonable to say that doing justice, whatever its principles might turn out to be, is the uncontroversial aim that justifies enforcing the law as we do.

This view of retribution as a kind of public virtue is, I think, seriously misleading. If really it were a virtue, there would be no need for any justification at all, but only an explanation of its place among the principles we live by. Compare doing justice by punishing crime with justice done in other ways. No justification is required for settling a dispute properly, for sharing out burdens and benefits in the right way, or for setting the right limits on the exercise of public power. Justifying punishment is, however, an obsessive concern that springs from feelings of repugnance as we continue to do what we feel we must in response to crime. What we properly call justice on such occasions is not punishing crime but rather the negative public virtues that are incorporated in measures to protect the innocent, to prevent disparity in sentencing, and to ensure that no one who is guilty gets more than his crime deserves. There is also one further negative public virtue here that is properly called justice: not letting those who commit crimes get away with them. Since the state keeps the hands of its citizens tied to prevent them from taking the law into their own hands it would amount to a gross abuse of power if the state itself then failed to maintain in operation a system of enforceable law.

Making sure that crime does not pay is easily confused with making the criminal pay for his crime. The first is preventing impunity, while the second is a retributive theme. Not letting one get away with it and getting even do have a certain affinity, and achieving the second will almost certainly entail the achievement of the first. The trouble is we hardly ever know how to get even with the perpetrator of the crime, whether on the victim's behalf or in a more objective way, and even if we did we are likely to find ourselves involved in unacceptable barbarity and obliged to take measures that far exceed what is necessary to prevent getting away with crime. It may well be that only the death penalty administered in an especially horrific way will allow us to get even for a particularly atrocious murder, but clearly something less than any death penalty at all will enable us to prevent the murderer from getting away with his crime. Capital punishment is only the most dramatic example of overkill in sentencing. After assessing the seriousness of the criminal conduct we regularly consider good reasons for making the sentence less than what the crime deserves so long as it does not allow the perpetrator to get away with his crime. Clearly it is something less than retribution at which we are aiming. I suggest it is whatever is necessary and sufficient to prevent impunity.

III

My claim is that law enforcement is justified by the need to prevent impunity. If that claim is to be accepted, I must present a case that impunity is intolerable and that the sort of system of law enforcement we rely on when crimes are committed is needed to prevent impunity. That case must be convincing beyond a reasonable doubt.

It seems to me a fact of social life that everyone finds impunity intolerable. It is bound to produce outrage, though for reasons we understand only dimly and imperfectly. The feelings of fear and anger that follow in the wake of crime are kept in check by enforcement of the law, and one must suppose that the general absence of an operating system for that purpose would have terrible consequences. The generally law-abiding attitudes that make life in society possible would disappear as perfectly decent people found they had to arrange for self-protection by any means that might be effective. Beyond that, people would have to pursue their own interests by whatever means were likely to prove successful in a world in which each person's power had no limits placed on it by law. In a world in which people are allowed to get away with their crimes there could exist only the rudimentary social co-operation that stems from offers that cannot be refused, threats that cannot be ignored, and any remnants of personal trust that might be able to survive in such a climate. It is, of course, the bleak landscape of man in a state of nature.

Fear and anger are the most prominent feelings in what is usually a strong and complex emotional response to crime. Law enforcement keeps those feelings within bounds and prevents acts of retaliation in the short term while maintaining respect for the law in the longer term. Both victims and others who share their feelings vicariously are satisfied. But satisfaction here does not mean any gratification that might be sought by the wanton imagination of the victim or those who identify themselves with him. In life we often require our feelings to give a good account of themselves, and consider them to be inappropriate as a moving force in responding to what produced them even though we recognize that as feelings they are themselves a wholly appropriate response to what produced them. We are more primitive than our legal system and rely on the law to help us behave in a civilized way. The result is a way of enforcing the law that represents a sufficiently stern response to the crime to keep the victim and those who put themselves in the victim's shoes from thinking that the perpetrator has got away with his crime, while still recognizing that a crime is, after all, only a crime and that those of us who commit crimes are no less human than those who don't.

We are of course put to the test when monsters are brought to book for their crimes and feelings run so strong that even after the depravity is explained and we are forced to see the perpetrator as a person again, we find ourselves thinking that his fate does not matter and that there is no place for humane considerations. There are those who carry out atrocities and who torture with pleasure the victims of some political regime. Others contrive hideous adventures in sadism and depravity on their own. There are those who kill or maim in cold blood as a vocation carried on to advance the objectives of a criminal organization. In these and many other cases we do pay a price for being civilized, and do to some extent let the perpetrator get away with his crime *morally*, though legally he has been made to pay the price that is required to prevent impunity.

At the other extreme are a great many crimes that just happen to be on the books. They are creatures of the law-making process rather than crimes that exist in their own right quite apart from the legal recognition they happen to enjoy. Some of these creations of the legal system are very serious crimes indeed. Spies, tax fraudsters, embezzlers, and even inside traders are tarred as criminals with much the same brush as burglars, rapists, muggers, and murderers, though the emotional response to the first group of crimes is much different and does not require the severe measures when sentence is passed that is needed to placate the fear and anger that the second group of crimes produce. The crimes that are crimes only because they are on the books must nevertheless be treated as much more than mere rule-breaking affairs with no victim to arouse our emotions or make claim upon the perpetrator's conscience. If they were not dealt with in a similarly severe way these crimes would be committed by many people who saw it in their interest to do so and thought they would not be caught. The same daunting system of law enforcement for crimes of both kinds results in both kinds being stigmatized in the same way as crime and in attitudes forming toward both that are sufficiently similar to serve the purposes at hand. But this plainly deterrent aim can not serve to justify law enforcement for the reasons already discussed.

In this perspective the criminal law appears to be a pretext for its own enforcement, and though it is true that it is also meant to make clear and to regulate, its main job is to provide a warrant for law enforcement to prevent impunity on those occasions when the law is broken. Other law-like systems do not have their rules playing the same role because there is not a need to prevent impunity.

One can imagine a religious group whose members are deeply committed to their laws and customs. Transgressions are bound to occur, but they are a problem only for the transgressor, who must reconcile what he has done with his deep commitment not to do it. He is helped by having his misdeed brought out in the open and recognized for what it is. But only expiation and reaffirmation are required, not law enforcement.

Obedience to the unenforced is the foundation of many less esoteric groups. Universities, clubs, and places of work assume that members of the group have an abiding attitude of conformity to the rules. Even though the rules may come under criticism and be changed, and even though they are enforceable, what they principally represent is an undertaking that is respected by members of the group as an indispensable condition of their membership.

At the other extreme are systems in which rules are made to be broken. Regimes of training to develop skill or discipline have rules that loom large and are enforced with particular zeal whenever an infraction is noticed, in order to achieve the purpose for which the system exists.

The criminal law occupies a middle ground. It does not expect obedience to the unenforced, much less the unenforceable, at least not by most people most of the time. On the other hand, though it takes itself very seriously and expects everyone else to as well, the law does not present itself with a chip waiting to be knocked off its shoulder. It tells people what they must and must not do (in case they didn't know already) and what can happen to them if they transgress. It also provides (and limits) the power by which enforcement of the law may be achieved. It seeks to keep itself credible through its enforcement and to maintain the general attitude of respect (or whatever else it is) that makes most people most of the time think it matters crucially what the law says when choosing what to do. Impunity would destroy the law as we know it.

Of course this might all be an illusion. Perhaps it really does not matter whether or not laws are enforced, either in the short run when rampant violence, ill-considered retaliation, and profound despair are the apparent dangers, or in the long run when social co-operation and living together peaceably would seem to be impossible without laws that are enforced. If there is any real case to this effect, the prevention of impunity is no longer the apparently uncontroversial goal that justifies law enforcement, and as far as I can see the whole business as we practise it would then indeed be an unjustifiable curtailment of liberty and imposition of suffering. Even now much of what we do is unnecessary to prevent impunity, and unless such practices are justified by equally uncontroversial goals they are a cause for reform in law enforcement.

IV

I want finally to suggest some items of practical advantage that follow from adopting this view of criminal justice as a working model.

If we adopt the model of anti-impunity, we feel more comfortable in mitigating the force of law enforcement. If our concern is simply not to allow people to get away with their crimes, we are free to admit various considerations to lessen the severity of a sentence and make it less than it would be if it were measured only by seriousness of the criminal conduct. If it is simply a matter of giving people who incur criminal liability what they deserve for what they have done, we automatically exclude many morally robust claims that are not relevant to the crime itself, and end up dispensing a much more damaging criminal justice than is needed to serve the requirements of law enforcement. It is not only the severity of sentences that is affected, but the modality as well. Innovative alternatives to custodial sentences that represent a great improvement over imprisonment can be prescribed only if we see that it is not a matter of measure for measure or of instilling dread in others, but simply a matter of making those who commit crimes accountable in a way that satisfies our social needs.

This leads to a longer-term consideration. The reforms in criminal justice that are clear in historical perspective mark a trend towards lower thresholds of impunity. As we understand more about ourselves and understand better how any of us might break the law, we see the needs of effective law enforcement satisfied by measures that in the past would not have been thought adequate. What is required to prevent the perpetrator from getting away with his crime is a decision supported by good reasons that provides comfort for those who are angry and fearful about the crime, though admittedly some will not wish to take this comfort. People do not always welcome the comfort that is provided, and it is possible to exploit the feelings that a crime produces for other ends. But those who have assumed a responsibility for not letting people get away with their crimes must remain uninfluenced by such exploitation and pay attention instead to the changing standards of enlightened public opinion.

The flexibility that this model allows is a reflection of the actual process of law enforcement, and this seems to me another of its virtues. Not only does it afford ample discretion in sentencing and other post-conviction dispositions, but it makes sense of features of the criminal justice process that otherwise seem either an impediment to effective law enforcement or irrelevant to it. Regulating proof beyond a reasonable doubt is only the first of many obstacles in the path of establishing criminal liability. Those who see retribution as the aim of this process and those who think punishment will deter crime often are understandably unhappy when the evidence clearly points towards guilt but some legal rule that has no bearing on guilt stands in the way of conviction. Once it is accepted that only the process itself is necessary to prevent people from getting away with their crimes, the system of law enforcement we have still appears a sensible social pursuit even though it is hedged about with various restrictions that otherwise must be deemed counter-productive.

A final point in favour of this model concerns attitudes and expectations. Most people keep their distance while at the same time indulging an almost morbid fascination with crime. There are very strong reprobative views regarding what has happened, and naïve hopes for a better future. On the other hand, those who come in contact with people who commit crimes and are acquainted with what happens to them after they are convicted find themselves beset by the urgent moral dilemmas that one would expect once such innocence is abandoned. They also find it impossible to imagine that somehow this process could ever succeed as an attempt to punish away crime. The modest but real goals of reform that match our moral growth and better understanding of the human condition are easily reconciled with the need not to allow people to get away with their crimes. This, I think, is a powerful recommendation for this model.

6

The Equality of Mercy

ROSS HARRISON[1]

The problem with which this paper is concerned can be brought out by considering four independently plausible, but mutually inconsistent, propositions. The first proposition is that states ought to be purely rational entities. All acts of states should be justifiable; that is, should be such that they can be supported by reason. States are different in this respect from individual people. Individuals are normally allowed some areas of absolute discretion, in which they are permitted to act in a completely arbitrary or irrational manner. But in states there should be nothing private, personal, or arbitrary; no whim, no play; everything which happens as a state action should happen for a reason.

The second proposition is that to act rationally is to act equitably, or (in one sense) justly. To act rationally is to act for reasons; and to act for reasons is to act on the basis of descriptions. Something or other about the situation gives the reason for action. But this thing, this description, is reapplicable. And where the description reapplies, so does the appropriate act. Therefore to act for reasons is to treat relatively similar cases in similar ways. But this is what it is to act equitably, or (in one sense) justly. So to act rationally is to act equitably.

Putting these first two propositions together we reach the conclusion that the state ought, of its nature, to act equitably, that is justly, or impartially. And so far, perhaps, so good. However, we now move to the third proposition. This is that we want those in power over us (the state's agents) to be merciful. Indeed, more than this, we think that this is a proper aspect of power, even of a purely rational power, even of God himself. In Portia's famous words we think that

[1] I am grateful to Hyman Gross for criticism of an earlier draft and have also benefited from D. J. Galligan, *Discretionary Powers* (Oxford, 1986) and Jeffrie G. Murphy and Jean Hampton, *Forgiveness and Mercy* (Cambridge, 1989).

> mercy is above this sceptred sway,
> It is enthroned in the hearts of kings,
> It is an attribute to God himself;
> And earthly power doth then show likest God's,
> When mercy seasons justice.

But now we reach the problem, which we can put in a fourth proposition. This is that something which is purely rational cannot be merciful. If it is rational, by proposition two, it proceeds equally, treating all cases and people alike. Yet if it is also merciful, then in particular cases the normal rules of justice have to be suspended, so that some people are specially treated. Instead of being treated justly, they are mercifully to be exempted from their just deserts.

So here we have the problem, following the course of the four numbered propositions. By number one, the state is rational; therefore, by two, it is just. Yet it should also, by three, be merciful. However, by four, this is impossible. So Portia's eloquent plea, just quoted, not only does, but also should, fall on deaf ears. As Portia herself says slightly later, in response to the request that she should 'to do a great right, do a little wrong',

> It must not be, there is no power in Venice
> Can alter a degree established:
> 'Twill be recorded for a precedent,
> And many an error by the same example
> Will rush into the state. It cannot be.

In other words, the similar treatment of similar cases, as enshrined in a doctrine of precedent, sets up the appropriate standard for states. It may be that individual people are allowed to depart from this standard and show mercy. In her famous speech, what Portia is actually doing is suggesting to Shylock that he might be merciful and drop his charge. She is not, that is, addressing the state, or its personal representative, the doge. She is addressing a private individual, Shylock. As a private individual, he could decide, arbitrarily, to be merciful. However, a state may not do this. States are bound by the principle of similar treatment of similar cases. If a state were to depart from its previous practice, that would be, in effect, to change the law; and so, if the present law was correct, error would rush into the state. Therefore a state cannot be merciful. If Shylock does not personally decide to drop his charge, then there is nothing the state can do about it. It must treat this case like the others, according to the law.

So much for *The Merchant of Venice*; and quoting *The Merchant of Venice* on mercy is as trite as referring to Pilate when discussing truth. However, the problem posed by the quotations is real, precise, and difficult. Neither the quality of mercy nor the quotations are strained. It would seem that the ideal of a state's rational behaviour, as exemplified by the all-wise lawgiver God, is to be both merciful and just. Yet the combination seems to be impossible. Precisely because the quality of mercy is not strained, equality of mercy seems to be disallowed. For to dispense mercy equally would be to (con)strain it. If a state behaves equally, it does not behave mercifully; if mercifully, then not equally. Yet the state is required to be both. Putting it another way, the state is required to be rational, therefore just. So mercy is impossible. Yet mercy is also required. Mercy, it seems, is both impossible and necessary. We obviously have a serious problem.

Arising as it does out of the four initial propositions, this problem can only be resolved or alleviated if something is made to give in one or more of these propositions. So let us look more closely at them, exploring for weaknesses. The first one, that the state is rational, may well seem very weak indeed, if not obviously false. The states we actually live in are all too frequently examples of manifest absurdity, and quite often examples of brutally immoral power. However, the first proposition is not descriptive but normative. It does not say that states are actually rational; it says that that is what they should be. So we are concerned not with what is actually the case but with how things would be if what was so was also right. We are concerned with the right, that is the justified, state. Yet, if it is justified, unsurprisingly, it is justified. The acts of a justified state have justifications, that is, reasons. So if the state is as it ought to be, then the state is rational. Far from being manifestly false, the first proposition is rather in danger of being tautologically trivial.

It may be trivial that the justified state is also a rational state; but, if it is trivial, it is also true; which is enough for present purposes. Perhaps it is also trivial that acting rationally also involves acting (in a certain sense) impartially or equally. However, if this is also trivial, it therefore is also true. So, even if trivial, in this way the first two propositions would be properly secured.

In fact, however, I think that neither proposition is trivial. This can be shown by two different directions of argument. On the one hand, it may be allowed that the conclusion of the state's impartiality is correct, but held that this is a significant and non-trivial result, being founded on something else than the state's rationality. On the other hand, it could be doubted whether it was possible for states or anything else to be impartial; hence the state's impartiality would not be trivial, because it would be false.

On the first tack, it may well be acceptable that the state should hold the ring between competing individuals. Individuals have particular interests. These interests conflict. Hence individuals are in competition. So it could be held that the duty of the state is to abstract from these particular interests and operate fairly, or impartially, with respect to these particular interests. This might be by restraining some; or by trying to construct a fair area of competition (a level playing-field). In neither case, even if the interests of some individuals benefit at the cost of others, is the reason for the state's action the interest of the benefiting individuals. Its reason, rather, is the desire to act impartially between them. But the reason for that is not trivial; nor does it follow just from the idea of rationality. Its reason, rather, is that the state is something in the position of an umpire as between competing individuals, and so ought to act fairly.

So, on the one hand, a non-trivial case might be made for the state's impartiality, based on its role as an umpire. But this case connects the idea of acting impartially with the idea of acting without particular interests. And this leads to the attack on triviality from the other flank. For if states are impartial, this seems now to be because they do not have any interests. Interests make agents partial; only those without interests can act impartially. So if states are impartial, this is only because they are very unlike normal agents. Normal humans have interests. They care for other humans, indeed love them. Love is personal; it is the admiration or attachment to something for its individual rather than its universal qualities. Love is partial. Love is merciful. But states are not people. They do not have love. They are impartial. In this sequence of thoughts, states only get to be impartial because they are completely inhuman, and have no interests. Even if this is true, it is certainly not trivial.

Indeed, once impartiality is connected to lack of interest, it is more plausible to suppose that no agent, whether state or individual, can lack interests. Hence it would seem to follow that no agent can be impartial. Then, to complete the attack from the second flank, the impartiality of states would be shown not to be trivial since it would have been shown to be false. Impartiality could not possibly be a motive for action, so impartiality is impossible: if impartiality is impossible, there is no point recommending it, either to states or to individuals.

The claim that nothing could be motivated by impartiality might start with the empirical observation that nothing actually is so motivated. In a world dominated by power and feeling, impartiality seems little sought after. People may piously mouth that it is a good, but they do not seem to pursue it. Indeed, it seems an abstract, or cold, virtue, with no obvious attraction. If to be impartial someone would have to have no particular interests, then it seems that it is a virtue which could only be pursued by merely hypothetical, wholly rational, people. Yet, lacking particular desires or interests, it is doubtful whether such people would have any motive for action at all. The impartial spectator is precisely that, a spectator; he is not an agent. Perhaps the impartial person is a purely hypothetical construct who has no actual self left to be interested in.

Some of the empirical basis of this argument may be granted. Our passions, and reasons for action, are such that we are interested in some people rather than others, love our friends and family more than the world at large, and in general have no incentive to act impartially. But this would not show that impartial action was impossible; only that it was unusual. It would be possible to imagine someone in love with justice, whose own particular thing was to act impartially, who got the sort of *frisson* of anticipation at the prospect of an impartial action that other people get at the prospect of food or sex. This is certainly possible. However, it is certainly also highly abnormal. So what this argument does is not to show that it is impossible to act impartially, but to cast doubts on the desirability (sanity, normality) of such action.

The problem of why someone should be impartial might just sound like a particular example of the old problem of why someone should be moral. This is not the case. Of course the standard problem of why anyone should be motivated to be moral is not easy; particularly if the only motivations permitted are self-interested ones. However, such self-interested motivations can in fact be suggested for most so-called moral actions. Not killing people, arguably, does give someone a better chance of not being killed himself; not stealing gives him a better chance of holding on to his own possessions; and so on. But not so with impartially. Impartiality is special. It is much more difficult to show that acting impartiality is in someone's interest. It is much more doubtful that treating people impartially increases one's chance of being treated impartially in turn; and, even if it did, it is not obvious that it is in one's interest to be treated impartially, in the way that it is obvious that it is in our interest not to be killed or to keep our possessions. If anything, it is in our interests to be treated mercifully; not to be treated impartially.

So, with impartiality, there does seem to be an especially difficult problem of motive. We return to the question of why anyone normal should be moved by something so cold and rational; something so intellectually inhuman. But this is just the answer. Rather than being repelled by rationality, remembering it will give us our motive. The connection between impartiality and rationality was asserted in the second proposition and, if this connection can be defended, we have our motive. Asking why people should be moral might be difficult enough; but asking why people should be rational has no answer but the obvious one: they could not have a reason not to be rational.

So the question of motive reduces to the validity of the second proposition, that impartiality, or a certain kind of equality or fairness in action, follows directly from the idea of acting rationally. And this proposition can be firmly defended. It is a property of a reason for action that it cites some property of the situation in which the action is recommended as giving the basis for that action. Because such and such a description is true, such and such a thing ought to be done. But the nature of descriptions is that they are reapplicable; they are universals which can be applied to more than one particular situation. Hence, if falling under this description gives a reason for action in one particular situation, it also gives a reason for action in all the other particular situations to which this description applies. Hence someone using this description as a reason for action is compelled by the very nature of reasons to treat like cases alike; which means that he is compelled to be impartial between them. Thus impartiality seems to follow from the mere nature of a reason. Either we are wholly irrational, or else we are forced to be impartial. So rather than being an abstract or doubtful virtue, impartiality becomes an inevitable one, stemming directly from our nature as rational beings.

Another way to put this is that impartiality is not a right or duty competing with others, which may have more obvious appeal, or might seem to be more defensible in terms of self-interest. Someone's humanity may be a reason for us not to kill him. This gives him a right not to be killed. But this is not a right competing with the right to be treated impartially. With this first right the second comes automatically.

For if his humanity gives him a reason not to be killed, then any other people's humanity equally gives them a reason not to be killed. If he has a right, therefore, then so also do they. If we recognize his particular right, we are therefore forced also to be impartial between his and these others' analogous rights. Rather than having to choose between his right and impartiality, the impartiality is forced on us.

So also for other reasons, and the specific rights which follow from them. If someone has a right to work because he is a citizen of a particular state, then any other citizen of that state also has a right to work; and someone recognizing his right is forced to be impartial between all these citizens. So impartiality is not a right or duty competing with others. It is prior to them; and this may explain its apparent invisibility when we first turned our attention to rights and duties. Or to put it another way: we do not need any special concentration on, or recommendation of, impartiality. Merely concentrating on, or recommending, other goods, or duties gives us all the impartiality we could require.

So part of the original problem came from taking the motivation to impartiality as being just like other motivations. However, if it is taken to be different in this way we can see how an individual can be motivated both to be impartial (that is, have a reason for acting impartially) and also have other, much more specific, motivations. We now seem to have moved to a position where, instead of impartiality being unnatural and impossible, it is inevitable and obvious, both for states and for individuals. This may seem to be too easy a disposal of the problem. Apart from anything else, if this solution is correct, it would seem to make it impossible to have conflicts between impartiality and other virtues. Yet, at least at the individual level, conflicts between impartiality and other reasons for action seem to be only too common. People are forced to decide between the treatment of strangers and the treatment of the family. Someone may be tempted by nepotistic impulses; this temptation may well be to do something wrong; yet it is not just the temptation to be irrational. So we seem to have made a mistake. Impartiality just does not seem to be as inevitable or as invisible as this account requires.

The objection can be met. The kind of impartiality being defended here is only the principle that the same kind of case should be treated in the same kind of way. The conflicts just considered, which seemed to create a difficulty, bring up the much more substantial and difficult question of what counts as a relevant consideration; that is, of which similarities are to be considered important and which not. Is it appropriate in considering a job that someone is one's cousin? Is it appropriate in spending money that it is being spent on family rather than strangers? These are the substantive questions which arise when impartiality seems to come into conflict with other interests (or goods). However, whatever the answer to these, if it is correct, then the same kind of case should be treated in the same kind of way. If it is appropriate to think that Jim has special claims because he is a cousin, then it is also appropriate to consider the special claims of cousin John. Precisely similar cases, if the action is justified, ought to be handled in similar ways.

This is all that is being considered here. But minimal as it is, it is enough. For the question of mercy is the question of whether the state may properly behave differently in two precisely similar cases. Is it, that is, to have a power of absolute discretion, a prerogative, so that it may decide differently in the two cases, even though (*ex hypothesi*, because there are no relevant differences) no reasons can be given for the divergence? Can the state just exercise its prerogative of mercy, decide, and that be the end of it, no reason being given; but none being required?

So, in this minimal sense, impartiality is quintessentially justified, rational, desirable. Rational agents, persons or states, have to act (in this minimal sense) impartially. The problem therefore now focuses back on the question of whether this has to form the whole of a state's appropriate actions. States may well be rational at times; but why may they not also play, just as individuals may? Why could they not exercise a bit of mercy whenever they felt like it, instead of proceeding according to the full rigour of the law? Why should not states love, forgive, forget; would they not be better; would they not indeed be more human if they did?

Now it may be thought that this can be caught by the first move made; that, trivially, it was only so far as they were justified that they were justified. Or, in other words, if no reason can be given, the action is (*ex hypothesi*) unjustified; hence it is something which could not be defended as legitimate state action. We are interested, it could be said, in justifiable state activity; it is only this which can be defended; and it is only this which, as theorists, we should recommend. Since an area of play, *ex hypothesi*, goes beyond justification, it is not something which, as theorists, we can defend or recommend. In our study of the state as it ought to be, all such play or arbitrariness cannot be considered and must be excluded.

However, this is too quick. This can be seen by considering the analogous claim about individual behaviour. Here again, it might seem that, as theorists of appropriate individual behaviour, we could only be interested in conduct for which reasons could be given. So again, it would seem, we could only defend the rational; and again mere arbitrariness and play would be excluded. But in fact this is not normally what we think. On the contrary, we think that it is fully defensible for individuals to exercise full discretion, to be as arbitrary as they like, over some parts of their conduct. Individuals are allowed whim, discretion, play. We normally think that it is perfectly appropriate for individuals to make their own decisons over certain areas; even if these decisions could not be independently justified. Sometimes, of course, it is because a decision has to be made, but it is quite arbitrary which is the correct decision; but we normally go much further than this. Even when we think one particular decision would be the correct or rational decision, we still sometimes think that an individual may, perfectly justifiably, make a different decision. In some cases, we think that it is perfectly appropriate and defensible for an individual to behave irrationally.

This is because of the value we place on individual autonomy. The clearest cases are those where the effects of the decision only concern the individual deciding and where he or she is of normal adult sense, and sound mind. Then we normally think that it is that individual's own risk and so they are entitled to decide as they will. For example, if someone bets on a race, we may think that the bet he makes, say on an outsider, is completely irrational, or unjustified as a bet. Yet, because it is his money, his risk, and his bet, we may nevertheless think that it is perfectly defensible for him to make it. He is entitled to be irrational, that is, not bet in the way that would be the most efficient way of minimizing his losses over a long run of bets. He is justified in doing something which, in itself, could not be justified.

There are several areas where we think in this way that it is right to allow individual discretion, or judgement, even though we also think that what the individual judges is wrong. These areas hence naturally lead to paradoxes unless handled carefully. There is the paradox of toleration in which I, being a tolerant man, think that people should be allowed to do what they think right; and yet I also think that Jones ought not to be allowed to treat people in the way he does. There is the paradox of democracy in which I, being a democrat, think that the majority view ought to be enacted; except, on this issue, I am in the minority, and hence think that the majority view ought not to be enacted. These can look like straight contradictions unless the reason why the action is justified is carefully distinguished from the reason why it is not justified. It is justified because it is the (free) decision of an autonomous moral agent, or of the majority, or whatever; that is, because of its source. It is unjustified because it involves cruelty, or unfairness, or whatever; that is, because of its content.

Once we have made such a distinction, we can see how something which could not be in itself justified, for example treating similar cases differently might, perhaps, be justified as the free, autonomous, act of a particular agent. In its content unjustifiable, it may, perhaps, be justifiable because of its source. So someone owed a debt by two, in themselves, exactly similar debtors might, perhaps, be entitled to waive the one and not the other. This is an exercise of whim, of arbitrary caprice; yet we may feel, just as with the betting case, that it is the individual's own loss, hence the individual's own decision. The unfortunate debtor, dunned with the full majesty of the law, can not complain that the creditor who brings the action let the other man off. That is, perhaps, his purely private business; and he need not say more by way of justification.

So we get back to the heart of the question. If individuals, perhaps, may exercise mercy in this way, why may not the state? If one is to be allowed discretion, why not the other? Why may not the state treat two exactly similar criminals differently, letting one off and punishing the other? And would the punished criminal have any more ground for complaint than the dunned debtor?

Obviously any answer to this involves finding some relevant difference between states and individuals. The most obvious one is that individual people can be seen and felt; states cannot. So it might be thought that, in some sense, individuals really exist but states do not; hence we are prepared to grant individuals moral autonomy, permitting them, in some cases, to act irrationally, because they really exist. States, however, which are invisible and do not really exist, may not be granted such rights of individual discretion or decision.

However, this is too simple. On the one hand, something does not just acquire rights or entitlement to moral respect, and hence autonomy, just because it is physical or visible. Stones, dogs, hands are all such; yet at least some of them do not possess rights. The right goes not with the hand, but with the person whose hand it is; which shows that something more is involved than physical flesh. On the other hand, something which is not visible can act and make decisions. It can enter into relations with individuals; hence it can acquire rights, responsibilities, obligations. It can be held liable; it can make contracts. So just because something is invisible does not prevent it having an autonomous power of decision. A state can do all these things. States, and public corporations, have legal rights, relations; they can act and be held liable for their actions. This is because they can act through their agents; particular people's acts become state acts because of these people's special positions, roles, or circumstances.

So if there is a difference between states and individuals, it must lie somewhat deeper than mere visibility, or lack of it. The question is not whether the state can, but about whether the state ought to have a separate area of decision-making, where it can act randomly. It is quite possible for the state to exhibit complete discretion, treating similar cases in radically different ways. For it will do this if its properly appointed agents, acting as agents of the state, do this. The problem is not whether it can but about whether it ought.

My claim is that it should not. Hence I have to find disanalogies with individual people. The chief reason given why individuals might be entitled to make their own decisions was that they carried the risk. But this is not true for states. No actions of states affect just states. They also affect its citizens; hence they are not purely self-regarding; hence every citizen has an interest in what states do. On certain, democratic, theories, this interest will also give them a right. Hence, on these theories, the actions of a state must be justifiable to its citizens; hence the state cannot be allowed pure discretion. Actions will not be good enough just because of their source. They must also be justified in their content. This means that the state is not allowed an area of play lying beyond any possible justification. It is not allowed mercy.

The assumption here is that, in the end, the state exists for the sake of the citizens, not the citizens for the state. This is a combined ontological and moral claim which, no doubt, does have connections with the greater visibility of one of these entities. More centrally, it arises from our particular perspective. We ourselves are citizens, not states. To give other people, other citizens, the right of autonomous decision is to give this right to entities like ourselves. Hence we can understand what the point is; we can see the reason. But to give this right to quite a different sort of entity (Martians; animals; trees) would involve a wholly different exercise of the imagination. We can't imagine what it is like to be a state, and so find it hard to appreciate why states should have autonomy (over and above any advantages this may give to its citizens). Perhaps, in the end, it is mere speciesism to assume that the state exists for us; like the speciesism of assuming that animals or trees exist for us. But, from our perspective, it is an absolutely natural assumption to make.

Once we defend the first two propositions like this, it is obvious which proposition in our original set has to give way. It is the third one, namely that mercy is a desirable property in a state or other authorities over us. Only by forgoing mercy can we enable the state (or other authority) to behave like a fully rational entity, accountable for all its actions to the people over whom it has power. Otherwise we have mere power without accountability.

This may seem to be a highly counter-intuitive result. It is not just in Shakespearian plays that we value mercy. And the connection with the supposed greatest, wisest authority of all, the Christian God, is also important. But for his mercy, no one would be saved; and whether we believe in God or not, the fact that this is the way that the Christian God is conceived should show us, if only as a thought-experiment, the desirability of mercy.

Furthermore, justifications in law tend to start from actuality. A first try at finding out how things ought to be is finding out how they are. And in the present English system there is an exercise of pure executive power, or prerogative, in the judgment and punishment of individual citizens. There is the prerogative of mercy, whereby the Home Secretary can overrule the highest court of the land, that is grant mercy to someone found guilty by it. The actual term of imprisonment served by someone sentenced to life imprisonment may also depend upon mere executive decision. Since such individual discretion exists in the present system, it is natural to think that it would be undesirable to remove it even if it were possible.

Yet if the argument of the first part of this essay is correct, there is no appropriate place for such mercy. Every use of power, of the power of states against citizens, should be subject to review. Review is only possible if it is possible to enquire into, and examine, the reasons for the action. And if the action is done appropriately and correctly for those reasons, then they will also apply in similar cases. In effect a regular procedure will have been instituted by the official from which departures in the name of mercy should not be permitted.

I suppose that the normal defence of the prerogative of mercy is that it allows an amateur, exercising common sense, to protect citizens from the absurdity of law. Hence, to suggest removing the prerogative of mercy may seem like a brutal assault on the security of the citizen. Unless the Home Secretary can defend us, it may be thought, we are at the risk of being abused by the legal system. But, if this is so, our final security rests on the government of men, not of law. It is very doubtful that this is the most reliable defence. Let us test this by taking a famous case where the prerogative of mercy was exercised, Dudley and Stephens (the trial of two shipwrecked sailors who ate the cabin boy).[2] Here it seems the legal establishment of the day were determined to uphold their conviction for murder, in the highest court of appeal, establishing that necessity was not a defence to murder in the English law. They also seemed determined not to execute Dudley and Stephens, once this had been established; so that the Home Secretary granted them what was effectively a pardon. But, in retrospect, it is hard to see the point of this procedure. Either necessity mitigated their offence or it did not. If it did, why was this not discovered or declared at the court which acted as the court of criminal appeal? If it did not, why was the Home Secretary letting them off when other murderers hung? So although the prerogative of mercy is a fact of the present law, more argument is needed to show its justification.

Another fact of present practice, it might be said, is that officials exercise discretion. Discretion neither can nor should be eliminated. However, as administrative law in England has caught up more fully with the power of officials, it has been rediscovered that discretion has been understood in more than one way in the history of English law. Such an august authority as Coke on Littleton said 'for as by the authority of Littleton, *discretio est discernere per legem quid sit justum*, that is to discern by the right line of law, and not by the crooked cord of private opinion, which the vulgar call discretion' (Co. Litt. 227b). I borrow the citation from Professor Wade, who has shown that this is merely one of a long line of judicial opinions with the same message.[3] Discretion is not arbitrary judgment, but, rather, the ability to discern correctly.

Of course, in any system of administration individuals will have to make decisions about individual cases. And this may well take them beyond the scope of rules which could be mechanically checked by a court. But, as will be discussed below, this does not take them beyond

---

[2] For a full description of the Dudley and Stephens case, see A. W. B. Simpson, *Cannibalism and the Common Law* (Chicago, 1984).

[3] H. R. W. Wade, *Administrative Law*, 6th edn. (Oxford, 1988), 396 n.

the scope of rationality (or of true discernment). It does not permit them to act arbitrarily. It would not permit them to take two exactly similar cases and impose a burden in one case and not the other as (arguably) a private citizen may with two exactly similar debtors.

Arguments about the need for a prerogative of mercy, or for arbitrary official discretion, are really often arguments about the need for flexibility. Certainly no legal system should be so rigid that it is forced into doing things which are manifestly and absurdly unjust in particular unforeseen cases. But this is an argument for providing a means for dealing with such cases inside the system, not for reaching outside it to arbitrary judgment. It is an argument for the final courts of appeal to have sufficient confidence on occasion to make the law, and themselves prevent manifest injustice. Take another case where the prerogative of mercy was used (or at least pardon was granted), which Roscoe Pound cites as a leading example of dispensing with a law.[4] Here the offender did something which was only an offence under an Act which he could not have known had been passed, being at sea at the time, and still at sea when the supposed offence was committed. This is the 1800 case of *R.* v. *Richard Bailey* (168 Eng. Rep. 651). Here we may agree that punishment would be unjust. But here again, it seems to me, this is something which the law should be able to decide for itself, without intervention of an extraneous political official. Given the date of this particular case this is in effect what happened. Bailey was formally found to be guilty in the final court of appeal but 'all the judges . . . met . . . and were of the opinion that it would be proper to apply for a pardon' (168 Eng. Rep. 653).

No doubt the central claim of this essay remains counter-intuitive. I shall therefore end by attempting to meet some further objections, or further amplifications of objections already mentioned. It might be objected that my concentration on law and rationality has meant that I have forgotten about equity. Yet, it could be argued, equity has always been brought in to modify the full rigour of the law. The original idea, which goes back at least to Aristotle, is that a general system of law will lead to injustice in particular cases. So there has to be some means of deciding these particular cases in which the full rigour of the law can be suspended so that justice may be done. Hence the development in this country of Equity, or decisions by the Lord Chancellor, alongside law. This, it may be thought, is the appropriate basis of mercy. It is the

---

[4] Roscoe Pound, 'Discretion, Dispensation and Mitigation: The Problem of the Individual Special Case', *New York University Law Review*, 35 (1960), 936.

intervention in particular cases, in the name of justice, to stop mechanical operation of rules of law which would be unjust in the particular case.

It is important to distinguish here between the mechanical operation of rules and the question of justice in the particular case. Obviously a simple or mechanically operated rule may not take appropriate account of the complexity or individuality of a particular case and, if applied, justice would not be done. This is because the case is importantly different from others which are, by contrast, appropriately covered by that rule. So the rule should not be applied in this particular case. But this, it seems to me, is quite different from saying that law should be suspended, or that a mechanism is needed outside the law which can suspend it. If this is the just decision in this particular case, then it will also be so in any exactly similar ones.

Of course, once a case is sufficiently fully described, no exactly similar one may arise. So this is another way in which it may seem that the effects of rationality which I have been stressing may be avoided. Particular cases elude general rules. Every one is idiosyncratic and must therefore be dealt with separately. However, even if every single case has a separate answer, this does not mean that reasons should not be used in reaching these answers. On the contrary. The reasons why a particular case should be treated differently from all others depend upon some property of this case which distinguishes it from all others. If they are bound by some rule and this one is not, this depends upon such a distinguishing property. But this property will also count with similar force in other cases where it applies. So the decision, if correct, should fit in with other decisions. It is not a complete one-off. It fits into a complete structure of rules and reasons, even if it is in itself highly idiosyncratic.

Particular, possibly unique, decisions have to be taken in particular cases. But this does not require purely arbitrary decision. What it requires is the trained application of the reasons of law to individual cases, such as is fostered by the Anglo-American common law tradition. Difficult cases should not be taken outside the law and handed over to political amateurs, in the name of justice. Rather, if justice is to be done, the decision made should be taken for reasons and be rationally defensible. Such a rational defence will include emphasizing all the special features of the particular case. Taken for reasons and rationally defensible, it should therefore be left to the experts in these sorts of reasons. It should be left to lawyers. So, rather than equity interfering with law, equity in its proper sense will be produced by the proper and careful application of case-law. And historically, of course, Equity, which may once have been deciding cases by the length of the Chancellor's nose, is now very much a part of (or very similar in its operations to) Law. In both decisions are bound by precedent.

Some of the objection to the mechanical operation of rules may remind people of Dworkin's attack on law as a system of rules.[5] But notice that Dworkin, of all people, does not think that this means that justice demands that gaps should be inserted in the law, gaps to be filled by mere arbitrary decision. On the contrary, for Dworkin hard cases have right answers. As well as rules there are principles. The perfect, fully trained lawyer, Dworkin's Hercules, can find this answer; and when he does justice will be done. It seems to me that there is nothing in these thoughts of Dworkin's which supports the idea that mercy should be allowed to intrude into the proper place of the law. It is an argument against rules, but it is not an argument against reason. Precisely the contrary. And, as I tried to show in the first part of this essay, it is reason which squeezes out mercy, not rules.

With these distinctions in mind, other objections based on the distinction between general rules and particular cases can be quickly dealt with. It might be said that the important quality needed in order that justice should be done is judgement, which is the correct assessment of the particular case. Whereas the promotion of reason only leads to algorithms, which are purely mechanical means of decision. But this is the same point as the one about the mechanical operation of rules; there is nothing in what I have said which excludes sensitivity to the particular case. Judgement is needed, but the best judgement is informed by, and sensitive to, reason. The best judgement is not just about one case in isolation, but is sensitive to the possible implications of that judgement on other cases.

This is the place, I think, to discuss some decisions of English administrative law which may seem to count against me. Decisions of licensing authorities have been held to be unlawful because of over-rigidity. That is, they have been objected to precisely because they were an attempt to follow rules and act consistently. So this would seem to show that I am wrong, at least if we again take the current law as a guide to how things ought to be. As Jenkins LJ put it in *R.* v.

---

[5] R. Dworkin, *Taking Rights Seriously* (London, 1977).

Flintshire Licensing (*stage plays*) *Committee*, 'the proper course is to consider each case on its merits. It seems to me that it [the objected to decision] wrongly pursues consistency at the expense of the merits of individual cases' ([1957] 1 QB 368). This is quoted with approval by Devlin in *Merchandise transport* ([1962] 2 QB 173 at 193).

These cases reveal differences between administrative and court procedure with respect to the correct use of precedents. Previous decisions of the same body have a greater force in the latter case than the former. But the central issue here is the one discussed already. It is that procedures should be sufficiently flexible to cater for the anomalies of particular cases. What is important in these administrative decisions is that the individual cases have been looked at sufficiently carefully to check whether or not they are similar to the ones already decided. That is, there is nothing wrong with the authority having rules and pursuing consistency providing it always checks in each particular case that the formulated rule really applies. As Professor Wade puts the point, 'it is a fundamental rule for the exercise of discretionary power that discretion must be brought to bear on every case'.[6] Or, as Devlin puts it, a 'tribunal may not . . . make rules which prevent or excuse either itself or the licensing authority from examining each case on its merits' ([1962] 2 QB 173 at 193). But this just takes us back to the objections to the mechanical operations of rules and a lack of sensitivity to the particular; there is nothing here in either the actual administrative law decisions against over-rigidity or their justifications which will form a defence of arbitrary judgement; or of mercy.

The final objection I shall consider comes from outside the law. The basis of all description, and hence of all rules and all use of reasons, is the application of universal terms to particular cases. Hence, philosophical views about such abstract questions as the nature of universals or the nature of meaning can have consequences for the possibility of such descriptions, or reasons. Suppose we take, for example, a Wittgensteinean view of language in which meaning is justified by use and the meaning of general terms cannot be provided by some talisman (some Platonic idea or formula or mental state) which guarantees correctness of application. On this view correctness consists in the actual course of application of words to particular cases. There is nothing beyond the particular applications which guarantees their correctness. On this view of meaning, it might be thought, there

---

[6] Wade, *Administrative Law*, 370.

would be no point talking about the power of description for the law, or about how reason connects particular cases together. All we have are individual applications, not pre-ordained by any talisman, which could go anywhere. In terms of the contrast used in this essay, it would seem that we have got all mercy and no reason. We just judge case by case and that is all.

However, even if we accept Wittgenstein, we still have the idea of following a rule. Wittgenstein's concern is to explain rule-following, not to abolish it. So there are still correct and incorrect uses of terms, and a means of distinguishing between them. This is because the application of terms to particular cases is a public practice. People agree in their applications. Hence we can still distinguish between getting it right and getting it wrong, even if there is nothing outside the actual applications to particular cases guaranteeing their correctness.

One way to illustrate this is by Wittgenstein's example of continuing a series.[7] Once we have a series of numbers, 2, 4, 6, 8, 10 . . ., we think that we can continue it. There is a correct and an incorrect continuation. Yet, for Wittgenstein, this is not provided by some external object (the idea of 'plus two' in my mind; a formula '+ 2'; a Platonic idea of twoness; or whatever). Correctness is, by contrast, constituted by the way that we together continue the series. We agree. And when we get to 1,000 we go 1,002, 1,004, 1,006 . . . However, if a group of people were instead to go 1,004, 1,008, 1,012 . . . it would be for Wittgenstein quite symmetrical: we would each think the other strange, but we could not reach for anything external to show who was right. But in fact such disagreement does not happen. Or so we suppose. Our way is to go 1,002, 1,004, 1,006 . . . And, once we are trained, we continue in our way.

Here we have a view of language which places extreme reliance on particular cases and removes the normal props for meaning. Yet even here we have the idea of correctness and the idea of rules. So even on this extreme view of language, descriptions can be given and reasons provided for judgement. The trained person operates in a certain way. The trained lawyer can apply certain terms, some of them technical, or with special meanings. Other lawyers agree. Hence, with a trained lawyer, these terms can be used to provide reasons. They show how

---

[7] L. Wittgenstein, *Philosophical Investigations*, tr. G. E. M. Anscombe (Oxford, 1953), i. ss. 139–242.

the particular case should be treated. So, even on a Wittgensteinian view of language, the arbitrary is extruded. There are constraints on what may properly be said and done by lawyers. Since the quality of mercy is not (con)strained, there is no space left, even on this radical view of language and meaning, for mercy.

7

Causation outside the Law

PETER LIPTON[1]

INTRODUCTION

In their important book *Causation in the Law*,[2] H. L. A. Hart and Tony Honoré argue that causation in the law is based on causation outside the law, that the causal principles the courts rely on to determine legal responsibility are based on distinctions exercised in ordinary causal judgements. A distinction that particularly concerns them is one that divides factors that are necessary or *sine qua non* for an effect into those that count as causes for purposes of legal responsibility and those that do not. Hart and Honoré claim that this distinction is often one of fact rather than of legal policy, and that the factual basis is to be found in the ordinary distinction we draw between causes and 'mere conditions'. If this claim is correct, we may hope to illuminate the legal distinction by articulating the principles behind the ordinary one. This is a challenging task since, as in the case of most cognitive skills, we are far better at making particular judgements than we are at stating the general principles that underlie them. Hart and Honoré devote the first part of their book to this difficult task.

We have, then, two large projects. One is to articulate our ordinary notion of causation, especially the distinction between cause and mere condition. This is the project of constructing an 'ordinary model'. The other is to argue for what we may call the 'shared concept claim', the claim that the concept of legal cause is based on the ordinary notion of causation, that 'causal judgements, though the law may have to systematize them, are not specifically legal. They appeal to a notion which is part of everyday life.'[3]

[1] I am grateful to Hyman Gross, Ross Harrison, Ingemar Lindahl, David Owens, Nigel Simmonds, and Bobbie Spellman for constructive criticism of an earlier draft of this essay.

[2] H. L. A. Hart and T. Honoré, *Causation in the Law*, 2nd edn. (Oxford, 1985).

[3] Ibid. p. lv. All in-text page references to follow are also to the 2nd edn. of Hart and Honoré, *Causation in the Law*.

This essay will focus on Hart and Honoré's ordinary model, rather than on their shared concept claim. In my judgement, Hart and Honoré's case for some version of the shared concept claim is strong, so they are right to maintain that a better understanding of our ordinary notion of causation will elucidate the legal situation. On the other hand, while their ordinary model has a number of admirable features, it also has several weaknesses that make it unacceptable as it stands. Hart and Honoré's style of presentation also makes it difficult to glean precisely what the content of their model comes to, in part because several of the model's features are not emphasized in their initial analysis of ordinary causal concepts, but only emerge in the subsequent discussion of the roles of causation in the common law. My plan for the following sections of this essay, then, is to present a compact sketch of their model, to canvass some of the difficulties it faces, and then to indicate the form an improved account might take. At the end of this essay, I will also suggest that a better understanding of ordinary causal judgements may have even more to tell us about the nature of causation in the law than Hart and Honoré suggest.

Before turning to the details of their ordinary model, however, I want briefly to consider the evidential relationship between that model and the shared concept claim, in the context of Hart and Honoré's general programme. It is natural enough to suppose that a model of our ordinary causal judgements should serve as a premiss in the argument for the shared concept claim. First we construct a good model of our ordinary notion of causation; then we may embark on the task of showing the extent to which causal judgements in the law fit the model. Hart and Honoré's presentation suggests this strategy. In the first part of their book, they construct an ordinary model; in the second, they try to show that many legal decisions show that courts apply the causal criteria their model describes (cf. p. xxxv).

This way of proceeding is legitimate, but it is an expensive way of justifying the shared concept claim. The main reason for this is the difficulty in constructing an adequate ordinary model, something Hart and Honoré emphasize. They go so far as to claim that the great gap between our ability to discriminate in practice between causes and mere conditions and our ability to explain the principles that guide us in these particular judgements reveals a 'pathological aspect' of both ordinary and legal language (p. xxxiii). As we will see, the battery of distinctions and nuances they find themselves forced to make in order to construct an ordinary model adequate to our actual judgements reveals just how difficult the project is. Our confidence in the correctness of a particular ordinary model should therefore in general be considerably lower than our confidence in the particular judgements the model is supposed to explain.

This suggests that the primary source of evidence for the shared concept claim is not to be found by determining the extent to which particular legal judgments are subsumed by the general principles of an ordinary model, but rather by the more direct route of comparing particular legal judgments with our ordinary causal judgements about the same cases. In other words, the main test of the shared concept claim ought to take the form of asking whether a court's decision to count one factor as a cause and another as mere condition in a particular case coincides with our everyday judgement about these factors. Indeed, I find it difficult to imagine how anyone could read the second part of Hart and Honoré's book without constantly performing thought-experiments of this kind. This procedure may seem disappointingly subjective, but it is no worse than appealing to an ordinary model, since the main evidence for the model can again only be our considered judgements about particular cases.

One of the prescriptive consequences Hart and Honoré draw from the shared concept claim is that the question of whether the harm suffered by a plaintiff was caused by the defendant's act is one that it is suitable to submit to members of a jury to decide by applying their ordinary notion of causation (p. 307). A member of a jury is of course unlikely to be familiar with a philosopher's ordinary model of that notion. What I am suggesting is that we too ought to act as a jury with respect to the shared concept claim, relying primarily on our ability to exercise the ordinary concept of causation rather than on the guidance of a philosophical model of that concept.

This in no way shows the project of constructing an adequate ordinary model to be unimportant, only that its primary role is not to support the shared concept claim. Instead, its main jurisprudential interest appears once we have convinced ourselves that the shared concept claim is sound. At this stage, we may apply an ordinary model to causation in the law, confident that the principles that underlie our ordinary causal judgements will elucidate the role of causation in the law. For this application to be fruitful, however, we need to construct a model that represents accurately our ordinary causal notions.

HART AND HONORÉ'S ORDINARY MODEL

What, according to Hart and Honoré, are the principles that govern our ordinary causal judgements? Their full account is complex and nuanced, but it has a clear core. Leaving aside cases of causal overdetermination (cf. pp. 122–5), where two or more factors are independently sufficient to produce an effect, a cause is a factor *sine qua non*, a factor without which the effect would not have occurred. We do not, however, treat every *sine qua non* as a cause. Some are not part of the causal history of the effect at all. Being coloured, for example, is not a cause of being green. Again, a flash of lightning does not cause the sound of thunder, since both are caused by the electrical discharge (cf. pp. 114–22). The cases that centrally concern Hart and Honoré, however, are factors *sine qua non* that do appear in the causal history of the effect yet are not ordinarily judged to be causes. When a house burns down, the presence of oxygen and the arsonist's lighting of the fire are both factors *sine qua non*, but only the latter would ordinarily be considered a cause of the destruction. Similarly, when a car is involved in an accident which would not have occurred if the engine was not running or if the brakes had not failed, only the brake-failure is a cause of the accident. The oxygen in the one case and the operation of the engine in the other, though both causally relevant, are mere conditions, not causes. Hart and Honoré are centrally concerned, not with the metaphysics of causation, but with a problem of causal selection. How, in ordinary thought, do we select causes from among those factors that are causally relevant? More specifically, the central question is this: what requirements must a *sine qua non* meet to be a cause and not a mere condition?

Hart and Honoré's answer can be resolved into three requirements that a *sine qua non* must meet if it is to count as a cause and not a mere condition. The first is that it must be either a voluntary human act or an abnormal condition, where a condition is abnormal if it is not 'present as part of the usual state or mode of operation of the thing under inquiry' (p. 35). In the examples of the fire and the automobile accident, this act or abnormal requirement correctly entails that the arsonist's act and the brake-failure are both causes, while the oxygen and the running engine are not.

This act or abnormal requirement, however, is still too permissive: not every voluntary act or abnormal condition is treated as a cause. The remaining two requirements are supposed to effect the necessary additional restrictions on the class of factors *sine qua non*. One of these concerns the relativity of causal judgements. When an abnormal situation or event is cited to explain why something happened, what counts as a cause is a highly contextual matter, relative both to the situation of the effect and to the interests of the enquirer. A condition that is normal in one situation may be abnormal in another. Thus the presence of oxygen may explain a fire if the fire takes place in a laboratory environment that was designed to be oxygen-free (p. 35). In cases such as this, the relativity is due to an objective variation in the local normal conditions: the normal environment of a house is different from the normal environment of a certain type of laboratory.

The requirement that a situation or event cited as a cause be abnormal, not simply in general but abnormal in the circumstances of the effect, is not yet an additional requirement for qualification as a cause; it is only a further specification of what is meant by abnormal. But there are also variations in causal judgements about a single case, variations that are due to interest relativity rather than to situation relativity, and this brings in the second requirement. Hart and Honoré illustrate the interest relativity of causal judgements with two examples:

> The cause of a great famine in India may be identified by the Indian peasant as the drought, but the World Food authority may identify the Indian government's failure to build up reserves as the cause and the drought as mere condition. A woman married to a man who suffers from an ulcerated condition of the stomach might identify eating parsnips as the cause of his indigestion: a doctor might identify the ulcerated condition of his stomach as the cause and the meal as a mere occasion. (pp. 35–6)

For the peasant, the government's food policy is part of the normal state of affairs and so a mere condition, whereas the World Food authority treats this as something unusual, since it distinguishes India from most other countries. For the wife, her husband's condition is normal, but eating parsnips is exceptional; for the doctor, the husband's diet is a normal part of most people's lives, while the ulcer is what distinguishes the husband from most people (pp. 36–7). The second requirement then, which we may call the relevance requirement, is that the cause, if it is of the abnormal variety, must also count as abnormal relative to the interest or point of view of the enquirer.

The third requirement for a cause is that the causal connection between the act or abnormal event and the effect not be defeated (Hart and Honoré say 'negatived') by an intervening act or abnormality. Although their precise conditions on defeat are complex, Hart and Honoré give two examples that clarify the process. In the first, an act's claim to be a cause is defeated by a subsequent act: 'A throws a lighted cigarette into the bracken which catches fire. Just as the flames are about to flicker out, B, who is not acting in concert with A, deliberately pours petrol on them. The fire spreads and burns down the forest. A's act, whether or not he intended the forest fire, was not the cause of the fire: B's was' (p. 74). Had A intended to destroy the forest, an act like his would normally be counted a cause of the devastation, but in this example B's subsequent act defeats the causal attribution. In a second example, the defeater is an abnormal coincidence: 'A hits B who falls to the ground stunned and bruised by the blow; at that moment a tree crashes to the ground and kills B. A has certainly caused B's bruises but not his death' (p. 77). A's act may have been both voluntary and a *sine qua non* of B's death, but it is still not a cause.

As a first approximation to this third requirement that a cause not be defeated by subsequent events, we might say that an act or abnormal event is only a cause if there is no subsequent *sine qua non* that is also an act or abnormal event. In other words, we might say that only the act or abnormal event closest to the effect is its cause. As Hart and Honoré show in detail, however, this is too simple, because not all intervening acts or abnormal events defeat. For example, if I leave my car unlocked overnight in New York City, the later act of a thief does not prevent my foolish behaviour from counting as a cause of the loss of the car. Again, to take another of Hart and Honoré's examples, '[I]f [a] defendant lights a fire knowing, through a reliable weather forecast, that an hour later a hurricane will pass through the district, the hurricane, however abnormal, will not negative causal connection between the defendant's act and the damage resulting from the conjunction of the hurricane and the fire' (pp. 170–1).

It is by no means easy to say in general and in detail what differentiates subsequent acts or abnormal events that are defeaters from those that are not. Hart and Honoré devote a great deal of care to this task. Their articulated account of defeaters comes close to the following. First, an act is defeated by a subsequent voluntary act intended to exploit the situation created by the initial act, provided that the original act does not provide an opportunity known to be commonly exploited (cf. p. 136). Secondly, an act or abnormal event is defeated by a subsequent *sine qua non* if the later factor is independent and abnormal or if the conjunction of the earlier and later factors is an unlikely coincidence, so long as the later factor is not foreseen by the agent (cf. pp. 162–3).

For Hart and Honoré, then, a *sine qua non* of an effect is only a cause if it is either a voluntary act or an abnormal event that is both interest-relevant and undefeated. This model brings out important features of our ordinary notion of causation and marks an advance on various earlier views, such as those that identified causes with factors that are initially unknown or that are susceptible to manipulation or control. In ordinary thought we do distinguish factors *sine qua non* that are causes from those that are mere conditions, and voluntary acts and abnormal events often qualify as causes. Moreover, our practice of causal selection is clearly highly sensitive to situation and interest, and the claims of an act or abnormal event to be a cause are often defeated by the sorts of subsequent factors Hart and Honoré flag. Nevertheless, the model does have its liabilities. In the next section, I will sketch what I believe is a better account of the principles that govern our ordinary causal judgements. First, however, we should consider some of the specific difficulties Hart and Honoré's model faces, taking their three requirements in turn.

The obvious weakness of the first requirement is that it rules out normal causes that are not voluntary acts. There are more of these than Hart and Honoré admit. As they rightly observe (pp. 9–10), in ordinary life we often want to know the causes of particular events that are themselves somehow abnormal, in contrast with scientific enquiry, where what are explained are typically general phenomena, and abnormal effects often require abnormal causes. Nevertheless, science has no monopoly on generalities. Many of our mundane beliefs are general judgements about what causes what, and the causes these judgements cite are seldom abnormal. A model of our ordinary notion of causation must allow for the beliefs that fire burns, sunlight warms, water quenches thirst, and innumerable other causal truisms at the heart of our ordinary conception of the world. Moreover, these general causal attributions have specific counterparts. We judge not only that rocks are warmed in the sun, but that this rock was so warmed. If we do not cite causal truisms when asked why an effect occurs, this is not because we deny that these ordinary factors are causes, but because we assume that our interlocutor already knows about them and so must be after additional causal information.

There are many other normal causes that are not voluntary acts, in addition to those cited in causal truisms and their instances. We sometimes cite a normal cause to explain a normal effect of a type that can be produced in a variety of ways. For example, people change jobs to make more money, to have more interesting work, to occupy a position with greater prestige, to live in a more attractive location, and so on. If we ask why Jones switched his job, the cause or causes will be whatever influenced him, however normal such influences may be. Again, it is normal for elderly people to die, and many of them die of pneumonia, but pneumonia may of course still be counted as a cause and explanation of Smith's death. Finally, acts may be causes even when they are neither fully voluntary nor abnormal. If I tell my young son that he dropped his food on the floor because he was not paying attention to the task at hand, I do not imply that this is an unusual state of affairs.

Hart and Honoré's first requirement is thus considerably too restrictive. I turn now to their second requirement, that the abnormality cited as a cause be relevant to the interests of the enquirer. The interest relativity of causal judgements is of central importance, but Hart and Honoré's analysis is not entirely adequate. The cases they discuss under this heading also further undermine the abnormality requirement. In the case of the husband's indigestion, what makes the parsnips or the ulcer explanatory causes is not that these factors are abnormal, since they would be explanatory even if the husband had parsnips with every meal and even if most people had ulcers. Similarly, in the case of the famine in India, both the drought and the failure to build up reserves would explain even if they were both the norm. Interest relativity thus cannot be explained by claiming that different people consider different factors abnormal, so we are left without an adequate account of the mechanism by which a variation in interests yields a variation in causal judgements.

This leaves the third requirement, that the abnormal event or act be undefeated. As we have seen, the main defeaters are coincidences and exploitations. Two difficulties here are that the coincidence condition is too weak, and the exploitation condition too strict. One sort of abnormal factor we would not count as a cause, although it is not defeated by the conditions of the third requirement, is illustrated by an example of irrelevant speeding that Hart and Honoré discuss at some length (pp. xxxviii–xxxix, 121–2). Suppose that Smith drives for a time at abnormally high speed, but then slows down and is later involved in a collision with a lorry at an intersection. In this case, where Smith's speed was normal at the time of the accident, we would not say that the prior speeding was a cause of the accident, any more than we would say this about the subsequent slowing down. Nevertheless, the speeding was a *sine qua non* of the accident since, had Smith not speeded, he would not have reached the intersection at just that unfortunate moment and so the accident would not have occurred. Yet, as Hart and Honoré themselves observe, this sort of factor is not defeated on the central conditions they give, specifically on the grounds of coincidence, since '[t]he difference between such cases of coincidence and the case of speeding is that in the latter it is irrelevant whether the conjunction of events required to bring about the accident is likely or unlikely' (p. xxxix). Irrelevant speeding is not a cause, yet it is a *sine qua non* that may satisfy all three of Hart and Honoré's requirements.

As Hart and Honoré observe (p. xxxix), what matters in the speeding case is not how common accidents are, or indeed how common are accidents with prior speeding, but rather whether the speeding increased the likelihood of the accident. In the example under discussion it did not, and this is why the prior speeding was not a cause. Conversely, in the more usual case where an accident occurs while a driver is speeding and is therefore unable to stop in time to avoid a collision, the speeding is a cause of the accident, even if the conjunction of events required to bring about the accident is unlikely. What counts is whether the accident was more likely with the speeding than it would have been without it. Only some factors *sine qua non* increase the likelihood of their effects. I will eventually argue that this is central to the distinction between causes and mere conditions.

The case of irrelevant speeding shows that the third requirement of Hart and Honoré's model is too liberal, wrongly counting mere conditions as causes. Some cases of exploitation show that it is also too restrictive, excluding genuine causes. Hart and Honoré discuss the following example: 'Defendant negligently left open an unguarded lift shaft; he was not liable to plaintiff when a lad, impersonating the lift operator and knowing the lift was not there, invited plaintiff to step into it, which he did, suffering injuries' (p. 137). According to their model, the lad's exploitation defeats the claim that the defendant's negligence was a cause of the injuries. This, however, seems the wrong result.

Perhaps we would not hold the defendant responsible, from a moral or a legal point of view, for the harm, and we would certainly blame the lad, but we might also say that leaving the shaft open was a cause of the harm. We would be particularly inclined to say this if we knew that the lad was only taking advantage of what was, for him, an irresistible opportunity for mischief, so that he would not have found some other way to harm the defendant had the lift shaft been properly closed off. The general point is that, *pace* Hart and Honoré, uncommon exploitation does not always defeat. Even though the neighbourhood in which I neglected to lock my car is uncommonly safe, if my car gets stolen, my neglect remains a cause of the loss.

In sum, all three of Hart and Honoré's requirements face difficulties. The first, that a cause be an abnormal factor or a voluntary act, wrongly excludes normal causes. The second, that the cause be relevant to the interests of the enquirer, fails to show how interests determine what will count as a cause. The third, that the cause be undefeated, both misclassifies some mere conditions as causes, as in the case of irrelevant speeding, and some causes as mere conditions, as in the case of the lad and lift shaft.

THE LIKELY DIFFERENCE MODEL

I will now sketch an alternative model of our ordinary practice of selecting causes from among factors *sine qua non* and argue that it improves on Hart and Honoré's account. This model is based on two conditions. The first—the increased likelihood condition—is that a cause significantly increases the likelihood of the effect; the second—the difference condition—is that a cause marks a difference between the situation where the effect occurs and a contrasting situation where it does not. These are both conditions Hart and Honoré themselves occasionally invoke, but in my view Hart and Honoré do not sufficiently acknowledge the central role these conditions play in determining our ordinary causal judgements.

The first condition of the likely difference model is that a cause, though it need not make the effect very likely, must significantly increase its likelihood. This condition is satisfied in ordinary cases where we count a *sine qua non* as a cause. If a successful arsonist started a fire in a house, his act significantly increased the likelihood that the house burned down. Similarly, if a house burned down because of faulty wiring, the wiring increased the likelihood of the accident, even if it did not make the fire very likely. Unlike Hart and Honoré's abnormality condition on causes, the increased likelihood condition is also satisfied by normal causes. When the warm weather caused the snow to melt, it of course raised the likelihood of the melting.

At the same time, the increased likelihood condition is not satisfied by every *sine qua non*. The irrelevant speeding case is a particularly clear illustration of the extra restriction that this condition imposes. If the only role of the initial speeding was to ensure that the driver was in the wrong place at the wrong time, we would not ordinarily judge the speeding to be a cause of the accident, even though it is a *sine qua non* of that accident. The reason, as we have seen, is that the speeding did not here significantly increase the likelihood of the accident. Of course speeding does in general make accidents more likely, but it did not do so in this case where the only role of the speeding was to get the driver to a particular point in the road earlier than he otherwise would have reached it, and where the risk of accident at that point is the same at different times (cf. p. xxxix).

It is not easy to say precisely which conditions we treat as given when we evaluate whether a factor significantly increased the likelihood of an effect. After all, if every other logically independent detail were held fixed, the irrelevant speeding would presumably raise the probability of the accident from zero to one. This suggests that we need to analyse the notion of increasing likelihood relative to an incomplete specification of the case at hand. We answer the likelihood question against a limited background, and the background we choose varies from context to context. Leaving situations of foreknowledge aside for the moment, what we usually do, I think, is this. We take the history up to the time of the candidate cause as fixed in all its detail, but then evaluate the increase of likelihood only relative to those independent aspects of the course of events between the candidate cause and the effect that we consider normal. We then ask whether, under these conditions, an effect of the type that occurred was significantly more likely with the candidate cause than without it.

This notion of increasing likelihood asks for further and more precise analysis than I can now provide. In particular, a full account would require a discussion of the way we determine the breadth of the type under which the effect should fall. The irrelevant speeding did not significantly increase the likelihood of an accident of the sort that occurred, yet speeding does increase the likelihood of some sort of accident. Moreover, as we will see in the case of foreknowledge to be discussed below, the parts of the history of an effect that are taken as given relative to judgements of likelihood varies to some extent with the context of enquiry.

Nevertheless, we can already see that the combination of incompleteness and generality in the conditions under which we evaluate likelihood explain how a factor can be a *sine qua non* yet not significantly increase likelihood. This may happen in two ways. The first, illustrated by the case of irrelevant speeding, occurs when an effect of the same type that occurred was just as likely without the candidate cause as it was with it. The second occurs when an independent abnormality intervenes between the candidate cause and the effect and, without the abnormality, the effect was not more likely with the candidate than without it. This is illustrated by many of the cases of defeat Hart and Honoré discuss. If Able knocks Baker to the ground, injuring him only slightly, and then a tree falls on Baker and kills him, Able has not caused Baker's death (p. 77). The falling of the tree was not part of the normal course of events subsequent to the knock and, without the tree, the knock did not significantly increase the likelihood of death, even though it was a *sine qua non* of Baker's death. A factor may be a *sine qua non* of an effect yet not substantially increase the likelihood of the effect because, unlike judgements of likelihood, a judgement whether a factor is a *sine qua non* of an effect prescinds neither from the specificity of the effect nor from any intervening abnormality.

To further articulate and defend the increased likelihood condition, consider some of the peculiarities of defeaters that Hart and Honoré describe. The first concerns a curious asymmetry in the power of an abnormal condition to defeat causal connection. Whether an abnormality defeats causal connection in ordinary thought depends on whether the abnormality occurs before or after the putative cause. Hart and Honoré illustrate this by considering two cases of falling trees:

Suppose plaintiff is run over through defendant's negligence. If on the way to the hospital he is hit by a falling tree, that is a coincidence. If, just previously to being run over, he was hit by a tree and severely injured, that is a circumstance existing at the time of the running over and will not negative causal connection between the running over and the victim's death, even if the victim would not have died from the running down but for the previous blow from the tree. (p. 172)

If the tree fell earlier, the driver killed the defendant, but not if the tree fell later (p. 179). In both common sense and the law, it appears that a subsequent abnormal condition defeats causal connection, but a pre-existing one does not. As Hart and Honoré remark (p. 172), this is an odd contrast. While the causal independence of the running over and the falling tree is clearly relevant and, one would have thought, their relative contribution to the death, the question of which came first seems besides the point.

The increased likelihood condition does, however, reflect and perhaps help to explain this initially odd contrast. It is only in the case where the tree fell first that we judge that the driver's act significantly increased the likelihood of death. This is so because, as I have suggested, the question of whether a factor increased likelihood is answered in a context that takes the entire history of the factor, abnormalities and all, as given, but prescinds from any independent abnormalities in the interval between that factor and the effect. Although we often judge whether an event increased the likelihood of an effect retrospectively, the notion of likelihood that is relevant to judgements of causation is usually an evaluation of how the situation stood at the time the putative cause occurred.

Another important contrast in defeaters that Hart and Honoré discuss and which their model reflects concerns foreknowledge. If someone leaves a small fire unattended, but a hurricane subsequently whips it up into a major conflagration, we would not normally say that the negligence caused the harm. But if the fire-starter left the fire because she knew, through a reliable weather report, of the abnormal winds to come, then her act is a cause (pp. 170–1). Like the asymmetry between earlier and later abnormalities, this is an odd contrast. It seems counter-intuitive to say that knowledge should affect judgements of causation in this way. The question of whether a fire causes a forest to burn down seems independent of the question of what a person happens to know about the weather. If we imagine that two people independently left fires burning, but only one of them knew about the winds to come, it sounds perverse to say that only the knowledgeable one caused the fire.

Nevertheless, I think Hart and Honoré are right about this contrast, and that the increased likelihood condition can be understood to reflect it. As we have seen, the answer to the question of whether a factor *sine qua non* increased the likelihood of an effect depends on what else we hold fixed. The fire substantially increased the likelihood

of the destruction given the winds, but not without them. The winds
are an abnormality that occurred after the fire was negligently left; so,
on the analysis I sketched above, we would ordinarily not include them
in the background against which we judge likelihood. What I want to
suggest now, however, is that we do include an intervening abnormality
in the background when it is foreseen by the actor. Considered simply
as a physical event, we would not say that a small fire, which would
have died out harmlessly without the subsequent abnormal winds,
significantly increased the likelihood of the destruction. Considered as
the act of a person with foreknowledge of the winds to come, however,
we would say that leaving the fire significantly increased the likelihood
of the destruction.

An actor's foreknowledge affects our judgement of likelihood rather
as if it brought the foreseen state of affairs back to the time of act, by
placing the future state into the background against which likelihood is
assessed. Thus the relativity of judgements of likelihood to background
accounts for the sensitivity of causal judgements to foreknowledge.
Moreover, this relativity is, I think, compatible with the confusion we
feel when asked to consider the cases of two fires, one left with
foreknowledge and the other not. When the two cases are placed side
by side, we are pushed to find a common background against which the
likelihood question is to be answered for both, and this makes us want
to say either that both fires were causes or that neither was.

Some readers will find this suggested relativity of judgements of
likelihood as unpalatable as the parallel relativity of our causal
judgements, but it does seem to be a feature of ordinary thought. The
situation is even clearer in cases where foreknowledge is exploited to
bring about an effect. If the fire was not left through negligence, but
with the intent of burning down the forest with the help of the
abnormal winds that were known to be coming, we are even more
strongly inclined to place those winds in the background and to say
that the act significantly increased the likelihood of the subsequent
destruction. Neither the intention nor the foreknowledge affected the
causal story from a physical point of view, but it does affect our
judgement of likelihood and so our judgement of whether the left fire
was a cause or mere condition. What we say is that the actor himself
knew that the fire would significantly increase the likelihood of what
ensued even though, had the small fire been undetected and naturally
caused, we would not say that the fire itself significantly increased the
likelihood of the destruction.

A third contrast concerning defeaters flagged by Hart and Honoré concerns the exploitation of previous negligence. They claim that this sort of exploitation normally defeats causal connection between the negligence and the harm. Thus, to take an example mentioned previously, when a lad causes someone harm by inviting him to enter a lift shaft negligently left unguarded, according to Hart and Honoré the lad's act defeats the claim that the harm was a consequence of the negligence (p. 137). By contrast, if negligence creates an opportunity known to be commonly exploited, the exploitation does not defeat the causal status of the negligence. If I leave my car unlocked in an area where car theft is known to be rife, my negligence is a cause of my loss. Here again, the increased likelihood condition provides a natural account. The negligence is a cause only if it significantly increases the likelihood of the harm. That is why the causal status of negligent acts is defeated by subsequent exploitation in some cases but not in others.

In the case of exploitation of negligence, the contrast that the increased likelihood condition underwrites is not quite the same as the one Hart and Honoré's model describes, but this divergence is to the condition's credit. According to the increased likelihood condition, the exploited negligence can be a cause even if it is not of a type commonly known to be exploited. Negligently leaving the lift shaft unguarded may significantly increase the likelihood of the subsequent harm even if the negligence is not known to lead to harmful exploitation and perhaps even if the risk of such exploitation is not all that great. This seems the right result: if the negligence significantly increased the likelihood, it was a cause. Conversely, if it did not do so, say because the lad was bent on harming the defendant and would almost certainly have found another way of doing so had the dangerous lift shaft not been to hand, then we would not say that the negligence was a cause of the harm.

I have argued that the increased likelihood condition captures much of what Hart and Honoré have to say about the way we ordinarily distinguish causes from mere conditions while avoiding some of the unattractive features of their model. The condition correctly relegates many factors *sine qua non* to the status of mere conditions, while providing a unified treatment of both acts and physical events and allowing for normal causes. It provides a natural account of the distinction between earlier and later abnormalities, and the peculiar influence of foreknowledge and intention on causal attribution. The increased likelihood condition also corrects Hart and Honoré's treatment of the situations under which the exploitation of previous negligence defeats causal connection.

The increased likelihood condition does not, however, completely account for the interest relativity of causal judgements. A particular person may treat only one of two factors as a cause, even though both significantly increased the likelihood of the effect. This is illustrated by the cases of the husband with an ulcer who eats parsnips and suffers indigestion and of the famine in India preceded by both a drought and a failure to maintain reserves of food. One reason both factors in cases such as these may increase likelihood is that we include one factor in the background when we evaluate the other. Thus the ulcer may increase the likelihood of indigestion, given the husband's diet, while the parsnips increase the likelihood given the ulcer. To account for the interest relativity of causation, I turn to the second requirement of my model, the difference condition.

This condition requires that a cause mark a difference between the situation where an effect occurs and a contrasting situation where it does not. The application of the difference condition is easiest to see in cases where causes are cited in explanations that are answers to what may be called contrastive why-questions. In many cases, when we ask why some effect occurred, our question does not take the simple form 'Why this?' Instead, it takes the contrastive form 'Why this *rather than* that?', where the fact to be explained is contrasted with a specific foil. The contrastive fact/foil structure of many why-questions helps to show why some factors *sine qua non* are treated as explanatory causes while others are not. To explain a fact in these cases, it is not enough to cite any causal factor: the cited factor, though it may be normal, must be one that marks a difference because there is no corresponding factor in the history of the foil. To explain why the plants in the front of my house are doing so poorly while the ones in the back are thriving, I cannot cite the fertile soil, if the soil is the same at both places. But the fact that only the plants in the back get steady light will explain this contrast, even though this light is not abnormal. Similarly, if Smith and Jones are both exposed to a disease but only Smith contracts it, the exposure will not explain this contrast. The fact that Smith was not inoculated will explain this, however, so long as Jones was inoculated, no matter how unusual such inoculations are. What counts is that the cause marks a difference between the fact and the foil, not that the cause be abnormal. At the same time, like the abnormality requirement, the difference condition shows why many causally relevant factors *sine qua non* are not ordinarily counted as causes. When we ask why one event occurred rather than another, we are looking for something that marks a difference between them, and many factors *sine qua non* of the first event will not do this.

A why-question does not have to carry an explicit or voiced contrast to be contrastive: the foil or foils may be obvious in the context. If I ask you why you were late for our appointment, I obviously want to know why you were late rather than on time, not why you were late rather than not showing up at all. Sometimes the full set of salient contrast only comes out when a proposed explanation is rejected, and the form this rejection takes confirms the importance of the difference condition. If you ask me why I went out to see *Candide* last night and I reply that I was in the mood for a musical, you may reply: 'Yes, but why did you go to see *Candide* rather than *Anything Goes?*' My original reply is rejected because it does not discriminate between what happened and a contrast that reflects the interests of the enquirer.

The difference condition gives a natural account of the types of relativity of causal judgements that Hart and Honoré discuss. The presence of oxygen does explain the fire in the laboratory, so long as the intended contrast is the absence of fires in oxygen-free laboratories or in the same laboratory at other times when oxygen is absent. In cases of interest relativity, a difference in interest corresponds to a difference in contrasts. The drought explains why the famine occurred this year rather than in other years when there was no drought, whereas the failure to build up food reserves explains why the famine occurred in India rather than in countries that did have such reserves. Again, the eating of parsnips explains why the husband suffered indigestion at some times rather than at others, while the ulcer explains why he suffered while other people do not. Hart and Honoré's abnormality condition does not handle these cases well, because the relativity in explanatory judgements is not due to a variation in judgements about what is normal. The relativity is due rather to a variation in the contrastive questions asked, specifically a variation in the foil. The difference condition accounts for this, since a factor that marks a difference between a fact and one foil will not in general do so when the foil is changed. The ulcer may seem no more normal for the husband's wife than for her doctor, but it still will not explain to her why her husband is sick at some times and not at others.

The difference condition helps to show why we are often so choosy about which factors *sine qua non* to count as causes: when we have a specific foil in mind, most causally relevant factors will not count as explanatory causes, even if they raise the likelihood of the effect, since they do not mark a difference between fact and foil. This selectivity is amplified by the fact that we tend to select foils whose histories are similar to those of the fact to be explained, so that most factors *sine qua non* will be shared and hence not explanatory. For example, we often ask a contrastive why-question precisely because we are puzzled that two apparently similar situations turned out differently. The difference condition also shows why, certain popular theories of explanation notwithstanding, a good explanation need not entail that the effect occurs. A cause that explains does not have to be sufficient for the effect, so long as it is causally relevant and marks a difference between fact and foil.

The second condition of the likely difference model, then, is that a cause must mark a difference between the effect and the contrasting cases. It is interesting to note that Hart and Honoré themselves appeal to something like the difference condition in defence of their basic abnormality requirement. They say that 'to cite factors which are present both in the case of disaster and of normal functioning would explain nothing: such factors do not "make the difference" between disaster and normal functioning' (p. 34), whereas '[w]hat is abnormal . . . "makes the difference" between the accident and things going on as usual' (p. 35). Once we introduce the notion of contrastive questions, however, we see that what makes a difference need not be abnormal, and that we can apply the idea of making a difference to provide an analysis of Hart and Honoré's insight that ordinary causal judgements are sensitive to the interest or point of view of the enquirer.

CONCLUSION

According to the likely difference model, only those factors *sine qua non* that both significantly increase the likelihood of the effect and mark a difference between the effect and salient foils will count as causes in ordinary thought. This model certainly needs more development than I have given it here. Further investigation is sure to reveal counter-examples to the simple formulation I have given and will require a more sophisticated account. There are also a number of issues of principle that demand attention. The difference condition shows how what counts as a cause is sensitive to intended contrasts, but this leaves the question, itself contrastive, of why we select one contrast rather than another in a given context. We also clearly need a fuller analysis of the concept of increasing likelihood. Finally, if we want a general account of causal judgement, we must also consider whether the scope of the likely difference model can be extended to cover situations where, as in cases of overdetermination, causes are not factors *sine qua non.*

Nevertheless, my hope is that this preliminary sketch of the likely difference model is sufficient to show that it improves on Hart and Honoré's account. The likely difference model gives a more unified picture of the way we select causes from factors *sine qua non,* avoiding the unnatural combination of abnormal conditions and voluntary acts, and their complex account of defeaters. The difference condition specifies a mechanism of causal triangulation that explains how variations in interests lead to variation in causes. The increased likelihood condition accounts for the difference that knowledge of a future abnormality makes to its status as a defeater and for the contrast between prior and subsequent abnormalities. Moreover, as we have seen, the model avoids at least three anomalies of the Hart and Honoré account. It leaves room for normal causes that were not voluntary acts. Pollution may be depressingly normal, but it may have significantly increased the likelihood that Smith, who lives in a city, contracted lung disease and may explain why he rather than farmer Jones did so. Second, as illustrated by the case of irrelevant speeding, it shows why an abnormal and undefeated *sine qua non* is not always a cause. Finally, it allows for cases, such as the lad and the lift shaft, where an uncommon exploitation does not defeat causal connection.

The likely difference model also explains why Hart and Honoré's account of our ordinary causal judgements so often gives the correct result in actual legal cases. When we consider the causes of a harm, we are often considering the causes of an effect which is itself abnormal, and abnormal effects generally do have abnormal causes, as Hart and Honoré's account suggests. When we ask why an abnormal event occurred, the natural foil will often be a normal state of affairs, and the factor that marks a difference between these cases will usually itself be a prior abnormality. Again, if the likely difference model is correct, it is hardly surprising that many acts will count as causes. When acts are means to intended results, they typically make the difference between the result occurring and not occurring, and they also substantially increase the likelihood of the result. Many unintended consequences will similarly have been made significantly more likely by the prior act.

Finally, Hart and Honoré's account of defeaters often gives the right result because these intervening factors prevent the candidate cause from significantly increasing the likelihood of the effect.

Hart and Honoré's overarching goal is to use a model of our ordinary causal judgements to elucidate principles of legal responsibility, by means of their shared concept claim that the judgements of causation in the law rest on largely the same basis as ordinary causal judgements. At the start of this essay, I argued that the primary support for the shared concept claim is to be found in the comparison of legal and everyday judgements in particular cases, rather than in the elevated comparison of general models of ordinary and legal causation. Nevertheless, it is worth noting that the likely difference model appears on balance to provide about as much support for the shared concept claim as Hart and Honoré's own account. Although we have found that the two models do give divergent answers in certain cases, on balance it seems that the answers given by the likely difference model are as much in line with judgements of legal cause as those given by Hart and Honoré's model. The case of the lad and the lift shaft does suggest that there may be more instances of ordinary causes that do not correspond to legal responsibility than Hart and Honoré acknowledge. On the other hand, the room the likely difference model leaves for normal causes and the way it excludes factors such as irrelevant speeding may leave even greater overlap between ordinary and legal judgements than there would be if Hart and Honoré's model were correct.

If the shared concept claim is sound, the distinction made by the courts between causes and mere conditions is neither arbitrary nor simply a product of legal policy. This, however, leaves open the important question of the extent to which the distinction is a matter of fact, a question which a good ordinary model ought to help us to answer. Hart and Honoré allow that the distinction between cause and mere condition is less a matter of fact than the distinction between those factors that are a *sine qua non* of an effect and those that are not (cf. pp. 110–11). The likely difference model supports this contrast and can be used to elucidate the non-factual elements. The distinction between causes and mere conditions is interest relative, in the sense specified by the difference condition. Moreover, our judgements of increased likelihood may vary, as we have seen, depending on the background we take as given and on how widely we characterize the type under which the effect falls. None of these three sources of relativity in the mechanism by which we make the distinction between causes and mere conditions appears to be in operation when we decide whether or not a factor is a *sine qua non.*

Both Hart and Honoré's model and my own are concerned with the practice of distinguishing among antecedently known causal factors those that are causes from those that are mere conditions. Both models treat the knowledge that a factor is causally relevant as given. This approach leaves to one side the evidential question of how we go about discovering or inferring what the causal factors or conditions *sine qua non* of an effect are in the first place. I conclude this essay with the suggestion that the features the likely difference model flags as central to the discrimination of causes and mere conditions are also central to the inference of causes from effects.

One account of causal inference that has recently attracted the support of a number of epistemologists and philosophers of science is known as Inference to the Best Explanation.[4] The governing idea of this account is that, while every effect could have had many possible causes, we are warranted in inferring just those that would, if present, provide the best explanation of our evidence. Faced with tracks in the snow of a peculiar shape, I infer that a person on snowshoes has recently passed this way. There are other possibilities, but I make this inference because it provides the best explanation of what I see. Having observed the motion of Uranus, the scientist infers that there is another hitherto unobserved planet with a particular mass and orbit, since that is the best explanation of Uranus's path. Given the data provided by autopsy, the coroner infers that a tap on the head was a cause of death, since that is part of the best explanation of the forensic evidence. To develop this account of inference, we need to say what makes one potential explanation better than another. This is a challenging project, but the features of marking a difference and increasing likelihood play a central role. When we ask a contrastive why-question, the contrast we choose often corresponds to a contrast in our evidence. Thus, if we want to uncover the causes of a famine in India, we may look to a country where there is no famine but which is similar to India in other respects. As we have seen, a good explanation of this contrast will cite some prior difference between India and the other country. My suggestion now is that the search for such explanatory differences is also a technique for discovering causes. The

---

[4] P. Lipton, *Inference to the Best Explanation* (London, 1991).

contrastive evidence of famine in the one country but not in the other supports the hypothesis that a prior difference was a cause. By contrast, it does not provide evidence for the causal role of any common factors, such as that both countries have large peasant populations, even though these shared factors may in fact be causally relevant to the famine.

The increased likelihood condition has a similar evidential role. In the case of irrelevant speeding, the speeding does not explain why the accident occurred, while factors that do increase the likelihood of the accident, such as brake failure or poor visibility, would help to explain it. Here again, a difference between explanatory cause and mere conditions corresponds to the difference between those prior factors the effect evidentially implicates and those it does not. The scene of the accident provides evidence for the presence of conditions that would have increased the likelihood of the accident, but not for factors such as the prior speeding which, though they might have been factors *sine qua non*, did not increase the likelihood of the accident.

The fact that the conditions the likely difference model employs to account for the distinction between causes and mere conditions are also in play when we use effects as evidence for their causes provides, I think, additional support for the model, by providing an independent argument that these conditions have a central role in our cognitive economy. The connections between the ordinary distinction between causes and mere conditions and the principles of causal inference also help to show why the ordinary distinction is neither arbitrary nor unimportant, by showing the role the distinction plays in the objective weighing of evidence. This also suggests a fruitful expansion of the scope of the project of investigating the foundations of our ordinary causal notions in order to cast light on legal matters. The principles of causal inference that the likely difference model reveals are not the exclusive province of ordinary thought. They are also central to scientific enquiry and to causal enquiries in legal contexts. So the model promises to elucidate aspects of legal evidence and inference, as well as of legal responsibility. This strongly supports Hart and Honoré's central contention that the careful investigation of everyday principles of causal judgement is an important source of insight into the application of causal notions in the law.

8

Fairness, Truth, and Silence: The Criminal Trial and the Judge's Exclusionary Discretion

T. R. S. ALLAN

In the leading case on the nature and extent of the judge's exclusionary discretion in the criminal trial,[1] Lord Scarman distinguished two faces of the common law. Its first, and sterner, face was that, generally speaking, all relevant evidence was admissible, however obtained. As Crompton J had brusquely asserted, 'It matters not how you get it; if you steal it even, it would be admissible.'[2] The second, and merciful, face of the law was the judge's discretion to exclude admissible evidence if the strict application of the law would operate unfairly against the accused. It is a familiar feature of the law of evidence in criminal cases that the effect of the rules may be adjusted in fairness to the defendant, although the scope of judicial discretion in that regard is deeply controversial.

In the broader context of the Rule of Law, J. R. Lucas has distinguished helpfully between the ideals of Legality and Equity.[3] A decision in accord with Legality is purely deductive, based on a finite number of features antecedently specified as relevant. It has the merits of certainty and predictability. Legality is not, however, to be equated with the Rule of Law: it is not identical with rationality, and is less just than Equity. Equity is more truly rational: it attempts to reach the right decision in all the circumstances, leaving the judge with wide discretion, subject only to treating like cases alike. Common law

---

[1] *Sang* [1980] AC 402. The parallel statutory discretion, under the Police and Crim. Evid. Act 1984, s. 78, will be mentioned below.

[2] *Leatham* (1861) 8 Cox CC 498, 501.

[3] J. R. Lucas, *The Principles of Politics* (Oxford, 1966), 133–5. See also id., *On Justice* (Oxford, 1980), 76–9.

adjudication, Lucas suggests, is characteristic of Equity—involving a limited number of persons, but an indefinite number of possibly relevant factors, justification for those selected being given *ex post facto*.

In the present context, the dichotomy between the rules of admissibility and the exclusionary discretion clearly corresponds to an analogous distinction between these ideals—within the framework of common law adjudication itself. The rules governing admissibility of evidence (both statutory and common law) may be viewed as constituting Legality. The discretion to exclude admissible evidence on grounds of fairness (under statute or at common law) cuts across these rules in the name of Equity: it permits a deliberate departure from Legality in pursuit of justice on the facts of particular cases.

I shall attempt, in this essay, to explore the connection between Legality and Equity in respect of evidence in criminal cases. I hope thereby to cast more light on the character of the judge's exclusionary discretion, and the part played in its exercise by the privilege against self-incrimination, or right of silence. I shall not resist the temptation, however, to offer more general reflections on the connections between Legality and Equity, and between law and morality, in the context of the criminal trial.

THE EXCLUSIONARY DISCRETION

The House of Lords, in *Sang*,[4] took a superficially restrictive view of the scope of the judge's discretion to exclude admissible evidence. Viscount Dilhorne expressly repudiated the claim, made by Lord Widgery CJ in a previous case,[5] that the discretion existed in respect of evidence obtained by trickery, deceit, unfair or oppressive conduct, or otherwise in a morally reprehensible manner. The court held that the judge was concerned, not with the way in which the evidence for the prosecution had been obtained, but rather with its use at the trial. None the less, the significance of the propriety of police methods could hardly be entirely denied. First, an exclusionary discretion was well established in respect of unfairly obtained confessions, even where, being 'voluntary', they were legally admissible. Secondly, Lord Diplock explained that earlier authority favouring a wider discretion, encompassing 'real' (non-confession) evidence, was based on the maxim *nemo debet prodere se ipsum*. There was an analogy with

---

[4] [1980] AC 402.   [5] *Jeffrey* v. *Black* [1978] QB 490.

confessions. The exclusionary discretion extended to 'evidence tantamount to a self-incriminatory admission which was obtained from the defendant, after the offence had been committed, by means which would justify a judge in excluding an actual confession which had the like self-incriminating effect'.[6] A defendant who was unfairly induced to provide an incriminating document, or submit to a medical examination, therefore came within the court's protection. The privilege against self-incrimination could be seen to provide the key to the nature and scope of the exclusionary discretion.

The underlying rationale of this branch of the criminal law, though it may originally have been based on ensuring the reliability of confessions is . . . now to be found in the maxim, *nemo debet prodere se ipsum*, no one can be required to be his own betrayer, or in its popular English mistranslation 'the right to silence'. That is why there is no discretion to exclude evidence discovered as the result of an illegal search but there is discretion to exclude evidence which the accused has been induced to produce voluntarily if the method of inducement was unfair.[7]

The value of the protection afforded the defendant by his privilege against self-incrimination has been much debated. It is not universally revered.[8] Its presence—for better or worse—as a major strand within the broader principle of fairness, as interpreted by English law, is none the less indisputable. It has been called 'a maxim of our law as settled, as important and as wise as almost any other in it'.[9] Once extended beyond oral and written confessions, strictly understood, however, it resists the straitjacket which Lord Diplock's analysis attempts to provide. In particular, his requirement of voluntary co-operation on the part of the defendant is hard to accept. It produces the strange result that the judge may exclude evidence of a medical examination to which the defendant was tricked into submitting; whereas evidence of an examination which he was unlawfully ordered to undergo must be admitted.[10] If it can plausibly be argued that the former is a case of breach of the privilege, and the latter not, the privilege begins to seem arbitrary. How can it be thought less *unfair* unlawfully to compel the accused to provide evidence against himself than to induce him to

---

[6] [1980] AC 402, 436.   [7] Ibid.

[8] See e.g. Adrian Zuckerman, 'The Right against Self-Incrimination: An Obstacle to the Supervision of Interrogation', *Law Quarterly Review*, 102 (1986), 43; Michael Menlowe, 'Bentham, Self-Incrimination and the Law of Evidence', *Law Quarterly Review*, 104 (1988), 286.

[9] *Scott* (1856) Dears & B. 47, 61 (COLERIDGE J).

[10] Cf. *Payne* [1963] 1 WLR 637 and *Apicella* (1985) 82 Cr. App. R. 295.

furnish evidence by means of inducements or deceit? Where the suspect mistakenly thinks himself bound to comply with a *request* for evidence, any distinction between induced co-operation and compulsion seems to collapse. In the High Court of Justiciary, Lord Cooper once held that evidence of fingernail scrapings had been wrongly admitted: there had been no use of force, but consent was of no avail unless given after fair intimation that it might be withheld.[11]

The privilege against self-incrimination entitles the suspect to resist interrogation: the police (or prosecution) have no right that he should speak. Any confession he makes may nevertheless be received in evidence on the ground that, by speaking, the defendant has waived his privilege of silence. There cannot be a true waiver, however, unless a confession meets the traditional standard of being 'perfectly voluntary'.[12] 'Voluntariness', despite much technicality, described the conditions under which an admission or confession could be fairly understood as a waiver of the defendant's privilege, exercised free from deception or pressure.

a confession will be rejected if it appear to have been extracted by the presumed pressure and obligation of an oath, or by pestering interrogatories, or if it have been made by the party to rid himself of importunity, or if, by subtle and ensnaring questions, as those which are framed so as to conceal their drift and object, he has been taken at a disadvantage, and thus entrapped into a statement which, if left to himself, and in the full freedom of volition, he would not have made.[13]

A trick violates the defendant's privilege since it provokes a waiver which cannot fairly be described as voluntary. The clearest example of an involuntary confession, however—and the plainest violation of the defendant's privilege against self-incrimination—is one obtained by torture or violence or oppression. When the privilege is extended to encompass evidence *analogous* to confessions, it must follow that, if obtained by similar means, its admission would equally violate the precept *nemo debet prodere se ipsum.* There is as strong an analogy between real evidence secured by force or oppression and a confession likewise obtained as there is between real and confessional evidence secured by inducements or threats falling short of oppression. And

---

[11] *McGovern* v. *HM Advocate,* 1950 SLT 133. Cf. *Callis* v. *Gunn* [1964] 1 QB 494.

[12] *Baldry* (1852) 2 Den. 430, 445. The common law rule operates to exclude 'statements that are not the outcome of an accused person's free choice to speak'. *McDermott* (1948) 76 CLR 501, 512 (DIXON J).

[13] *Johnston* (1864) Ir. CL 60, 83–4 (HAYES J).

evidence obtained by oppression is, quintessentially, evidence obtained without the voluntary co-operation of the accused: it 'imports something which tends to sap, and has sapped, that free will which must exist before a confession is voluntary'.[14]

If, therefore, we accept Lord Diplock's persuasive analogy with the right of silence in respect of all evidence obtained from the defendant, it seems that we can consistently do so only by rejecting his condition of voluntary co-operation. To the contrary, evidence involuntarily obtained—whether by deceit or guile or simple coercion—would fall naturally within the ambit of the exclusionary discretion. We are, it seems, driven to accept something like the principle of Scots law, in which 'irregularities require to be excused, and infringements of the formalities of the law ... are not lightly to be condoned.'[15] The court is unlikely to be able to resist some scrutiny of police procedures, or to decide their effect on the trial by invoking predetermined and arbitrary rules. The discretion cannot be so easily confined:

Whether any given irregularity ought to be excused depends upon the nature of the irregularity and the circumstances under which it was committed. In particular, the case may bring into play the discretionary principle of fairness to the accused which has been developed so fully in our law in relation to the admission in evidence of confessions or admissions by a person suspected or charged with a crime.[16]

THE PRINCIPLE OF FAIRNESS

Much discussion of the fairness principle has been bedevilled by an attempt to distinguish between the trial and pre-trial proceedings—as though the gravest improprieties in the course of preparation of the prosecution case might be succeeded by an impeccably fair trial. The distinction is mistaken, and the associated notion of fairness fundamentally flawed. Conflicting perceptions of procedural fairness gave rise, in *Sang*, to a diversity of judicial opinion regarding the scope of the exclusionary discretion. There was unanimous emphasis on the judge's primary concern with the use of evidence at the trial. Lord

---

[14] *Priestly* (1965) 51 Cr. App. R. 1 (SACHS J).

[15] *Lawrie* v. *Muir*, 1950 SLT 37, 40 (LORD JUSTICE-GENERAL COOPER).

[16] Ibid. Although the Scottish cases envisage an *inclusionary* discretion, it was suggested in *King* [1969] 1 AC 304, 315, that 'the same end is reached in both jurisdictions though by a slightly different route.' For similar criticism of the reasoning in *Sang*, see P. G. Polyviou, 'Illegally Obtained Evidence and *R. v. Sang*', in C. F. H. Tapper (ed.), *Crime, Proof and Punishment* (London, 1981), 226.

Diplock's speech reflected that unanimity in asserting that it was 'no part of a judge's function to exercise disciplinary powers over the police or prosecution as respects the way in which evidence to be used at the trial is obtained by them'.[17] But this agreement could scarcely conceal an underlying divergence of views about the extent to which the 'pedigree' of evidence affected the justice of the trial. Lord Scarman's speech neatly captured the crucial ambiguity:

Each case must, of course, depend on its circumstances. All I would say is that the principle of fairness, *though concerned exclusively with the use of evidence at trial*, is not susceptible to categorisation or classification, and is *wide enough in some circumstances to embrace the way in which, after the crime, evidence has been obtained from the accused.*[18]

There is sometimes said to be a right to a fair trial in the sense that there is a right not to be wrongly convicted.[19] It may be said in its defence that there is a special moral harm done to the individual in such circumstances, over and above any punishment officially inflicted.[20] This does not, however, exhaust the sense in which common law grants the defendant a fair trial. Fairness of course includes, as a major component, the adoption of procedural conditions designed to secure an accurate assessment of guilt or innocence. But the governing idea is not satisfied by punctilious adherence to Bentham's principle of 'rectitude'.[21] The common law embraces a wider conception of fairness or justice, which imposes constraints on the way in which the defendant may be treated by the criminal justice process. No lawyer doubts, for example, that the judge's duty to ensure a fair trial extends beyond his concern with the quality of the evidence. His exclusionary discretion is not restricted to the rejection of evidence whose probative force is outweighed by its likely prejudicial effect on the jury. There has long been recognized the power to exclude a wholly reliable confession on the ground that it was unfairly obtained. If there is a special moral harm involved in the (mistaken) conviction of the innocent, it must stem from the defendant's dignity and autonomy as a moral agent. Unjustified conviction, and unmerited punishment, denies that status, violating the integrity of his relations with the state

[17] [1980] AC 402, 436.
[18] Ibid. 456–7 (emphasis mine).
[19] See e.g. D. J. Galligan, 'The Right to Silence Reconsidered', *Current Legal Problems*, 41 (1988), 69; Adrian Zuckerman, 'The Right against Self-Incrimination'.
[20] Ronald Dworkin, *A Matter of Principle* (Oxford, 1986), 79–84.
[21] See Michael Menlowe, 'Bentham, Self-Incrimination' (n. 8 above).

and with his community. That same moral status—entailing a sense of the respect due to someone in virtue of his humanity and his membership of the community—generates ideas about how he should be treated by those in authority. It is for similar reasons, Lucas suggests, that a judge, before sentencing a convicted prisoner, asks him if he has anything to say; 'for even a convicted prisoner, although altogether subject to the coercive power of the State, is still a human being, not a sack of potatoes.'[22] There are standards of justice and fairness which are thought to regulate the relations between the offender and the state, and which are quite independent of the issue of guilt or innocence.

In the present context, any sharp division between trial and pre-trial procedures seems artificial and morally arbitrary. The fairness of the trial must be determined in the wider setting of the criminal justice process. There is no valid sense of 'fair trial' which exists in abstraction from the process of collection of evidence and preparation of charges. A 'fair trial' on the basis of evidence forced from the accused under torture, or obtained by wholesale seizure of his personal papers and effects, without legal authority, is—in the underlying common law conception—simply a contradiction in terms. His guilt may be established beyond reasonable doubt, but he has not been fairly tried. His dignity and autonomy have been blatantly flouted: he has been treated not as an end in himself, as his moral status would require, but rather solely as a means to society's ends in curbing and punishing crime. The Police and Criminal Evidence Act 1984 encapsulates this interdependence of propriety and fairness: section 78 permits the exclusion of evidence where it appears that, 'having regard to all the circumstances, including the circumstances in which the evidence was obtained', its admission 'would have such an adverse effect on the fairness of the proceedings that the court ought not to admit it.'[23]

Although an important goal, truth is not the only value which the system of criminal justice serves. The interests of truth or accuracy march hand in hand with those of justice, in the wider sense of fairness; and though these values are often in harmony, they will sometimes conflict. The rejection of incriminating statements obtained under pressure, or in response to inducements, may serve equally the goals of truth and justice. In other cases, reliable confessions may be

---

[22] Lucas, *Principles of Politics*, 132–3.
[23] S. 82 preserves the exclusionary discretion at common law. The precise relationship between the two discretions remains obscure.

excluded in deference to justice or fairness. The clearest example is the rejection of improperly obtained confessions, when their reliability is established by the consequent discovery of incriminating real evidence: the discovery of the stolen goods, made in the light of the confession, is admitted, but the confession itself (and perhaps therewith all connection with the defendant) excluded.[24] And, no doubt, the discovery itself might be excluded in the judge's discretion if fairness sufficiently required it.[25] Indeed, it is sometimes difficult to distinguish fairly between confession and subsequent discovery, whatever the cogency of the latter may be. The High Court of Justiciary once held it wrong to admit evidence that, following an inadmissible confession, the accused had pointed out the purse of a murder victim in a cornfield on the ground that it was 'part and parcel of the same transaction as the interrogation'.[26]

The right to a fair trial, the fundamental right secured by the system of criminal justice, amounts to the right to be treated in a way which properly reflects these different criteria. It is a right to the appropriate mix of truth and justice: the rules of evidence designed to secure a reliable verdict are qualified in deference to the accused's right to be treated with respect and dignity. Morality and history combine to fix the appropriate balance between the claims of justice and truth. Lord Wilberforce drew similar conclusions, based on the adversarial nature of common law adjudication, in respect of the rules of discovery of documents in civil proceedings. The plaintiffs were prima facie entitled to the disclosure of documents 'necessary . . . for disposing fairly of the cause'.[27] There were, however, limits to the court's powers to compel such disclosure. 'In a contest purely between one litigant and another . . . the task of the court is to do, and be seen to be doing, justice between the parties—a duty reflected by the word "fairly" in the rule. There is no higher or additional duty to ascertain some independent truth.'[28]

Properly understood, the exclusionary discretion exists to safeguard the integrity of our system of criminal justice. It is in that broad sense that it serves to secure the defendant a fair trial. Fairness demands that the adversarial nature of the criminal trial be protected from abuse;

---

[24] Police and Crim. Evid. Act 1984, s. 76 (4), (5); *Warwickshall* (1783) 1 Leach 263.
[25] Cf. A. Gotlieb, 'Confirmation by Subsequent Facts,' *Law Quarterly Review*, 72 (1956), 231.
[26] *Chalmers* v. *HM Advocate* 1954 JC 66, 76.   [27] RSC, Ord. 24, r. 13.
[28] *Air Canada* v. *Secretary of State for Trade* [1983] 2 AC 394, 438.

and the defendant's privilege against self-incrimination is a well-established feature of our adversary procedure. The United States Supreme Court called it 'the essential mainstay of our adversary system'.[29] The accused's right of silence has hitherto applied equally before as during the trial.[30] There is (generally) no compulsory procedure for discovery. The Crown may seek to obtain incriminating evidence from his lips, his person, and his premises only in strict compliance with legal rules and standards. Where evidence is obtained in breach of those standards, the adversary process is undermined. The trial itself is simply the consummation of a process of investigation and interrogation, whose integrity is flouted if police or prosecution are allowed to cheat to the defendant's disadvantage.[31]

Lord Scarman succinctly summarized this broader conception of the right to a fair trial:

What does 'fair' mean in this context? It relates to the process of trial. No man is to be compelled to incriminate himself: *nemo tenetur se ipsum prodere.* No man is to be convicted save on the probative effect of legally admissible evidence. No admission or confession is to be received in evidence unless voluntary. If legally admissible evidence be tendered which endangers these principles . . . the judge may exercise his discretion to exclude it, thus ensuring that the accused has the benefit of principles which exist in the law to secure him a fair trial; but he has no power to exclude admissible evidence of the commission of a crime, unless in his judgement these principles are endangered.[32]

The dependence of fairness on the nature of the adversary process, viewed as a whole, is illuminated by Brennan J's dissenting judgment in *Baker* v. *Campbell*.[33] The majority of the High Court of Australia held that documents to which legal professional privilege attached could not lawfully be made the subject of a search warrant issued under s. 10 (*b*) of the Crimes Act 1914. Although Brennan J dissented on the issue of construction, he held that the scope of permissible

---

[29] *Miranda* v. *Arizona* 384 US 436, 460 (1966).

[30] Judicial comment may sometimes be made, however, on the defendant's failure to testify; and the law seems likely to be amended to permit adverse inferences to be drawn from silence before trial, in certain cases, as was recommended by the Criminal Law Revision Committee (*11th Report* (1972), Cmnd. 4991). Adverse inferences may sometimes be drawn already from failure to provide evidence: see e.g. *Smith* (1985) 81 Cr. App. R. 286; Police and Crim. Evid. Act 1984, s. 62.

[31] Cf. A. J. Ashworth, 'Excluding Evidence as Protecting Rights' [1977] Crim. LR 723, 725. (It is doubtful, however, whether the fairness principle protects more concrete rights in quite the way Ashworth envisages.)

[32] [1980] AC 402, 455.   [33] (1983) 49 ALR 385, 418.

seizure was none the less limited ·by the requirement of reasonable grounds for belief that material seized 'will afford evidence' of the commission of an offence. He considered that documents which were brought into existence by or on behalf of a litigant, for the sole purpose of use in legal proceedings, would not be received as evidence of the commission of an offence. Their reception would deny the accused a fair trial.

That conclusion was surely correct. The defendant's entitlement to legal advice is an important adjunct of his privilege against self-incrimination, ensuring that any waiver is freely made with full understanding: 'voluntarily, knowingly and intelligently'.[34] It is said to be one of the primary objects of legal privilege that the defendant should be encouraged to speak freely to his lawyer.[35] If, then, his confidential communications are subsequently admitted in evidence, the state takes unfair advantage of him: the inducement to frankness constitutes a trap. Whatever the rule of admissibility in such circumstances, as a matter of strict Legality—and the authorities conflict—Equity surely demands a firm response. The interests of justice compel an exercise of the exclusionary discretion in the defendant's favour: reception of such documents would constitute an abuse of the legal process, undermining the integrity of the trial. As Brennan J stated the point: 'Even if the prosecution were authorised to gain custody of documents which had come into existence "merely as the materials for the brief", a court before which such documents might be tendered in evidence would be bound to reject them lest its own adversary procedures be subverted.'[36] The judge suggests here that the evidence is rejected on the grounds of the public interest in protection of the court's procedure, rather than in deference to the litigant's interests. But it seems plain, on closer inspection, that this separation of public and private interests is quite artificial. Integrity and fairness are interdependent and at one:

The purpose of the privilege is the facilitation of access to legal advice, the inducement to candour in statements prepared for the purposes of litigation,

---

[34] Cf. *Miranda* v. *Arizona* 384 US 436, 444, 469 (1966).

[35] *Waugh* v. *British Railways Board* [1980] AC 521, 531; *Grant* v. *Downs* (1976) 136 CLR 674, 685.

[36] (1983) 49 ALR 385, 427–8 (GIBBS CJ and MASON J, who also held that privileged documents could lawfully be seized, expressly reserved the question whether the power extended to documents brought into existence for the purpose of obtaining legal assistance and representation at a pending criminal trial).

and the maintenance of the curial procedure for the determination of justiciable controversies—the procedure of adversary litigation . . . If the prosecution, authorised to search for privileged documents, were able to open up the accused's brief while its own stayed tightly tied, a fair trial could hardly be obtained; in a criminal trial, to give the prosecution such a right would virtually eliminate the right to silence.[37]

The right of silence is sometimes defended on the ground of privacy, which in turn protects personal identity and autonomy. The imposition of a duty on the suspect to explain and justify his actions or intentions would strike unacceptably at the core of privacy fundamental to individual personality.[38] The argument suggests an underlying rationale common to the right of silence and, more generally, to the privilege against self-incrimination. It equally suggests a common foundation with rules limiting the scope of permissible seizure of real evidence from the defendant's premises. The United States Supreme Court has made that connection, linking the Fourth and Fifth Amendments. The right to a fair trial included 'the right not to be convicted by use of a coerced confession, however logically relevant it be, and without regard to its reliability';[39] and the same principle applied to what was 'tantamount to coerced testimony by way of unconstitutional seizure of goods, papers, effects, documents, etc.'

We find that, as to the Federal Government, the Fourth and Fifth Amendments and, as to the States, the freedom from unconscionable invasions of privacy and the freedom from convictions based on coerced confessions do enjoy an 'intimate relation' . . . They express 'supplementing phases of the same constitutional purpose—to maintain inviolate large areas of personal privacy'.[40]

The value of privacy fails, however, to provide a convincing justification of the right of silence in English law. The logic of the Supreme Court's reasoning led to its adoption of an exclusionary rule: the protection of privacy demanded the rejection of all evidence obtained in breach of the Fourth Amendment. Although English law refuses to admit an involuntary confession, or one which fails to meet the present statutory conditions,[41] it fails to acknowledge a similar rule

---

[37] Ibid.

[38] See e.g. Galligan, 'Right to Silence' (n. 19 above).

[39] *Mapp* v. *Ohio* 367 US 643, 656 (1961).

[40] Ibid. 656–7, citing *Bram* v. *US* 168 US 532, 543, 544 (1897); *Feldman* v. *US* 322 US 487, 489, 490 (1944).

[41] Police and Crim. Evid. Act 1984, ss. 76, 77.

excluding unfairly obtained real evidence. The privilege against self-incrimination is protected only by an exclusionary discretion. It is true that *Sang* recognized the analogy with confessions, and it may be argued that that analogy properly extends as far as evidence improperly seized from the defendant's premises, as well as his person. None the less, an exclusionary discretion whose exercise depends on all the circumstances of the particular case seems a poor instrument for protecting privacy. The common law, in its British instantiation, accepts that the legitimacy of police methods may depend on the offence in question. There are no universal barriers erected against invasions of privacy: 'The position of the accused, the nature of the investigation, and the gravity or otherwise of the suspected offence, may all be relevant.'[42]

Nor may the privacy rationale be saved by confining it to confessions. As we have seen, the fairness principle readily encompasses real evidence, obtained from the defendant, and cannot naturally be restricted to incriminating statements alone. The Supreme Court had itself been 'unable to perceive that the seizure of a man's private papers and books to be used in evidence against him is substantially different from compelling him to be a witness against himself'.[43] Even if fingerprints and bodily samples, on the one hand, could in theory be sharply distinguished from incriminating statements, on the other, that is not the theory of the common law. The exclusionary discretion applies the principle of fairness selectively to both.

If, as it seems, the courts have firmly denied any disciplinary basis for excluding relevant evidence, an approach based generally on protecting ordinary civil rights seems a doubtful substitute. It fails to explain, in particular, why evidence obtained by trickery (when the confessions analogy applies most readily) is sometimes rejected, while the fruits of unlawful searches and seizures (however personal or intimate) have generally been received. And if the law is protecting such rights, they are the rights of the guilty alone. The rights of an innocent suspect may be violated by unlawful police methods, but it is usually the guilty who are caught by stratagems of deceit or guile. For example, in Barker[44]—where the Court of Criminal Appeal held that

---

[42] *Murphy* [1965] NI 138, 149 (LORD MACDERMOTT).

[43] 367 US 643, 662 (1961) (BLACK J, citing *Boyd* v. *US* 116 US 616, 633).

[44] [1941] 2 KB 381. See JTC, 'Evidence Obtained by Means Considered Irregular' *Jur. Rev.* (1969), 55.

evidence of tax fraud, provided by the defendant in response to an implied promise of immunity from prosecution, was wrongly admitted—the defendant's guilt was plainly an essential constituent of the trick. The ordinary civil rights of both innocent and guilty enjoy other means of protection; and the advantage which the exclusion of evidence affords the guilty must be defended independently.

The guilty defendant is as much entitled to a *fair trial*, however, as the innocent. The principle of fairness requires that the adversarial procedure of the criminal trial, including therein the pre-trial processes of investigation and interrogation, is not tipped too far to the defendant's disadvantage. It affords only weak, and incidental, protection for his rights to liberty, property, or privacy. A wrongful arrest or illegal search cannot be cured by excluding their fruits from the subsequent trial. If, however, the right of silence, suitably extended, assists in maintaining an equitable balance between suspect and state, the exclusion of evidence becomes an appropriate remedy. *Unfairness* lies precisely in the reception of evidence obtained in breach of the precept *nemo debet prodere se ipsum*, broadly interpreted. This is the sense in which police misconduct or impropriety may undermine the fairness of the trial. It is a mistake to think that the right to a fair trial collapses into a set of more specific rights (though it includes the privilege against self-incrimination, narrowly understood). It is essentially irreducible—confronting the detailed circumstances of a particular case in all their moral complexity.

However, the integrity of the trial is not endangered by the admission of evidence resulting from every minor irregularity: technical or trivial illegalities committed by zealous officers acting in good faith can sometimes be excused. It does not follow from the courts' repudiation of the 'disciplinary' basis of exclusion that the deliberateness of any impropriety becomes irrelevant. Even on a 'protective' basis—protecting rights—it remains a significant feature of the moral context.[45] Deliberate disregard of settled rules and standards does special injury to the integrity of the trial; and evidence may be excluded accordingly. It is a matter of equitable balance; and the discretion serves in place of an exclusionary rule to permit calculations of degree. 'Fairness does not require such a rule and common sense rejects it.'[46]

---

[45] *Pace* Ashworth, 'Excluding Evidence' (n. 31 above), 730–1.
[46] *People* v. *O'Brien* [1965] IR 142, 159–60.

LEGALITY AND EQUITY AND THE UNITY OF LAW AND MORALITY

Lord Scarman, in the passage already cited from *Sang*, attempted to provide guiding principles for the interpretation of the broader principle of fairness. While accepting Lord MacDermott's view that unfairness could not be closely defined,[47] he was naturally unwilling to leave the matter entirely at large. 'One must,' he considered, 'emerge from that last refuge of legal thought—that each case depends on its facts—and attempt some analysis of principle.'[48] It is an interesting question how far the trial judge may properly be denied that refuge. Justice may sometimes be denied the litigant if freedom to meet the moral complexity of the particular case is denied the judge. Those of their Lordships in *Sang* who embraced Lord Widgery's dictum, favouring an open-ended judicial discretion, were surely wiser than their brethren who repudiated it. If the claims of Legality and Equity stand in perpetual opposition, it is hard to resist the conclusion that the latter must ultimately prevail. And notwithstanding the great authority of the House of Lords, it is reasonable to suppose that the claims of fairness must sometimes deny the suggested limits of the exclusionary discretion.

Two principal limits were proposed. First, the fairness principle applied only to evidence obtained from the accused himself (possibly including his premises). Lord Fraser thought it hard 'to see how evidence obtained from other sources, even if the means for obtaining it were improper, could lead to the accused being denied a fair trial'.[49] Secondly, the principle extended only to evidence obtained after commission of the offence: a wider discretion would undermine the substantive law, which does not recognize entrapment as a defence to a criminal charge. It is not difficult to see how the more fundamental moral principle could challenge these constraints in particular cases. Are there no possible circumstances in which the use of 'third-degree' methods against third parties could be held to undermine the fairness of the defendant's trial—perhaps against a close friend or member of his family? And could no case of entrapment, however morally repugnant, ever justify the rejection of evidence against the accused—where the judge could receive it only at the price of undermining the integrity of the trial?

---

[47] See n. 42 above.　　　[48] [1980] AC 402, 452.　　　[49] Ibid. 450.

It is only necessary to put the questions to demonstrate the vulnerability of the suggested limits, whatever their practical value for the general run of ordinary cases. One cannot legislate (even judicially) for exceptional cases; and that, of course, is precisely the strength of the common law: the rules may often be adapted to meet new contingencies, responding to factors whose relevance has now become apparent; or the rules may sometimes be overridden to meet the justice of a particular case. In either case, we appeal beyond the rules to more fundamental principles.[50] The law then proves flexible enough for underlying moral principle—in this case, the principle of fairness—to be brought directly to bear on the facts of unusual, and unanticipated, cases. And where statute adopts a general moral principle, as in s. 78 of the Police and Criminal Evidence Act, there is similar scope for flexible interpretation in response to unforeseen events.

Conflicting views have been expressed in the Court of Appeal about whether the section could be applied so as to contravene the substantive rule in respect of entrapment, even if the common law discretion is more restricted.[51] It may perhaps be denied that the case of entrapment constitutes an instance of unfair self-incrimination. Any trickery or deception occurs before the offence is committed: it leads to the commission of an offence, rather than to discovery of the culprit after the crime. But when tested against the more fundamental standard of fairness, of which the privilege against self-incrimination forms a central strand, the distinction seems unpersuasive, even arbitrary. It seems clear that the court's discretion cannot be neatly circumscribed by any such boundaries, conveniently settled in advance of future cases. The circumstances of entrapment may clearly produce unfairness; and the court's discretion to impose a lenient sentence upon conviction will not always be sufficient to do justice. The view, expressed in one case, that 'the unfairness inherent in entrapment arose not from the evidence given of the offence but from the entrapment itself' is quite confused.[52] It makes the mistake, already identified, of attempting to sever the collection of evidence from the circumstances of the defendant's trial. Morally, they cannot be so easily distinguished.

---

[50] Cf. Lucas, *On Justice*, 78.

[51] Compare *Harwood* with *Gill and Ranuana* [1989] Crim. LR 285; 358.

[52] *Harwood* (n. 51 above). The same error vitiates WOOLF LJ's confused attempt to distinguish *Mason* (n. 75 below) in *Marshall* [1988] 3 All ER 683, 685, where he refused to acknowledge (apparently even in principle) that the admission of evidence obtained by police officers acting as *agents provocateurs* could affect the fairness of the trial.

Neither discretion—common law or statutory—can be easily confined within a narrow compass; and the statute wisely directs the court to have 'regard to all the circumstances'. Legality, in the form of the entrapment rule, stands inviolate; but its result may on occasion be eclipsed by Equity in the circumstances of the particular case. The substantive rule is not abandoned, or even modified, but overridden on the grounds of justice. As Lucas explains: 'Justice is not comprised by conformity to rules, which, being general, cannot accommodate the circumstances of every case . . . Ideally, a just decision should be based on all and only those factors relevant to the particular case.'[53]

Moreover, it is quite conceivable that the circumstances of entrapment might one day invoke the court's power to dismiss the charges altogether as an abuse of process. The courts carefully deny any general jurisdiction to review the propriety of the decision to prosecute, seeking to preserve a strict separation of powers between judge and prosecutor. As Lord Scarman firmly insisted,

The role of the judge is confined to the forensic process. He controls neither the police nor the prosecuting authority. He neither initiates nor stifles a prosecution. Save in the very rare situation . . . of an abuse of the process of the court (against which every court is in duty bound to protect itself), the judge is concerned only with the conduct of the trial.[54]

The qualification, of course, is of great significance. The separation of powers cannot be absolute for the same fundamental reason that there can be no watertight division between investigation and trial. The judicial power to stop a prosecution derives, as Lord Devlin explained, from the 'inescapable duty to secure fair treatment for those who come or are brought before them . . . The courts cannot contemplate for a moment the transference to the executive of the responsibility for seeing that the process of law is not abused.'[55] It may be true, as Lord Scarman asserted, that the rights to prosecute and to lead admissible evidence are not—in general—subject to judicial control. But in the last analysis, when the facts of the particular case seem to warrant it, all questions of law and jurisdiction must acknowledge a superior moral requirement. All are subject to the overriding, and ultimately irreducible, binding principle of fairness.

We are forced to conclude that there is an important sense in which, once embraced, a general moral principle supporting the right to a fair

---

[53] Lucas, *On Justice*, 78. [54] [1980] AC 402, 454–5.
[55] *Connelly* v. *DPP* [1964] AC 1254, 1354. See also *Barton* (1980) 32 ALR 449.

trial occupies the whole field. Every legal rule, substantive or procedural, may be enforced or applied only in accordance with, and so far as is compatible with, that basic principle. And the relevant moral requirements are crucially dependent on all the detailed circumstances of the particular case, and on the impression these make on the mind of the (particular) trial judge. It is a rule of practice in criminal cases that several defendants, charged with a single offence, should ordinarily be tried on a single indictment: it is considered desirable that the same verdict should be returned and a similar punishment ordered against all those concerned in the same offence. The rule applies even where it may result in inadmissible evidence (such as a co-defendant's statement) being heard by the jury. Its application is ultimately circumscribed, however, by the fairness principle: 'Of course if a case is strong enough, if the prejudice is dangerous enough, *if the circumstances are particular enough*, all rules of this kind must go in the interests of justice.'[56]

M. J. Detmold has deprecated talk of principles on the ground that it is better to speak of reasons; but he concedes that they are harmless enough as loose references to classes of reasons.[57] Principles are universalized reasons. Detmold rightly insists, however, that law is a practical activity, and that cases are decided on the basis of reasons for action. And only facts are reasons for action: practical judgement is determined by particular facts. A conception of practical judgement as based on universals, he argues, would be incorrigibly theoretical.[58] A judge decides a hard case—one not settled simply by rule—by weighing relevant reasons for action; and the weight of a reason for action means the degree of passionate response to the fact which constitutes it.[59] The futility of attempting to escape the particularity of facts no doubt explains the Court of Appeal's recent refusal of counsel's invitation to tie the hands of the trial judge. It was stated to be 'undesirable to attempt any general guidance as to the way in which a judge's discretion under section 78 or his inherent powers should be exercised. Circumstances vary infinitely.'[60]

What, then, is the nature of the judicial discretion to exclude relevant evidence on the grounds of fairness? In what sense, if any, is

---

[56] *Lake* (1976) 64 Cr. App. R. 172, 175 (emphasis mine).

[57] M. J. Detmold, *The Unity of Law and Morality* (London, 1984), ch. 4. It follows that the principle of fairness, while not reducible to other principles, is strictly speaking reducible to reasons.

[58] Ibid., ch. 1.   [59] Ibid. 73.   [60] *Samuel* [1988] 2 All ER 135, 146.

the judge's (subjective) moral response to the circumstances of the case conditioned or structured by law? What defence can be made of Lord Scarman's view that 'The accused is to be tried according to law. The law, not the judge's discretion, determines what is admissible evidence'?[61] First, it is clear that the exclusionary discretion is a weak discretion.[62] The judge has no *choice* about whether or not to reject improperly obtained evidence: it is his duty to do so where he concludes that its admission would undermine the fairness of the trial.[63] As Dixon J explained (in the High Court of Australia) in respect of the discretion to exclude confessions, 'all that seems to be intended is that he should *form a judgement* upon the propriety of the means by which the statement was obtained by reviewing all the circumstances and considering the fairness of the use made by the police of their position in relation to the accused.'[64] The standard of fairness, however, is necessarily a matter of his personal moral judgement. Moreover, there can be no distinction here between his moral and his legal judgement. As Detmold explains the point, to see the value of a principle one must be committed to it, and to be committed to assigning it some weight, which will be infinitely variable over particular cases.[65] But a person has only one capacity to weigh reasons: legal reasons are therefore indistinguishable from moral reasons.[66]

It is important, however, not to forget that the judge's primary responsibility is to preserve the integrity of the trial. His (necessarily subjective) response to the facts of the case occurs within a highly elaborate legal structure. He does not decide whether, in the abstract, the defendant has been fairly treated; he is concerned only with the fairness of the defendant's trial, broadly understood. It is a question of whether evidence has been obtained 'by conduct of which the Crown ought not to take advantage'.[67] We may safely assume that the judge accepts the fairness of the process of criminal justice *in general*: it would otherwise be impossible for him (honestly) to sit in judgement. He will recognize that there must be a balance of interests between

---

[61] [1980] AC 402, 454.

[62] Ronald Dworkin, *Taking Rights Seriously* (London, 1977), ch. 2.

[63] It follows that the difference between the Scots inclusionary, and English exclusionary, discretions is largely one of emphasis. The *admissibility* of evidence is, strictly speaking, ultimately dependent on an exercise of 'discretion' in *both* jurisdictions. Cf. *King*, n. 15 above.

[64] *McDermott* (1948) 76 CLR 501, 513 (emphasis mine).

[65] Detmold, *Unity*, 85.

[66] Ibid. 155.   [67] *King* [1969] 1 AC 304, 319.

prosecution and defence:[68] the right to a fair trial exists to safeguard and monitor the balance, not to disturb it. He will understand, in that sense, Lord Scarman's assertion that 'the prosecution has rights, which the judge may not override.'[69]

The requirement of a balance of interests should not be misunderstood. It is not suggested that the judge should engage in some nice adjustment between competing public policies, comparing the dictates of criminal justice with those of public order.[70] (Although the nature of the offence may naturally be relevant to the acceptability of the means of investigation, the court need not seek to weigh the conflicting demands of deterrence, retribution, police discipline, liberty, etc.) Individual rights cannot be subsumed within ordinary utilitarian calculations of that kind.[71] Nor would such calculations be suited to judicial resolution.[72] Moreover, the requisite balance of fairness may not subsequently be qualified in deference to overriding public interests. Though the test of fairness entails a balance between the claims of truth and justice, it cannot itself be traded off against the public interest in preventing or punishing crime. There can be no question, as is sometimes thought, of weighing unfairness to the accused against the importance of securing convictions against the guilty.[73]

On the contrary, the relevant right, the right to a fair trial, is unconditional and absolute. A balance of procedural fairness between prosecution and defence is what the right itself requires; and evidence whose admission would undermine the fairness of the trial must be excluded. Its admission, where fairness dictates exclusion, would deny the defendant that respect and dignity which it is a basic moral purpose of the process of criminal justice to secure. It is quite in order, then, to claim that the accused is tried according to law. The judge's discretion, though demanding personal moral evaluation, is exercised within powerful constraints: it is a (passionate) response to all the facts of the defendant's case made in the light of the judge's knowledge, understanding, and experience of the criminal trial.

The last point deserves elaboration. Though the exclusionary discretion is exercised within the context of the English criminal trial,

---

[68] *Hughes* [1988] Crim. LR 519.   [69] [1980] AC 402, 455.

[70] Cf. *Bunning* v. *Cross* (1978) 141 CLR 54, where the High Court of Australia rejected the fairness criterion in favour of 'broader questions of high public policy'.

[71] Dworkin, *Taking Rights Seriously*.

[72] Cf. Polyviou, 'Illegally Obtained Evidence' (n. 16 above), 246.

[73] *Pace* Z. Cowen and P. B. Carter, *Essays on the Law of Evidence* (Oxford, 1956), 92.

as it is currently understood, it does not follow that the propriety of the judge's decision can easily be *demonstrated*. It is not merely that the decision is so heavily dependent on contingent facts. It is also the case that the judge must employ an expertise born of close familiarity with criminal procedure, and long experience. He can be expected, of course, to identify the principal factors in the case relevant to his decision; and he should be able to distinguish other cases on rational grounds. It would not otherwise be possible for his decision to be corrected, as it may be if necessary, on appeal. 'Granted the infinite complexity of human affairs, we can never hope to specify all possibly relevant factors, but can expect a man who differentiates in his treatment or evaluation of two cases to say, at least approximately, wherein the difference lies.'[74]

There will sometimes indeed be only one reasonable exercise of the judge's (weak) discretion. A deceit practised on the defendant's solicitor, which sharply erodes the value of independent legal advice, might be thought a clear example. A confession obtained in such circumstances could hardly be admitted consistently with acknowledging the right to a fair trial.[75] The judge's expertise is not, however, a simply technical one, and its ingredients cannot easily be stated, at least not comprehensively. Once again, Detmold assists us here. A lawyer's ability to weigh reasons (for example, that the suspect's interrogation was oppressive, or that he was tricked into making a confession) is a product of his education, including his exposure to legal institutions. And education cannot be reduced to the simple conveyance of information.[76] The reluctance of the Court of Appeal to substitute its own judgment on the facts for that of the trial judge, when the latter has not mistaken the (ordinary) limits of his discretion, is therefore well grounded. The Court of Appeal, Criminal Division, has no monopoly of legal education.

If, then, Equity cannot easily be circumscribed, or its content definitively stated, it operates in harness with Legality. It qualifies Legality, but does not (wholly) supplant it. The fairness discretion operates within a framework of rules, and departures from the rules could scarcely be justified by reasons which deny the justice of the criminal law as a whole, or the legitimacy of an adversarial criminal procedure. (There would ultimately be no objection in principle; but any consensus about the nature and purpose of the criminal trial—and

---

[74] Lucas, *On Justice* (n. 3 above), 44.
[75] *Mason* (1988) 86 Cr. App. R. 349.   [76] Detmold, *Unity*, ch. 4.

of the judge's role—would disappear: it would not be a trial at common law.) Within those very broad constraints, which help to define the character of the judicial task, however, the relation between Legality and Equity is infinitely flexible. It would be surprising, no doubt, if the exclusionary discretion were invoked (for example) in *every* case of entrapment: Equity would then seem quite at large, and the sense in which a trial was conducted in accordance with Legality would be seriously weakened. That consideration, however, could hardly weigh with the judge who must conduct a particular trial. He must apply the principle of fairness in that single case, where the relevance of entrapment to the exercise of his discretion, sensitive to the particular facts, cannot justly be denied.

Moreover, the principle of fairness cannot be confined to instances of police malpractice or misconduct. A judgement of fairness in such cases assumes, as a background judgement, that the trial is otherwise fair. The judge would have no reason to preserve the integrity of an unfair trial. (It is not clear that such an objective would make any sense.) In *Sang*, Lord Scarman affirmed that the exclusionary discretion was 'a general one in the sense that it is to be exercised whenever a judge considers it necessary in order to ensure the accused a fair trial'.[77] It follows that a rule of law might properly be overridden in any appropriate case—and perhaps thereby even rendered quite redundant, if it seemed invariably to work injustice. A statutory rule of evidence, whose formal authority the courts could not of course deny, and whose content could not be adapted (by interpretation) to conform to underlying principle, would seem a prime example. If this looks like judicial exercise of a suspending power, in violation of Legality, it is none the less demanded—legally and morally—by the judge's overriding duty to ensure a fair trial.[78]

Generally, a common law rule will be brought into harmony with underlying notions of justice and fairness by development in successive cases: an unjust rule will be distinguished or overruled. (One would expect a rule that entrapment was no defence to a charge to be

---

[77] [1980] AC 402, 452.

[78] See *O'Connor* and the discussion of Police and Crim. Evid. Act 1984, s. 74, which may result in the defendant incurring the burden of proving his innocence: [1987] Crim. LR 260–3 (note by J. C. Smith). Smith observes that the unfairness is inherent in the statute, but denies that s. 78 gives the court a suspending power. The Theft Act 1968, s. 27 (3), permitting evidence to be given of the defendant's previous convictions of theft or handling (or possession of stolen goods on other occasions) provides another example: see *Bradley* [1980] Crim. LR 173; *Perry* [1984] Crim. LR 680.

abandoned if it persistently caused injustice.) A judicial refusal to develop the law, on the ground that legislation is a better, because more radical, means of reform, is therefore unjust. A judge who considered that the rule against hearsay (which the courts have refused openly to change[79]) prevented the admission of cogent evidence vital to the accused's defence would be obliged to deny (or adapt) the rule— whatever the strength of its formal authority. He is bound to protect the fairness of the trial, and his duty admits of no exceptions.

It may now be objected that the fairness principle is circumscribed by the scope of the exclusionary discretion, and has no wider function. But such a limit is obviously morally arbitrary, and therefore not available. It is hard to see how the fairness principle could apply only to the *exclusion* of otherwise admissible evidence, but have no relevance at all to the *admission* of evidence normally excluded. The principle of fairness which informs the judge's exercise of his exclusionary discretion cannot logically be insulated from other aspects of the trial: a judgement of fairness inevitably puts every rule in issue, at least potentially.

In some circumstances, perhaps quite exceptional, an exclusionary rule (like the hearsay rule) may produce manifest injustice. How in such circumstances could the judge be satisfied that the defendant has been fairly tried? A judge who applied an exclusionary rule to frustrate a defence which might be well grounded in fact would necessarily do injustice. It would make no sense to claim that the trial was legally fair, but morally unfair: his legal duty, as trial judge, is to ensure that morally, taking all relevant circumstances into account, the defendant is fairly tried. The fairness principle itself, which resists a distinction between law and morality, commits the judge, if he is rational, to a moral judgement of that kind. It follows that a case like *Myers*,[80] which denies the court's freedom to modify an exclusionary rule of evidence, even in fairness to the accused, must be wrongly decided.

These reflections provide support, in the present context, for Detmold's contention that the judge's moral responsibility is inescapable. He takes full moral responsibility for his (legal) decision. Perhaps this conclusion simply reflects the special character of the English (and

---

[79] In *Myers* [1965] AC 1001, the House of Lords held that the hearsay rule could now be altered by Parliament alone. In practice, the Court of Appeal has permitted various covert new exceptions (generally assisting the prosecution) in an effort to do justice in particular cases.

[80] See n. 79 above. Lord Pearce, dissenting, objected that the decision might prevent the admission of cogent evidence for the defence.

Scottish) criminal trial, which acknowledges the principle of fairness? No doubt, the judge's exclusionary discretion could be abrogated by statute. The law of evidence could be reduced to a series of (statutory) rules. It is not, however, conceivable that Parliament could legislate to abolish the right to a fair trial. And in so far as that right, properly understood, forbids the use of illegal or unfair police procedures, its effect on the conduct of the trial itself could hardly be eliminated. No doubt, if the jury failed to express its outrage by taking a merciful view of the facts, the judge's attitude to serious police misconduct might be reflected in his sentence. (It is accepted that entrapment may be a proper ground for leniency.) In the absence of an exclusionary discretion (or an exclusionary rule), the power to halt a prosecution as an abuse of process might be more readily invoked. It is because the right to a fair trial derives from the defendant's right to be treated with dignity and respect that it is (legally and morally) absolute. He cannot, in any circumstances, be treated less favourably.

These conclusions reflect the dependence of the Rule of Law on considerations of legitimacy. A rigid adherence to strict Legality, in disregard of the claims of Equity, will ultimately destroy Legality and thus be self-defeating. A system of criminal jurisprudence which, whatever the rigour of the courts' adherence to legal rule, failed to meet widely acceptable minimum standards of justice and fairness would forfeit all legitimacy. If the ordinary rules of evidence provide the general context for the application of the principle of fairness to the facts of any particular case—the aim is to protect the integrity of the criminal trial as it is presently conducted—the principle must none the less address the moral standards and perceptions of justice of the whole community.[81]

[81] Cf. Richard May, 'Fair Play at Trial: An Interim Assessment of s. 78 of the Police and Criminal Evidence Act 1984' [1988] Crim. LR 722, 730: 'The concept of fair play which is at the heart of this section is very much part of our culture.'

9

The Theory of the British Constitution

PHILIP ALLOTT

To make us love our country, our country ought to be lovely.

(Burke, *Reflections on the Revolution in France*, 1790).[1]

I

Rivalled only by the constitutions of the Church of Rome, of China, and of France, the British constitution is the most interesting example of a constitution available for contemporaneous study. With fourteen centuries of continuous and well-documented development, it is a unique living specimen of the long-term self-socializing of the human species.

Study of the British constitution is a less proud tradition. Cloudy and confused since the earliest days, the constitutional self-awareness of the British people has been distorted over the last two centuries by a series of developments whose significance goes far beyond the problems of the British constitution.

The adoption in 1787 of a document entitled the Constitution of the United States of America and the prestige which rapidly attached to that document, especially in the minds of those familiar only with the evils of pre-revolutionary regimes, caused an ancient idea to degenerate into a dangerous modern doctrine. The idea was that the constitution of a state is to be found in the distribution and control of public power by the law. This became the idea that the constitution of a state is its legal constitution. And that in turn has become the idea that the nature of a society is determined by its legal constitution.[2] During the

---

[1] *The Works of Edmund Burke* (Bohn's Standard Library; London, 1899), ii. 350; Burke, *Reflections on the Revolution in France* (Everyman edn.; London, 1910), 75.

[2] It is true that Aristotle defined a constitution as 'the arrangement of magistracies in the state, especially of the highest of all'. *Politics* (tr. Jowett; Oxford, 1905), 3. 6. 1, p. 112. But he also used the word in other senses in the *Politics*, and the theme of the

nineteenth century, many other developments contributed to this unfortunate simplification: the adoption of written constitutions as the symbolic but tangible embodiment of successful revolution; the Hegelian separation of the idea of the state as rational universality from the idea of civil society as natural collectivity; the development of the Rule of Law and *Rechtsstaat* principles as the guarantees of constitutionality; the revolutionary vigour of the British legislature and the assertion of its so-called sovereignty or supremacy; the intense development of the study of legal history, including legal constitutional history as a major element, and of anthropology, including the study of primitive legal institutions as a major element; the establishment of Constitutional Law as a primary category in the new taxonomy of law.[3]

Such developments were accompanied by a paradoxical development in other social studies. The study of the historical development and the social role of ideas, at one time identified by the term Ideology, had been a promising initiative stemming from the eighteenth-century Enlightenment. The idea of an 'idea' could still be questioned.[4] But ideas were clearly worthy of special attention, since ideas are located at a place of great interest, the point of intersection of the social, the philosophical, and the psychological. It seemed possible that a phenomenology of mind, to adopt and adapt Hegel's term, could give to humanity a potentially useful capacity to transcend its own mental activity, perhaps even to judge and to reform such activity on a continuing basis.

The whirlwinds known as Marx and Freud swept through the human mind like conquistadors (to use a metaphor which Freud

book is precisely that a legal constitution is related systematically to much else: human nature and potentiality, the ethical aim and the circumstances of the particular society, political practicality.

[3] 'Besides the civil and the penal, every complete body of law must contain a third branch, the *constitutional*. The constitutional branch is chiefly employed in conferring, on particular classes of persons, *powers*, to be exercised for the good of the whole of society, or of considerable parts of it, and prescribing *duties* to the persons invested with those powers.' Bentham, *Principles of Morals and Legislation* (1780/89; Oxford, 1879), 334. Dicey's discussion of the matter ('Outline of the Subject' in *An Introduction to the Study of the Law of the Constitution* (1885)) finally established the credentials of the new branch of law. Maine's *Ancient Law* (1861) was especially influential in propagating the idea that social change could be presented as change in legal structures.

[4] 'But Johnson was at all times jealous of infractions upon the genuine English language, and prompt to repress colloquial barbarisms . . . He was particularly indignant against the almost universal use of the word *idea* in the sense of *notion* or *opinion*, when it is clear that *idea* can only signify something of which an image can be formed in the mind.' Boswell, *Life of Johnson* (1795), ed. Chapman (Oxford, 1980), 873.

himself used, although not explicitly about himself), leaving the study that was ideology as a gentle, if persistent, side-stream,[5] and carrying off the word 'ideology' to do mercenary service in a very different cause. It is right that we still wonder at the manic intellectual energy of Karl Marx, fired by an understandable obsession with early Victorian industrial capitalism, and at the manic intellectual energy of Sigmund Freud, fired by an understandable obsession with *fin de siècle* sexuality. They had the practical effect, among many other effects, of illuminating and, at the same time, of distorting, possibly beyond repair, the relationship of the social, the philosophical, and the psychological. They achieved this effect by the great social power which came to be attached to their ideas, a power which must be explained not only in terms of the unquestionable explanatory value of their ideas and the force of their personalities, but also in terms of the pathological social situations into which their ideas erupted.

A consequence of these developments was that law, sociology, economics, history, psychology, and philosophy retreated into their separate realms, to lead their essentially separate existences, brought together in occasional conflict, as one discipline invaded another in order to demystify or to deconstruct it, and in occasional alliance, as neighbouring disciplines used the copula 'and' to form academic joint ventures of a temporary and tentative kind.

Had such developments not occurred, we might have expected that the study of all the phenomena of mind—social, philosophical, psychological—would have proceeded in a fruitfully integrated fashion. We might have expected that there would be a discipline known as Jurology—the study of law as a total phenomenon, social and philosophical and psychological. The maxims of prudence of such studies would not have been difficult to state. To study social structures without studying law is as sensible as studying human physiology without studying the human skeleton. To study law without studying its social and psychological setting is as sensible as studying plant physiology without studying the soil medium. To study philosophy without studying social structures and psychology is as

---

[5] The valiant stream of Ideologists from 1750 to the present day may be said to include: Bayle, Voltaire, Condorcet, Schelling, Hegel, Coleridge, Destutt de Tracy, Carlyle, Arnold, Ruskin, T. H. Huxley, Froude, W. James, Unamuno, Benda, Cassirer, Marcuse, Arendt, Popper, Steiner, Foucault, Gay. They treat ideas transcendentally (new ideas about ideas), not merely as history or academic routine and, although *parti pris* on important issues, not merely for polemical purposes. They are a continuing Enlightenment.

sensible as studying music without ever hearing the sound of a musical instrument. To study the British constitution as if it were merely a legal phenomenon is as sensible as studying love as if it were merely a matter of physiology. A constitution is, on the contrary, a total social process, the self-constituting of a human society. To study the sickness of a constitution is to uncover the sickness of a society.

II

A human society is a society of human beings constituting themselves as a society. As human beings, they have the form of consciousness which is characteristic of human beings. Human consciousness includes reflexive consciousness, that is to say, the capacity of consciousness to consider its own functioning. So it is that a society is able, as part of the self-constituting of society, to consider what it is for human beings to conceive of themselves as a self-constituting society. Because human consciousness can reflect on its own activity as consciousness, we can treat the act of society-constituting as an act itself capable of being conceived in consciousness. In other words, we can transcend in social consciousness a process in social consciousness. Consciousness can ask of itself the question: what does consciousness do in conceiving of a society by constituting that society in consciousness?

Reflexive consciousness is layered, in the sense that consciousness can consider its own activity and then consider itself considering its own activity, in a process of self-enriching abstraction which can apparently be continued indefinitely. Consciousness can conceive of the consciousness necessary for the self-constituting of a particular given society (practical theory). Consciousness can conceive of the consciousness necessary for the self-constituting of societies in general (pure theory). And consciousness can conceive of the consciousness necessary for the forming of social consciousness in general (transcendental theory). Consciousness can also go on indefinitely considering as an object of its consideration each successive self-considering of consciousness, considering even the nature of consciousness in general (meta-transcendental theory to the nth degree).

It is the function of the social enterprise known as philosophy to organize such reflexive activity of consciousness. Philosophy is consciousness forming itself for itself. One of the tasks of philosophy, throughout the whole of its recorded history, has been to consider the role of consciousness in relation to the self-constituting of society. And yet, notwithstanding an effort so long sustained, philosophy has not found any generally accepted answer, whether at the practical or at the pure or at the transcendental level, to the problem of how consciousness should conceive of the self-constituting of society in consciousness. There is no reason to believe that, short of divine intervention or the collapse of all philosophy into physiology, any such answer will ever be found. However, at the end of the twentieth century, we are privileged to have available to us a highly developed self-consciousness of such consciousness. Given the intensity of philosophical activity over the last ten centuries and especially over the last two centuries, we can transcend the problem and its possible solutions in a way which far surpasses that which was possible for any of our predecessors. But our self-confidence necessarily includes the self-tempering knowledge that, in the future, others will certainly surpass even our enlightenment.

If we consider the work of self-conceiving consciousness at the transcendental level (answering the question: what is it to conceive of a self-constituting society in consciousness?) we find that there have been generated a number of philosophical strategies or approaches. They are strategies which have seemed to be distinct from each other, mutually incompatible, perhaps even mutually antagonistic, at least in dialectical tension with each other. It is the purpose of the present essay to suggest a unifying view of how we may conceive of a society constituting itself in consciousness, and then to verify and exemplify that view in considering the particular instance of social self-constituting which is the British constitution, so that, finally, we may be in a position to diagnose the current condition of self-constituting British society.

III

1. We have learned that it is possible to conceive of social self-constituting *phenomenologically*. A constitution of a society can be seen as a Husserlian constituting in the mind. That is to say, it is a process which generates something which is neither merely the matter of a hypothetical actual social world nor merely an event of free imagining. A constitution—like a person or a table or a dream—is a forming of that which consciousness conceives as not-consciousness into something which consciousness conceives as present-within-consciousness. It is something which contains the subject (the consciousness)

and the object (not-consciousness) in a form which is neither the one nor the other but which would not be as it is without the one and the other.

And the constituting in the mind is not merely for-that-mind. It is intersubjective. That is to say, it is a knowing rather than merely an imagining. It presents itself as something which is constituted for-mind rather than for a particular mind. Consciousness is itself a constituting by consciousness of precisely the same kind (intersubjective subject–object). And consciousness presents itself transcendentally to itself as something which is not merely the activity of this-consciousness. The subject of intersubjective constituting is any subject, no subject in particular. The object of intersubjective constituting is constituted as a sharable object, and such constituting is, in that sense, a mode of knowing.

To adopt a Hegelian mode of expression, the constituting of a given society is the actualizing of the universal which is a constitution, with a view to actualizing the possibilities of that universal in the particular of an actual constitution.

2. We are also able to say that the constituting of a society is a Diltheyan *interpretation* and a Habermasian *communication*. There are constitutional events—a king makes a coronation oath, a parliament enacts a statute, a voter marks a ballot-paper. But what makes such events into constitutional events is the constitution. A constitution contains all that is necessary to make events into constitutional events. A constitution is thus a world of significance, a significant reality. A constitution is a system of signifying.

In order to be a system of signifying, the constitution is in a reciprocal relation of communication with that which it makes significant. The constitution—like other social processes of signifying—speaks of itself in speaking of society, speaks to itself in speaking to society. In seeing itself by seeing society, the constitution enables society to see itself in seeing its constitution. A constitution—like other social processes of signifying (religion, art, morality)—is a mirror of a mirror which, nevertheless, generates an image which is not merely the image of a mirror. Society and society's idea of itself form each other in forming themselves and, in so doing, they secrete the constitution by which they are constituted.

3. Thirdly, we may say that there is a specific device which consciousness uses in the constituting of the constitution for-mind and

in the self-constituting of a particular society through signifying communication with itself. That device may be understood in terms of the Kantian *idea-of-reason* or the Weberian *ideal-type* or what might be called the *organic metaphor* of the structuralists.

It is a device which is far more than merely a device. It is so central to the self-constituting process of social consciousness as to suggest that it forms part of consciousness in general considered transcendentally.

A constitution is not merely a report or a description, historical or sociological. A constitution is not merely a set of prescriptions or rules or aspirations. But a constitution manages to be both things in being neither, and to be more than both things. In generating an idea-of-reason or an ideal-type or an organic metaphor, the mind installs within itself something which is a hypothetical reality with a view to action. It is not itself a rule of action. It is not itself a representation of reality. But it manages to function as both because of a particular feature of the functioning of consciousness, namely that human willing takes place within the reality which human consciousness conceives. So, to conceive, even hypothetically, of a reality-with-a-view-to-acting (for example, the social contract or the general will or market forces or state or nation or race or class) is to will-by-knowing. Such a reality is not merely a Vaihinger fiction nor the calculated deceiving of Machiavelli's Prince nor the calculated social poetry of a Sorel. It is not that we behave as if it were our reality. A reality-with-a-view-to-acting is real when it is the reality within which we act.

To conceive of a constitution—say, the British constitution—is thus to conjure up the reality which is a constitution as the reality within which we make our acts of will, the reality which we make real by our acting. We will the constitution by an act of knowing.

4. We are able also to conceive of a self-constituting society as a self-forming realm of Aristotelian/Kantian *necessity*. In constituting itself in consciousness, a society seems to be constituting itself in obligation, constructing an ever more dense web of self-constraint. The artistic freedom of the self-imagining society is a freedom to submit to its own idea of itself. The will of society, the general will, wills its subjection to its own will. Society conceives of itself as if its social reality consisted of obligation.

Every social process within self-constituting society, with the possible sole exception of art, is presenting reality to consciousness in terms of obligations. Mythology, religion, morality, natural science, the humane sciences, law—as each of them develops in the self-constituting of society, it helps to make ever more substantial the social reality which is the reality-for-society, the reality within which all free willing and acting within society takes place. Society makes for itself an artificial necessity-for-willing, as if in imitation of the apparent necessity-for-acting of the physical world.

Law seems to be a first among equals among the manifestations of society's artificial necessity. The special magic of the law is the way in which it carries the process of social self-constituting from society's past into its future. The transformation of society's past into society's future is through the operation of law as it takes effect in society's present. Law mediates what-was and what-might-be through what-is, but it does so, specifically and directly, in relation to social willing. Legal relations of all kinds speak of social willing in the past, but they speak to the future by constraining the willing and acting in the present of those who are subject to such relations.

IV

The four strategies of philosophy so far considered are not fortuitous products of the work of more or less professional philosophers. Since their production has been part of the social process which they were considering, we may say that they are themselves aspects or *moments*, to use another Hegelian expression,[6] in the self-contemplating of human self-socializing. In seeking to find a new integration of that process here and now in the present essay—an endeavour which is itself an episode in that same self-contemplating—we may now choose to say that, seen as significant moments of a process which is the self-constituting of a society, they can be related to each other as follows:

Moment 1. The self-constituting of a society is conceived as a form of self-contemplation. Society knows itself as social consciousness. The constitution as consciousness.

Moment 2. The particularizing of the universal self-conceiving of society is conceived as its communicative actualizing in a particular society. Society knows itself as a self-forming self within social consciousness. The constitution as communication.

---

[6] The word is used by analogy with its use in mechanics: a measure of the tendency of a force to cause a body to rotate. It is used in the present context to stand for a particular tendency to cause the development of ideas.

Moment 3. The particular actualizing of a given society is conceived as a reality-for-itself. Society knows itself as a particular self-forming self within social consciousness. The constitution as reality-modelling.

Moment 4. The reality-forming of a particular self-constituting society is also a reality-constraining, the forming of something which constrains itself to be what it is in order that it can continue to be a particular society. Society chooses to be a particular self-forming self within self-forming consciousness. The constitution as artificial necessity.

So it is that a particular constitution, say the British constitution, may be described as the self-choosing self of British society, forming itself within the self-forming consciousness of British society.

Such self-constituting moments are thus being treated as necessary moments in self-constituting social consciousness. But they are not by themselves sufficient to cause the self-constituting of a given and unique society. Social consciousness must perform one more trick to make possible the self-constituting of a particular unique society. It remains to know how a particular society forms its unique self-consciousness in relation to its unique material situation. It remains to know how a specifically British society formed a specifically British society.

5. The problem of self-constituting society as a self-constituting *totality* is a problem to which philosophy has devoted particularly intense effort. Once again, we may see moments in the process of society's transcendental self-contemplating. But it is impossible to do more here and now than to catalogue the moments of exceptional human self-illumination. They must be abstracted from a continuous and unending process of human self-contemplating.

(5.1) With Montesquieu we were at last enabled to conceive of a particular society's constitution as a unique totality, mediating between the universal nature of law and the unique circumstances of the given society as people, place, climate, resources, culture, history.

(5.2) With Kant we were at last enabled to conceive of a particular society's constitution as a totality of obligation, a seamless web of obligation, so that all aspects of the artificial necessity of a society could be presumed to be the fruit of a common source in self-constituting consciousness (practical reason).

(5.3) With Hegel we were at last enabled to conceive of a particular society's constitution as a totality within an infinitely larger totality, the totality of the total human social process, the total process of the universe of all-that-is (society as state as spirit).

(5.4) With Savigny we were at last enabled to conceive of a particular society's constitution as integrated into the totality of the development of a self-knowing people through time (the spirit of a people).

(5.5) With Marx we were at last enabled to conceive of a particular society's constitution as the transcendental aspect of the totality of the actual world-transforming activity of the society (society as economy).

(5.6) With Freud we were at last enabled to conceive of the macrocosm of a particular society's constitution as integrated totally into the microcosm of actual human psychology, its dynamic, and its pathologies (human nature).

(5.7) With Wittgenstein we were at last enabled to integrate the total phenomenon of a particular society's self-communicated constitution into the total phenomenon of language, a social phenomenon like any other.

Moment 5. The reality-forming of a particular society takes place within a reality which seems to have an actuality transcending consciousness because it has been made by the physical world and/or made by the past, including past states of consciousness. Each society is a unique self-forming self within self-forming consciousness and within all that it finds to be actual. The constitution as natural necessity.

Such learning cannot now be unlearned. It can only be surpassed. We can no longer regard a constitution merely as the chance residue of a time-ordered series of historical events—the deposing of a king, the throwing off of some foreign domination, the expansion of the national territory, some revolutionary redistribution of power, a particular victory of a class or an idea. We now have no choice but to consider a particular constitution, even the British constitution, as an idea which is also an organism, a programme which is also a personality. A constitution is not an arrangement of institutions. It is a dialogue between consciousness and circumstance.

V

The British people suppose that the British constitution is nothing less than the social genome of the British people. We feel that, in the very genes that makes us what we are as persons, we have inherited the self-acquired characteristics of the British people. We feel that the constitution has made us as we have made the constitution. Surely the personality of the British people has made the constitution of the British people, and the constitution of the British people has made the personality of the British people.

And yet the first surprising characteristic of the specimen of human self-socializing which seems to be the self-constituting of the British people is that there is no British people to constitute. The English, the Welsh, the Scots, and the Irish and all the other subordinate cultural groups who have participated in the forming of the constitution (from the ancient Britons, the Celts, the Romans, the Angles, the Saxons, the Danes, and the Normans, to all the other individuals and groups who have come from elsewhere to live in the British islands) do not know themselves as a unique totality otherwise than as members of a constituted totality, a totality which is not a people but a society. And, to make matters worse, each of the contributing peoples has generated its own cultural romance, to emphasize its specific virtues and the virtue of its specificity. Only the legally constituted society which has recently come to be known by the uncomfortable name of the United Kingdom of Great Britain and Northern Ireland has generated no cultural romance of its own.

The second surprising characteristic is that there is no place which is the specific and integral location of the British people. The several Roman provinces, the Anglo-Saxon kingdoms, the pan-European system of the Roman Church, the obscure and changing involvement with the monarchy of France and with parts of geographical France, the obscure association with the Channel Islands and the Isle of Man, the assimilation of Ireland, the assimilation of Wales, the establishment of overseas colonies, the separation from Rome, the personal union with Scotland, the association with Hanover, the parliamentary union with Scotland, the formation of Great Britain, the formalization of the British Empire, the dissociation and partition of Ireland, the formation of the United Kingdom of Great Britain and Ireland/Northern Ireland, the formalization of the British Commonwealth and then of the Commonwealth, the independence of the overseas territories, adherence to the constitutional system of the European Community. The constitutional geography has changed like the form of a lively micro-organism. And, to make matters worse, the peoples of the different geographical areas have each generated a poetry of place to sacralize their counter-constitutional homeland. Once again, it is only the territory of the society which has come to be known as the United

Kingdom of Great Britain and Northern Ireland which has inspired no poetry of place.

The absence of a British people and the absence of a British place might have pleased Aristotle, since they suggest that our One is a fruitful Many.[7] But they are only the first of a series of absence–presences which seem to be structural idiosyncrasies of the British self-constituting. They are absences whose function is to make their absence felt.

The British people have found a specific series of Others, absent friends and rivals whose assigned role seems to have been to help to form the British self by dialectical opposition, appropriated in order to be alienated, alienated in order to be appropriated. The Other has been a series which has included successively the Romans, the Celts, the Angles and Saxons and Jutes, the Danes, the Vikings, the Normans, France (so near and so far), the Scots, the Irish, France again, Holland, Spain, the American colonies, the United States and all other former colonies (the disinherited heirs), France yet again, Europe (meaning continental Europe), Germany (our formidable north European culture-cousins), the European Community, so-called immigrants of all kinds, not to say so-called foreigners in general.

We are not merely ethnically mongrel as a constituted people. The culture of the British islands has been formed under the powerful and all-pervading influence of all that has, at different times, been perceived as Other. Without all that is subjectively not-British there would have been nothing that is subjectively British. The British are a figment of their own imagination, but they have always found it easier to imagine the not-British. The intermittent and multifarious intervention of foreign bodies has irritated into existence a vague and inarticulate and tenuous and fitful image of a rather admirable Anglo-Saxon/English/British self. What seems like British xenophobia is better seen as a hesitant autophilia.

The most notorious absence of the British constitution is the absence of a written constitution or even of any established notion of higher law or fundamental rights. Indeed, there seems to be an absence of any articulated and readily ascertainable legal constitution

---

[7] 'The error of Socrates must be attributed to the false notion of unity from which he starts . . . For there is a point at which a state may attain such a degree of unity as to be no longer a state, or at which, without actually ceasing to exist, it will become an inferior state, like harmony passing into unison, or rhythm which has been reduced to a single foot. The state, as I was saying, is a plurality.' Aristotle, *Politics* (tr. Jowett), 2. 5. 13, p. 64.

of any kind. But equally notorious is the fact that the absence of a materially formulated legal constitution has not prevented the British from believing that they have a legal constitution. That certainty manifests itself intermittently, but especially when the constitution is thought to be in danger. The British are most certain about their constitution whenever they think they may be losing it.

In this perverse comedy, foreign kings have played a leading role. The Anglo-Saxon/English/British citizen-selves have found themselves to be legal subjects of a procession of kings who could all be seen, if need be, as Other—Danish, Norman, French, Welsh, Scottish, German. This fact has given us a splendid power over our monarchs. It has enabled us to represent the constitution as something that is above and beyond kings, something that foreign kings cannot understand, since it is written in the hearts and felt in the bones of the British people. To make the monarch constitutional we have had to make the constitution magical. On three occasions we have dispensed with kings who did not respect a constitution which, we were rather surprised to hear ourselves saying, makes kings kings and must, if need be, unmake them.[8]

The result has been that a coherence of the legal constitution has been generated as a sort of back-formation from the real-world constitution of everyday public life. Again and again, judges and politicians, in particular, have invoked the constitution by invoking the ancient rights and liberties of the English people. They are rights and liberties which are said to go back to King Edward and King Alfred and beyond, into the mists of tribal law.[9]

The strange fact is that, although no one has ever formed any clear idea of what precisely those rights and liberties might be, the idea of their existence has played a role similar to that of a written constitution, especially a written constitution which contains fundamental rights—the role of something transcendental, in relation to everyday lawmaking and law-executing. In their multiplicity and their

---

[8] Richard II (1399), Charles I (1649), James II (1688). Other cases of premature termination of a king's reign did not have the same constitutional significance.

[9] 'So I have here collected the dooms [decreed laws] that seemed to me the most just, whether they were from the time of Ine, my kinsman [*c.*688–95], from that of Offa, king of the Mercians [757–96], or from that of Aethelbhert [king of Kent, 560–616], the first of the English to receive [Christian] baptism . . . I, then, Alfred, king of the West Saxons, have shown these [dooms] to all my witan, who have declared that it is the will of all that they be observed.' Dooms of Alfred (871–901). C. Stephenson and F. G. Marcham, *Sources of English Constitutional History* (New York, 1937), 10.

metaphysicality the ancient rights and liberties seem, nevertheless, to imply some hypothetical unity contained in a hidden constitution, of which the everyday constitution is a this-worldly shadow, integrated by the unifying effect of the ideal constitution. Because they are traditionally formulated in legal terms (rights, liberties, privileges), they seem to share in the artificial necessity of the law, and so give the past a hold over the future. But they manage to do so by moving from the past to the future without entering the present. They are not a source of law in the lawcourts, to be applied in everyday decision-making. The function of the natural–customary laws of the British implied legal constitution has been to be unactual but active. *Pace* Hegel, we may say that, in the depths of the British legal constitution, the rational is not actual, but the actual is made rational by the non-actual.

A particularly intriguing absence–presence of the British constitution is a concept of the state. As compared with constitutions in continental Europe, we have not developed a systematically significant concept of the state as the locus of all public power within the legal constitution. We have not even developed an equivalent of the useful French notion of *le pouvoir* (*le pouvoir constitué* in the influential formulation of the Abbé Sieyès)—the Other which exercises actual public power in relation to the Self of the people, within what may be called the *real* constitution, the constitution as it is implemented daily in the struggle of social life, constituted power as it is actually applied to change the lives of the citizens. The word 'state' has had many uses down the centuries. In recent times, the uncomfortable adjectival use of the word has increased—state schools, state industries, state pension. But such uses have not integrated themselves into a reified constitutional substance.

The absence of a structurally significant concept of the state is a familiar fact which is generally assumed to be of relatively little significance. When it is set against the equally familiar fact that the British system contains quite as much organized public power as, say, the French or the German systems, then the presence of the fact and the absence of the concept become crucially significant. To unravel that significance is to penetrate into the depths of the constitutional mystery, not only a mystery which is full of the absences that are also presences, and the others that are also the self, but a mystery in which light is also a form of darkness.

The absence of all absences in our constitutional order is the absence of rational constitutional consciousness. The British constitution is characterized by an intellectual insouciance which must be classed as pathological. The crowning of Henry VII with a crown plucked from a thorn-bush on Bosworth Field (1485) is as poetically apt a symbol of a particular constitutional ethos as is the scene of Bonaparte taking the crown from the Pope to crown himself as Emperor in the cathedral of Notre-Dame (1804).[10]

Despite the intellectual and practical interest of foreign observers in such things as feudalism in England or Magna Carta or the Bill of Rights or the role of a constitutional monarch or the *inter se* relationship of the members of the former British Commonwealth, the British themselves have shown remarkably little sustained interest in such things. That is to say, they may have shown some academic interest but they have shown very little existential interest. It has not seemed to be necessary for the satisfactory constituting of British society to form a satisfying view of such abstract matters, or even of a whole series of less abstract matters which could seemingly not be left, given everyday practical necessity, in a state of radical confusion—the constitutional relationship of the English and French domains of the Anglo-French or Franco-English kings, the precise legal status of Magna Carta and the Bill of Rights (law or not law, fundamental law or not fundamental law), the nature of the Crown as a trinity of quasi-persons, the presence or absence of a constitutional separation of powers, the legal effect of so-called constitutional conventions, and very many other questions of structural importance.[11]

The intellectual detachment extends even to problems of ultimate social values, the constitution-forming ideas which reflect the ideal of a society as it constitutes itself, dynamically and progressively, as a

[10] Apart from the Pope's blessing, Napoleon was fortified by a witty *senatus consultum*, which 6 months before the coronation, had declared him to be 'hereditary emperor of the French by the grace of God and the will of the people'. Henry's initiation of the House of Tudor was the subject of a charmingly disingenuous subsequent statute made by a parliament which he had summoned: 'to the singular comfort of all the king's subjects . . . and in avoidance of all ambiguities and questions: be it ordained, established, and enacted by authority of this present parliament that the inheritances of the crowns of the realms of England and of France . . . be, rest, remain, and abide in the most royal person of our now sovereign lord, King Henry VII.' *Statutes of the Realm*, ii. 499; Stephenson and Marcham, *Sources*, 298.

[11] It is only very recently that the courts have reconceived the so-called Prerogative of the Crown. It is no longer supposed to be some sort of Sovereignty of the Executive but merely the collective name for the residual inherent powers of the Crown, which are, as legal powers, subject to the control of the courts. There remain many other unresolved structural questions.

society. Once again, foreign observers have shown more interest in the contribution of British experience to the development of the idea and the practice of constitutional monarchy or representative government than have the British themselves. The irony of the American Revolution was lost on most Englishmen, as the American colonists were obliged to teach the English about the ideal principles of the British constitution.

The American Revolution made an idealized version of the ideal English constitution into the legal constitution of a re-constituted society. English schools, to this day, do not teach the theory and practice of the constitution as a core subject at primary or secondary level, let alone the ideas and the ideals of liberal or social democracy.

VI

Of all the strangenesses of the British constitution, the strangest and the most challenging is a notorious feature which takes us to the heart of a constitution's darkness.

The British people, as they constitute the society which constitutes them as a people, communicate with themselves in a familiar fog of half-formed ideas and a half-forgotten past. But that is not all. The British people communicate with themselves in and through fantasy.

The British constitution is articulated around the fantasy of an absolute monarchy. It is a fantasy of palaces and glass coaches and orders of chivalry, a fantasy in which the representatives of the people present Humble Addresses to Her Majesty, and statements of government policy are published By Command of Her Majesty, in which the monarch reads the government's programme for the parliamentary session seated upon a gilded throne, in the presence of tiaraed duchesses and earls in ermine, overheard by the representatives of the people who remain standing. It is a fantasy in which legislation becomes law when the monarch assents, an assent in the form of a performative statement, but a statement which communicates the exact opposite of the truth: *La Reine le veult.* In fact the Queen, as a person, wills nothing at all.[12] Such an untrue performative statement is, perhaps, the most appropriate symbol of the British constitution. The British constitution rests upon a fantasy which is, and is known to be, a lie. The self-conceiving consciousness of the British people (moment

---

[12] The same applies to formulas which refer to the Queen's pleasure. No doubt Her Majesty is not always pleased to do what she is pleased to do.

1 in section IV above) communicates with itself (moment 2) by forming a reality (moment 3) which is an arduous rule-filled game (moment 4) but which is, and can easily be seen to be, a baroque unreality (moment 5).

There are many possible explanations for the presence of a fantasy constitution at the heart of the British constitution. The first is that it is the intrusion of the ideal constitution into the legal constitution. By the ideal constitution is here meant the self-constituting of a people conceived in terms of their highest social values and aspirations. The fantasy monarchy would then be a poetic image of an ideal absolute monarchy—the monarch as *parens patriae* and friendly shepherd of the people[13]—which the legal constitution then modifies in the light of some other ideal considerations, such as the high values known as political freedom or self-determination or equality.

Another possible explanation is a modification of the first. It is the view that our constitutional history is the history of the whittling away of absolute monarchy in the name of political freedom. This Whig view is the explanation which the British people, in their intermittent moods of self-admiration, would most like to believe. It implies that the fantasy elements of the present form of the constitution are vestiges, residues left by history, harmless and entertaining but instructive and minatory. It ignores the fact that we have never had a clearly articulated absolute monarchy. What we have had is weak kings who went too far, strong kings who sponsored useful social change, and many indifferent kings who were an irritant or an irrelevance.

A third possible explanation is a variation of the first two. It is that the British people have sought to tune their constitution like a lute, blending this and that—church and state, nobles and commons, the dignified and the efficient.[14] So it is that we have been able to secure both the positive aspects of an absolute monarchy, especially its numinous metaphysics, and the positive aspects of a republic, in terms of decisive popular government, without the negative aspects of either, avoiding especially the follies of grandeur which would beset a monarchical president. But this flatters the self-creating rationality of

---

[13] Aristotle, *Ethics*, tr. Thomson (Harmondsworth, Middlesex, 1953), xi. 248.

[14] As one specimen of countless such encomia, we may cite Blackstone: 'And herein indeed consists the true excellence of the English government, that all the parts of it form a mutual check upon each other . . . Like three distinct powers in mechanics, they [king, lords, commons] jointly impel the machine of government in a direction . . . which constitutes the true line of the liberty and happiness of the community.' *Commentary on the Laws of England* (1765; 16th edn., London, 1914), i. 153.

the British people and mistakes a rationalization for an explanation. It also requires that the monarchy should be seen as dignified and the government should be seen as efficient, a rare conjunction.

This leads to another popular variant—that the British constitution is the work of the cunning of unreason, the accidental residue of history, what Jeremy Bentham called a chance medley, without any rhyme or reason other than that which someone may choose to impose on it retrospectively for their own self-interested purposes. Edmund Burke, clairvoyant outsider from our other island, called it the happy effect of following nature. He advised us to understand the constitution so far as we are able, 'and to venerate where we are not able presently to comprehend'.[15] Alexander Hamilton contrasted a constitution made by accident and force with a constitution, such as the American, made by reflection and choice.[16] To use a concept of Heidegger, our constitution would, on this view, reflect the *Geworfenheit* of the human condition, the existential situation into which the British people simply find themselves thrown.[17]

A fifth possible explanation is that the monarchy is the unity of our multiplicity, the One which acknowledges and negates our Many. The multiplicity of British society is not only ethnic and regional. It is economic, reflected in radical disparities of living conditions and life-opportunities. It is cultural, organized as what can be seen, from different perspectives, as a class-system or a caste-system or a tribalism, defined by countless factors of birth and education and behaviour. It is semiotic, impeding communication across frontiers of vocabulary, dialect, semantics, and symbolization. The fantasy monarchy then provides a Saussurian sign, whose function is to be accepted as a focus of shared meaning, a focal totem, the sharing being more important than the meaning. It is an organic metaphor which is beyond dissection, analysis, or explication, a windowless monad, to use Leibniz's concept as a metaphor, a substance which is not formed from substance. It is a simple, to use the herbalist's term for an uncompounded substance. For the British monarchy, to be is to seem to be.

This suggests one further possible explanation—the Monarchy as

---

[15] Burke, *Works* (London, 1872), iii. 114.

[16] A. Hamilton, *The Federalist Papers* (1788), No. 1.

[17] It is tempting to follow the existentialist analysis further. There seems to be a fear of freedom and of nothingness in so much of the bad faith and the play-acting of the British constitution (see sections VIII and IX below).

Noble Lie. It is an explanation which is worthy of further consideration, if we are to put ourselves in a position to understand, let alone to treat, the sickness of British society which is the sickness of its self-constituting.

VII

Plato evidently intended that an ultimate constitutional story should be believed not only by the ruled class but also, preferably, by the ruling class as well.[18] The idea that all public power in Britain derives from, and is exercised in the name of, the monarch seems to be believed by those who exercise public power and by those who have public power applied to them. It might even be said to bear at least a family resemblance to the noble lie specifically proposed by Plato in the myth of the Earthborn, which was designed to suggest that the native land of a particular nation was native in the ultimate sense that the people were the descendants of people who had physically emerged from the land itself. Monarchy-born public power seems, through the hereditary principle, to be in direct line of descent from the misty origins of British society, with the possible admixture of sources still more exotic (the Round Table, the lost tribes of Israel, Noah, Adam). And, at the coronation, we allow for the possibility that a king may, after all, have a special relationship with a King of all Kings. Such ideas make possible a belief that public power is essentially supersocial, in the sense that it is derived from something beyond the everyday arrangements of society. In the words of Bagehot: 'The English Monarchy strengthens our government with the strength of religion.'[19]

To sustain its story-book earthborn monarchy in the face of the actual distribution of political power, the British constitution has worked a particular wonder in the form of four bizarre idea-complexes which strain rationality to its limits. The fantasy absolute monarchy has generated a shadow—an absolute presidency. And that shadow has been sustained by three typical dream-work creations—a sanctified contradiction, an unpersoned person, and law which is not law. The

---

[18] *Republic*, 414b ff.: in Shorey's translation, the notorious phrase is given as *opportune falsehood*. *Statesman*, 269b ff.

[19] W. Bagehot, *The English Constitution* (1867; Oxford, 1928), 35. Bagehot also purported to believe that 'The best reason why Monarchy is a strong government is, that it is an intelligible government' (ibid. 30). If so, then it is a case of Milton's 'darkness visible' (*Paradise Lost*, I, l. 61) rather than Goethe's 'darkness which gave birth to light' (*Faust*, I, l. 1350).

absolute presidency is Prime Ministerial Government. The sanctified contradiction is the Sovereignty of Parliament. The unpersoned person is the Crown. And the law which is not law is Constitutional Conventions.

The irony of the expression *the sovereignty of parliament* appears on its very face. The characteristic pretension of monarchy is attached to something which detached itself from monarchy, and grew strongly through opposition to the pretensions of monarchy. The imaginative *tour de force* which is the concept of *the Crown* is achieved by detaching fundamental legal capacities from the monarch, and attaching them to a non-substance which carries the name of the most substantial symbol of the monarch. The *absolute presidency* is created by entrusting the absolute powers of the monarch to persons who are mere members of parliament but who act in the name of a monarch who has no absolute powers. *Constitutional conventions* then organize the real relations of these actors through rules whose essential nature is not to be legal rules, but whose effect is to make possible all legal rules. Such is the manic ingenuity of our constitutional wonderland.

This set of interlocking devices has given rise to the ultimately unfathomable status of the Executive branch in the British constitution.

(1) The government-from-parliament has, at least in the eyes of conventional schoolroom history, taken over from the government-from-the-palace. But, never having had a cathartic revolutionary moment—a 1776, 1789, 1848, 1871, 1917, 1933, 1949, 1968, 1989— we have had to be content with a permanent and unfinished slow-motion revolution.[20] This has engendered a permanent and nagging and unfocused grief in our constitutional consciousness, an inarticulate sense of a usurpation by an imposter, mingling with the pride we may have in the winning of what we may conceive to be an increase of our political freedom. Like Oedipus, we seem to have killed our father the king, only to find ourselves living in representative democracy with our mother (who is also reputed to be the Mother of Parliaments). And yet, like Hamlet, we also find that our mother is continuing to live with a king who is not properly a king.

---

[20] The rebellion of the middle classes which ended in 1649 was too equivocal in its origins, too protracted in its execution, and too anomalous in its immediate consequences (the Protectorate) to count as a satisfactory modern revolution. The so-called Glorious Revolution of 1688 might better be regarded as a media event *avant la lettre*, full of hypocrisy and ambiguity and playing to the gallery, the kind of other-deceiving which becomes self-deceiving.

(2) The government-from-parliament seems to have taken the government-from-the-palace into its service, borrowing the magic of monarchy, using for its own purposes the power and prestige of monarchy and such obedience and loyalty as it may still summon from the deepest genetic recesses of our social consciousness.

(3) The government-from-parliament willed itself into existence by convincing itself of the existence of the ancient rights and liberties of the English people. But those rights and liberties had the dialectical function of *controlling* the power of the powerful. They were not a *source* of the power of the powerful. Another nagging tension in our social consciousness is thus a dull sense that the ancient rights and liberties are somehow and paradoxically being abused so as to generate a new form of abusive and excessive power, the power of the government-from-parliament.

(4) These considerations help to explain how, to this day, the people do not regard the government-from-parliament as the Lord's Anointed, whatever its reflected glory of majesty, whatever its participation in the deepest structures of constitutional consciousness. To this day, the government-from-parliament seems to be Them and not Us, an Other and not part of the Self, more government-of-the-people than government-by-the-people. Whatever it is, Her Majesty's Government is apparently not the People's Government.

(5) However, these considerations also help to explain why extreme criticism even of the government-from-parliament seems to be accompanied by a slight *frisson* of impiety. In an unarticulated way, we feel that we may be breaking a taboo which hedges a king. And the government-from-parliament may even make so bold as to present a threat to its power or authority (from extra-parliamentary opposition, from the European Community, or from international systems in general) as a wanton threat to all that is constitutionally most precious.

(6) All the above engenders a phenomenon which may be called the Cromwell Conundrum. The hallowed phrases *Her Majesty's Government* and *Her Majesty's Ministers* are used as labels for the Executive branch of our government, labels for the government-from-parliament. The titles are gems of the art of equivocal constitutional rhetoric.[21] Are

---

[21] Another splendidly poetic trope is the negation-of-the-negation *Her Majesty's (Loyal) Opposition* to describe the absolute-presidency-in-waiting, whose systematic function is not to challenge the absoluteness of the presidency but to legitimize it, by making clear that the only alternative is more of the same, the appearance, but not the substance, of a dialectic.

these people courtiers masquerading as parliamentarians or are they parliamentarians masquerading as courtiers? Is Thomas Cromwell pretending to be Oliver Cromwell or is Oliver Cromwell pretending to be Thomas Cromwell?

In the light of all this, it is not difficult to understand why there has been no written constitution.[22] And the otherwise outrageous insouciance of all those involved as to the theory of what is going on also becomes more easily comprehensible. A subtlety of theologians would find difficulty in untying the mystical knot to identify the attributes of the trinity of monarchy, presidency, and parliament—to say how the legal powers of the second person proceed from the fantasy powers of the first inspired by the notional will of the third. It even becomes clearer why there is no specific nation or people to be constituted, and no specific constitutional geography. The frontiers of dream-worlds are always undefined. A dream-world Island Race (identity otherwise unspecified) occupying a dream-world Sceptred Isle (location uncertain) is summoned up in song and story and polemic to embody the virtues and the achievements of the unseen constitutional wonder-workers. And the Island Race displays this surprising trait that, despite the intelligence and creative energy that they deploy in other fields, they have a passionate uninterest in the theory of their own society. They repress theoretical thought about their social selves, as if it were a sin of the mind.[23]

No doubt self-constituting human societies, like humankind in general, cannot bear too much reality. But such a degree of unreality at the heart of a social personality suggests something wrong in the process of social individuation. Moment 3 (in section IV above) of self-constituting social consciousness has made possible, in the fantasy monarchy, an idea-of-reason which defies reason and an organic

[22] The present writer witnessed (in the mid-1960s) an incident in the Fourth (Dependent Territories) Committee of the UN General Assembly, when the constitution of a soon-to-be-independent British colony was being considered. A Soviet delegate, objecting that it was a strange sort of democracy where the Governor-General could appoint and dismiss the Prime Minister, assent to legislation, etc., was told that he would not actually do these things, except in the sense permitted by (unenacted) constitutional conventions.

[23] Lord Chancellor Ellesmere's might be taken as the representative voice of intellectual repression. 'I will not stand to examine by human reasons whether kings were before laws or laws before kings, nor how kings were first ordained, nor whether the kings or the people did first make laws, nor the several constitutions and frames of states and commonweals, nor what Plato or Aristotle have written of this argument.' Case of the Postnati (1608); T. B. Howell, *State Trials* (London), ii. 690.

metaphor which has taken on a life of its own. Using that phenomenon, moment 5 has then made possible a unique totality, a soul or spirit, a spirit of our laws, a specific self-constituting of the British people. Why is it that the natural necessity within which the British people must constitute themselves has generated so strange a totality in comparison with that of so many other, otherwise comparable, republics and monarchies? To switch to a Freudian from a Jungian track, what is the repressed reality that is generating such unreality? What is the truth from which the British people are hiding?

VIII

The *unconscious constitution* is the self-constituting of a society which occurs at the place where the personality-constituting of the individual human psyche meets the society-constituting of social consciousness. The strange self-constituting of the British people has its roots in the unconscious constitution. And as with the analysis of the psychology of the human individual, so with the socioanalysis of a society, we must approach an understanding of the problem of the unconscious constitution by considering the society's behaviour, by looking at what has been referred to above as the *real constitution*, the everyday process of the self-constituting of a society, as actual willing and acting take place under or in accordance with the rest of the constitution, including the legal constitution. We discover the real constitution by asking tough questions. Echoing Lenin: who whom? Echoing Lasswell: who gets what, when, how?

The who-what-whom we have found is that an absolute presidency is, to borrow an image of Francis Bacon's from another context, leading a fantasy absolute monarchy around like a captive in a procession, parading it and humiliating it. And we also found that such a performance had been achieved and acclaimed as the constitutionalizing of the monarchy in the name of the rights and liberties of the English people. The question is: in whose interest has it been to treat the monarchy like a performing bear in the name of the constitution?

Through the history of our real constitution, one social group after another has used the idea of political freedom as the basis of its claim to take a leading part in forming the will of society. They have been typically, but not always, groups with an economic identity, handing on the baton of self-interested political freedom from one to the other, from the eleventh to the twentieth century. The robber-baron feudal landowners, the newly educated and newly self-confident prelates and other clergy, the burgess merchants involved in long-distance trade and requiring legal certainty and economic freedom, the guild crafts-men with a bankable (and legally protectable) monopoly, the liberated religionists (liberated from Rome) for whom toleration and persecu-tion were the light and the shadow of their new freedom and for whom religious freedom was in a continuum with economic and political freedom, small-scale country potentates with land-based privileges requiring legal protection, the progressive farmer-landowners for whom freedom was especially a freedom to be cost-efficient at whatever cost to others, the impresarios of the Industrial Revolution, the small-scale entrepreneurs of the new industrial economy, shop-keepers supplying the new urban masses, the directors of the new capitalist world economy, the newly educated bourgeois bureaucracy, the capitalist technologists of mass production and research-and-development, the managers of the industrial–commercial–financial corporate bureaucracies.

In the life of the real constitution, that group is most significant which, at a particular time, contains the highest social energy, especially frustrated social energy. And that group seeks to seize psychic power, in the name of political freedom, and then political power, power over the process of social will-formation. The result has been that the idea of political freedom has been installed in the ideal constitution as a very high social value, seemingly unassailable.

Freedom is to social philosophy what sexuality is to individual psychology. Sexuality is the self-reproductive capacity of the human being. All the rest is the work of consciousness. Freedom is the self-creating capacity of society. All the rest is the work of consciousness. The work of consciousness produces the totality which is the personality of a particular human being. The work of consciousness produces the totality which is the constitution of a particular society. Society constitutes the self-creating of the human being by constituting human freedom in society. Each is part of the self-creating of the other. Society is the violation of freedom and society is the means of freedom.

Freedom is a postulate which is counterfactual but unavoidable. It is a characteristic product of moment 3 (in section IV above) which, once formed, becomes part of the artificial necessity which we create for ourselves by Moment 4. It is a counterfactual postulate because all our knowledge and experience demonstrates to us the utter necessity of the natural order of the physical universe (including our species inheritance of physiology and our personal genetic inheritance) and the virtual necessity of our social and psychological universe, where we are the by-products of our circumstances. But it is an unavoidable postulate because our human consciousness happens to operate by presenting the becoming of our lives as a self-directing becoming, as a matter of making choices, generating action as a product of a self-forming process called willing: individual and social willing. For a human being to live is to choose. To be human is to be obliged to be free.

Much unfreedom has been done in the name of freedom. The idea of moral freedom has generated the idea of sin. The idea of political freedom has generated the idea of the will of the people. The idea of freedom of belief has generated the idea of orthodoxy. And then the derived ideas become the master ideas. The idea of sin is used to oppress the moral individual. The idea of the will of the people is used to oppress the social individual. The idea of orthodoxy is used to oppress the believing individual.

A socioanalysis of a society must deal with that society's struggle with the problem of freedom, just as the psychoanalysis of an individual must deal with that individual's struggle with the problem of sexuality. The pursuit of happiness of the individual human being is the same pursuit of happiness as that of the society. As with sexuality, so with freedom, the pursuit of happiness is a social struggle within the consciousness of the individual.

In the everyday practice of the real constitution of a society, the fantasies and deceptions and obsessions of that society at the level of self-constituting consciousness are actualized in countless forms of social suffering of individual human beings—poverty, sickness, indignity, injustice, discrimination, crime, torture, genocide, war, and on and on. No human society is without social suffering, and doubtless no human society ever will be. No human society is socially healthy, and doubtless none ever will be. The social struggle, like the struggle with the pain and sickness of the body and the mind, is unavoidable and never-ending.

As in the case of individual psychology, the struggles of a society with the problem of political freedom have also been the source of social progress. The struggle which a society presents to itself as a struggle for freedom is also a struggle which stimulates into life, and then fills with energy, a great deal of society's most fruitful self-constituting. Sexuality, repressed or released, may enslave or it may energize a person. Freedom, suppressed or released, may enslave or it may energize a people.

At the level of social performance, measured in terms of the potentiality of the British people and the performance of other comparable societies, it is difficult to avoid the impression that British society is not all that it might be, that it is underachieving, that it is, overall, second-rate. Worse still, the British people seem to have come to regard the inferiorities of British society as natural phenomena.

The immigrants who have entered our society over the last hundred and more years have served as providential redeemers—in academic scholarship, scientific research, the fine arts, literature, music, sport, and even in the traditional areas of British excellence—finance, commerce, and industry. It is chilling to think what would now be the state of British society if this Other had not come to improve our Self, if they had not chosen to make their home in this strange land.

The ethos of the second-rate is accompanied by specific social phenomena which are reminiscent of the disabling neurotic behavioural complexes of human individuals, perversions which have their roots in the social unconscious: the marginalizing of women; the hegemony of the economic, with its supposedly natural egoism, over the social and even the moral; the tribalism of a cultural caste-system which Marx misconstrued as an economic class-system; the provincialism of a country whose imperialism was even a sort of imperialism of disdain, disdain for other so-called races and peoples.

The unhappiness of British society is revealed in the perversions and anomalies of the current state of British self-constituting, but it is rooted much more deeply. It seems to be an existential unhappiness, going to the root of the unconscious struggle of human self-creating within social self-constituting.

IX

The truth from which the British people have been hiding is the state, and the rape of society by the state. The anaesthetizing fantasy constitution and the perpetual transubstantiating of the signs (*king, council, ministers, cabinet, parliament, lords, commons, the judges, courts, church, sovereignty, supremacy, law, custom, convention*) have had the effect of wrapping the problem of power in a cloud of equivocal unknowing. The problem of the state, of the nature of public power and its relation to the power of the human individual, has been hidden behind an obsessive concern with the identity of the power-holders. Freedom, the self-creating capacity of the individual, has come to be nothing but the residue left by the activity of the power-holders, orphaned of its true parents, which are the pursuit of individual happiness and the pursuit of the happiness of society. The problem of who is to be powerful has left no room in our self-constituting consciousness for the problem of what power is and what it is for. Put in schematic terms—the dilemma of the Self and the Other has taken precedence over the dilemma of the One and the Many.[24]

Britain's permanent slow-motion revolution has been a constant retelling of an old story, as compared with the revolutionary discontinuities of other societies which, in redefining and redistributing the powers of the state, have had to face explicitly the problem of the power of the collectivity in relation to the individual. It is this contrast, between British and, say, American and continental European experience, which enables us to diagnose the problem in the unconscious self-constituting of the British people which seems now also to be the problem of all advanced democracies.

Society, a one comprising the many (each of which is one), constitutes itself in dialectical opposition to the individual. The self-constituting of society meets the self-creating of the individual. Every society is a particular compromise between totalitarianism and anarchy, oppression and liberation. The idea of the state, a moment 3 organic metaphor in the self-communicating consciousness of society, substantiates the power of the collectivity. But it does so not only in relation to the individual citizen. It substantiates public power also in relation to society seen as a totality, society which is more than the sum of public power. The state by negation affirms the integral society, the society which is not merely the state.

In the British constitution, the state, which is an absence, is not, and has not been, substantiated separately from society in self-constituting consciousness. This has meant that the power of the collectivity (the power of the one over the many of the citizens) has been able, more or less imperceptibly, to transubstantiate itself so that it has seemed to become equivalent to society. The integral British society has tended to become the society of public power.

---

[24] For further discussion of the role of such dilemmas, see P. Allott, *Eunomia: New Order for a New World* (Oxford, 1990), pt. 1.

Victorian Britain, neurotic as it was in its own way, at least had the virtue that, for a while, it worried about the problem of being an integral society, about the threat to culture from the latest manifestations of British philistinism. And it seemed to hanker after the life of the integral society in its rather frenzied interest in religion, morality, natural history, art and the arts, history and the new humane sciences.

The British people could not understand the immoderate grief of Queen Victoria at the early death of her husband. Prince Albert, a German, came bringing a German ideal of an integral society united in self-perfecting. He came to what must have seemed a rough, uncultured society, an East Prussia or even a Russia of the West, the outer-edge of civilization, with a middle class confident in the excellence of their trade and industry, an upper class excelling in self-indulgence and field sports, a working class reduced to a state of urban and rural servitude, and an intellectual class which managed to combine crude Humean scepticism with peculiar certainties. Albert's death was a portent of the demise of the possibility of an integral British society united in self-perfecting.

Real-world developments conspired to prevent any possibility of re-constituting the integral society through its own efforts. The needs of war, of a declining economy, of the end of Empire swept the unacknowledged state to an easy victory over an enfeebled society. The triumph of the state is our secret shame.[25] Parliament, which could be a communal self-communicating of a people, became a system for the mass production of law at the prompting of the unstate. Politics became a form of unstate-sponsored entertainment, generating another form of fantasy constitution, the mediatic constitution, formed through the self-communing of the mass media. Economic activity, having become an end in itself in the form of a model of reality (moment 3) labelled capitalism, with its own laws of nature and its own natural law, in the form of a self-justifying morality, was subjected to the hegemony of politics and became the principal henchman of the unstate. Academic study retreated into a shadow-world of insignificance from

[25] Bagehot describes the close union of executive and legislative as the 'efficient secret of the English [*sic*] Constitution' (*English Constitution*, 9). British public life specializes in an elegant variation of the secret of Polichinelle. After a secret is disclosed it may still be treated as if it were a secret. Two pillars of the constitution (sometime Lord Chief Justice and Lord Chancellor respectively) have spoken the secret of the absolute presidency: G. H. Hewart, *The New Despotism* (London, 1929); Hailsham, *Elective Dictatorship* (London, 1976).

which it would be lured from time to time by the siren voice of the unstate to become one more of its paid acolytes.

So it is that the rich peculiarities of the British constitution are the colourful mask which conceals an interesting fact. The state is the non-existent subsociety of a British society that no longer exists.

At the very end of Plato's *Republic* is placed the story of the warrior Er, who found some useful wisdom in rather odd circumstances.[26] He learned that we choose our destiny. In choosing the happiness which we will pursue, as individuals and as societies, we choose our own necessity. It is possible that the British people now have the opportunity to choose a new constitution.

X

There is reason to believe that the coming-to-consciousness of the sickness of democracy is the coming-to-consciousness of a change of eras. In Hegel's depressing image, as we paint the grey in grey of the British constitution, we may sense that we are describing something which is already dying.[27]

There have been three periods in British constitutional history:

1. 500–1000—*Germanizing*—when the foundations of our language, law, and institutions were laid;

2. 1000–1500—*Gallicizing*—when we were locked in a turbulent embrace with the land and the culture of France;

3. 1500–2000—*Europeanizing*—when we joined in the post-Renaissance, post-Reformation culture of Europe.

It seems now that we are entering a fourth period:

4. 2000– ?—*Globalizing*—when we re-constitute ourselves as part of the self-constituting of Europe and of the international society of the whole human race.

To treat the sickness of British society is now no longer a matter only for the British people. The problems of the self-constituting of British society are the problems of social affluence. It is a luxury, by comparison with the suffering of very many other societies across the world, if we are able to speak of our social suffering at the same time

---

[26] *Republic*, 614b ff.

[27] 'One word about giving instruction as to what the world ought to be. Philosophy in any case always comes on the scene too late to give it.' Hegel, *Philosophy of Right* (1820), tr. Knox (Oxford, 1942), Pref. 13.

as we acknowledge so much evidence of social progress, especially in the material living conditions of the mass of the people. And, if we seek to diagnose and treat that suffering, we should acknowledge that we do so not only in the interest of the self-constituting British people but also in the interest of all other peoples who have been influenced by our example in the past, not to speak of all those peoples whose self-constituting has been irrevocably modified by the forceful intrusion of British and other European peoples.

It is obvious that to adopt a written constitution would be worse than doing nothing. It would mean adopting the crudest kind of Freudian therapy to deal with an essentially Lacanian problem. If a written constitution enacted the constitutional conventions, it would fix in amber a current and, it may be hoped, transient distribution of public power. If it did not enact them, it would fix in amber the mirages of the fantasy constitution. It would stifle the process which has been referred to above as the process of transubstantiation, in which the forms remain as the substance changes, and which at least allows for endless and subtle constitutional change.

Above all, it would consecrate and consolidate still further the power of the legally constituted state over the integral society of the self-perfecting spirit. It would consecrate the idea that the constitution is the legal constitution, and the legal constitution is the determinant of the self-constituting of society. What we have found in the present study is that the self-communing of social consciousness, considered in section IV above, has, in constituting the unique British society, generated one constitution which is many—legal (past social willing made present in legal relations); real (the day-to-day struggle to have and to exercise social power); ideal (the potentiality of society conceived in the medium of value); fantasy (shared self-delusion); unconscious (social consciousness within personal psychology); mediatic (social constituting play-acted as entertainment).

A constitutional convention to draft a British constitution would be a theatre of the absurd. The French Revolution was not made in the posturings of lawyers and priests in the Convention and the Assembly. It was made in the *cahiers de doléances* from the provinces and in the cries of the starving peasants, calling for a new regime of social aspiration and not merely for a new regime of politics. The Russian Revolution was not made in the Soviets of Workers' and Soldiers' Deputies or in the successive Soviet constitutions. It was made in periodic challenges offered, down the centuries and to the present day, to the regime of bureaucracy and police and Church in the name of so-called Westernizing social ideals. The German Revolution was not made in the *Grundgesetz* of the Federal Republic but in the catharsis of Weimar and the Third Reich, as the German people learned that the integral society could become a society of disintegration through bad politics and a society of constitutional tyranny through the blood and iron of the total state.

Macaulay professed to believe that 'the history of England is emphatically the history of progress.'[28] Since his day British society has undergone a permanent and diffuse revolution of more than 160 years. The British people might make a further contribution to human self-socializing if they were able now to lead the way to a society reconstituting itself in such a way as to transcend politics, in the name of the integral society of the self-creating human social personality. Such a development would call for self-surpassing lucidity in the face of the dis-integration which is at the heart of the present constitution, a dis-integration which is not merely social but also moral. There is a miasma of dishonesty, pretence, and self-deception which derives from the condition of the constitution and which pervades the whole of British society, distorting its aspirations and dissipating its energies. The efficient cause of the sickness of British society is self-disabling self-delusion, the self-constituting of an as-you-like-it people.[29]

It is in this sense that the problem is Lacanian. It is not a matter of rearranging our relationship to our constitutional parents, especially if the new *modus vivendi* were to be worked out under the domination of those parents. It is a matter of how we present and represent ourselves to ourselves in the self-communing which is at the heart of our self-constituting as a people. Our anguish is an inarticulate feeling that democracy as currently conceived is distorting our self-creating, our self-perceiving even, as human beings. Our freedom has been perverted. We are not creating ourselves in the creating of our society.

---

[28] Review of Mackintosh's *History of the Revolution in England, in 1688*; in *Edinburgh Review*, July 1835; reprinted in *Lord Macaulay's Essays and Lays of Ancient Rome* (London, 1885), 322. 'To us, we will own, nothing is so interesting and delightful as to contemplate the steps by which the England of Domesday Book, the England of the Curfew and the Forest Laws, the England of crusaders, monks, schoolmen, astrologers, serfs, outlaws, became the England which we know and love, the classic ground of liberty and philosophy, the school of all knowledge, the mart of all trade' (ibid. 323).

[29] It is tempting to regard Shakespeare's comedy as an extended metaphor of the British constitution, a forest with poetry in the trees. 'No, truly, for the truest poetry is the most feigning' (*As You Like It*, III. iii). Calderón's *Life Is a Dream* and *The Great Theatre of the World* can also cause a shock of the familiar in an English breast.

We are being re-created by the state to serve a society which we have not made. Democracy newly conceived will not be a matter of elections or of the appropriate distribution of public power. The new democracy will be the actualization of our ideal constitution, the integration of the pursuit of the happiness of the human individual with the pursuit of the happiness of human society. It is the self-creating of the human being within the self-constituting of society. And in that new society, the monarchy will find its transcendental function and its dignity—no longer as a plaything of the state machine, but as the living embodiment of the integral society of the British people, the self-communing society of the spirit and the mind and the heart.

Such a revolutionary change will require also a coming-to-consciousness of what may be called the generic constitution of a society, the constitution of constitutions, the constitution of the integral society, flowing from the nature of self-constituting society in general.[30] And a leading principle of that constitution is that all public power, having been conferred by society, is accountable to society in its exercise, not merely the power of the legal institutions of the state but also the public power of religion, of commercial and industrial corporations, of all forms of public mind-forming. All social power is capable of being used for the oppression of the human individual. The struggle against the oppression of all forms of public power is the next frontier in the permanent revolution which is democracy.

Such a re-constituting of British society will now also necessarily involve a revolutionary re-constituting of the European Community and of international society. In the eyes of many of its subject citizens, the European Community must seem like a pre-revolutionary *ancien régime* racket, a Hegelian state without a Hegelian civil society, let alone an integral society of the kind considered in the present study, a thirteenth state-apparatus colonizing the twelve national societies. It contains an arrogant king (an areopagus of national executive branches known as the Council), a time-serving parliament, and an impatient bureaucracy. Soon, outdoing Caesar and Charlemagne and Napoleon, it will march into Scandinavia and then, perhaps, into Eastern Europe and even Russia, bringing its religion of the mixed economy (capitalism plus bureaucracy) to those long-suffering peoples.

It follows from all that has been said above that the remaking of the European Community will not be a matter of tinkering with the powers

---

[30] For further discussion of the generic constitution, see Allott, *Eunomia*, ch. 11.

of the European Parliament, integrating financial services and central banks, removing frontier controls. To take the so-called European Community beyond its 1687, 1788, 1916 will be the work of the transcendental European Community, the integral European society which must re-imagine itself into existence, communicate with itself in order to reconstitute itself as a society. The ground for optimism lies in the fact that a self-conscious Europe, a true European Community, has pre-existed the so-called European Community by centuries, if not millenia, a consciousness which inspires itself into intermittent activity in the life of the spirit, the Europe of religion and art and literature and music and philosophy and science and law, the Europe of countless proud peoples, each with their own form of self-communicating consciousness.

Re-constituted British society will constitute itself also in relation to the international society of the whole human race, the self-constituting of humanity as a society. It is an ancient problem which has now become urgent, as capitalism and technology and mass culture sweep across the face of the world, with all their life-enhancing and life-threatening effects. The future of humanity as a species now rests on the capacity of human consciousness not only to constitute each human individual as self-creating personality but also to constitute all human beings as society. The new democracy will be a globalization which is also an individualization, re-humanizing humanity in the name of the One of humanity which is also the teeming billions of the Many of humanity, every one of whom is a unique One of human personality.

CONCLUSION

A society seeks its self-perfecting by creating itself as an integral society in consciousness. The legal constitution is a manifestation of the integral society. British society has made for itself a fantasy constitution, which has actualized itself in what masquerades as a legal constitution. The integral British society is a shadow thrown by the fantasy legal constitution which has become the plaything of the politics of public power. To cure itself, British society must refocus its self-consciousness on the integral society of self-perfecting, re-constituting itself within the integral societies of Europe and of the whole human race.

10

The Territorial State

THOMAS BALDWIN[1]

Max Weber famously defined states as human associations that successfully claim the monopoly of legitimate use of physical force within a given territory.[2] Modern theorists and critics of the state who start out from Weber's definition typically concentrate on the first part of it—the claim to a monopoly of the legitimate use of force. Thus Michael Taylor starts his discussion in *Community, Anarchy, and Liberty* with the Weberian definition,[3] enters a few critical reservations concerning it, and concludes that 'What is left of the Weberian account is the notion of a concentration of force and the attempt by those in whose hands it is (incompletely) concentrated to determine who else shall be permitted to employ force and on what occasions.'[4] What is manifestly lacking here is any reference to the territorial aspect of Weber's definition. This absence reflects Taylor's interests; but my aim in this essay will be to discuss precisely that aspect of the Weberian definition which Taylor and others neglect, the claim to a territory.

The territory of a state is, for Weber, that area of land within which a 'human association' has a monopoly of the legitimate use of physical force. Other theorists adopt a definition more closely tied to legal concepts: thus for Kelsen 'the territory of a State is in reality nothing but the territorial sphere of validity of the legal order called State'.[5] This difference reflects the different approaches to political theory of a sociologist and a legal theorist; but the underlying idea of a territory as

---

[1] I am much indebted to Kurt Lipstein, Brenda Almond, Peter Nicholson, Quentin Skinner, John Dunn, Martin Hollis, Sam Black, and an anonymous referee for help and comments on earlier versions of this paper.

[2] This is an abbreviation of the lengthy definition Weber advances in *The Theory of Social and Economic Organisation* (New York, 1964), 154–6; cf. n. 3 below.

[3] M. Taylor, *Community, Anarchy, and Liberty* (Cambridge, 1982), 4–5; I have copied Taylor's abbreviation of Weber's definition.

[4] Ibid. 5.

[5] H. Kelsen, *General Theory of Law and State*, tr. A. Wedburg (Cambridge, Mass., 1949), 208.

the area of the earth's surface within which a political authority is supreme is shared, and is enough to work with at present. It is of course not required that a territory be a geographical unit; a single territory can have non-contiguous spatial parts (as Pakistan used to have).

Intuitively, there is little doubt that possession of a territory is considered essential to the recognition that a suitably organized community constitutes a state. The foundation of the state of Israel is usually dated from its acquisition in 1948 of control over a territory, and debates about the establishment of a Palestinian state focus on the need to provide adequate territory for it. Nor is the point just one of common-sense intuition: J. G. Merrills writes in a recent handbook on international law that 'For legal purposes states are primarily territorial entities';[6] and A. James begins a recent discussion of international politics by declaring that 'The hundred and seventy or so states which engage in international relations have several characteristics in common. Perhaps the most fundamental is that they are all territorially based.'[7] At the start of this century there was some debate on the issue. W. E. Hall wrote:

Abstractly there is no reason why even a wandering tribe or society should not feel itself bound as stringently as a settled community by definite rules of conduct towards other communities, and though there might be difficulty in subjecting such societies to restraint, or, in some cases, of being sure of their identity, there would be nothing in such difficulties to exclude the possibility of regarding them as subjects of law, and there would be nothing therefore to render the possession of a fixed seat an absolute condition of admission to its benefits.[8]

To this W. Willoughby responded that if the area of land over which the tribal society wanders is regarded as part of the territory of another state, then we are not likely to regard the tribal society as constituting a state; whereas if the area of land in question is not already part of the territory of another state, then we will regard it as the territory of the society in question in so far as we regard the tribal society as constituting a state at all.[9] And as far as our normal judgements are concerned Willoughby seems right.

    [6] J. G. Merrills, *Anatomy of International Law* (London, 1981), 45.
    [7] A. James, *Sovereign Statehood* (London, 1986), 13.
    [8] W. E. Hall, *A Treatise on International Law*, 8th edn. (Oxford, 1924), 18–19.
    [9] W. W. Willoughby, *The Fundamental Concepts of Public Law* (New York, 1924), 64–5, 310.

What none of this justifies, however, is the assumption that the territorial conception of the state has legitimate application. We can extend Willoughby's line of thought to argue that if some political societies have territories, then, given the finite area of land available, all had better have them; but the initial premiss remains to be justified. Within international law one finds a list of criteria concerning the acquisition of territory which descend from Roman law; these concern such matters as discovery, occupation, prescription, cession, and conquest. But the application of these criteria in situations where there is a territorial dispute is not always straightforward—as in the case of the Falkland Islands/Islas Malvinas. And once questions are raised about the application of these criteria, questions arise about the choice of them in the first place: what should be our attitude to, for example, discovery and conquest? Rousseau asks:

When Nuñez Balbao, standing on the seashore, took possession of the South Seas and the whole of South America in the name of the crown of Castille, was that enough to dispossess all their actual inhabitants, and to shut out from them all the princes of the world? On such a showing, these ceremonies are idly multiplied, and the Catholic king need only take possession all at once, from his apartment, of the whole universe. (*Social Contract*, i. 9, tr. G. D. H. Cole; London, 1913)

As well as questioning the criteria employed within international law, we can call into question the status of international law itself and that of organizations such as the United Nations. We like to look scornfully at the Papal Bulls of 1493 by which Alexander VI divided the new world between Spain and Portugal. Palestinians take a similarly dim view of the role of the United Nations in resolving in 1947 in favour of the partition of Palestine.

A suitable symbol for the difficulty in gaining a clear understanding of the matter is the puzzling etymology of the word 'territory' itself. It is, obviously enough, the English translation of the Latin word *territorium*, which was employed to describe the area of land surrounding a town (*municipium*) which was under the latter's jurisdiction. But what is the origin of this Latin word? The obvious answer would appear to be that it comes from the word *terra*. But, as the *OED* observes, if that were correct, it should be spelled *terratorium* (so that we would have 'terratory'), a spelling which is indeed employed in the medieval period. The actual spelling of *territorium* suggests, instead, derivation from *terreor*—to frighten, via *territor*—one who frightens, to *territorium*—a place from which people are frightened off, which would at least fit within Austinian jurisprudence, and would give it the same etymology as 'terrorist'.

Another puzzle concerns the historical background to the territorial conception of the state. It is often said that this conception is characteristic of post-medieval Europe, of the decline of the Holy Roman Empire and the rejection of the juridical claims of the Papacy; and that the Peace of Westphalia of 1648, which brought an end to the Thirty Years War, is held to be especially significant in this respect. Thus T. A. Walker wrote that 'International Law as matter of *scientific* appreciation, resting upon Territorial Sovereignty, dates from the Peace of Westphalia, 1648.'[10] Now there is certainly something to this thesis: Huber's famous, and influential, work on 'The Conflict of Laws' (of 1689) begins by noting that 'since the breaking up of the provinces of the Roman Empire, Christendom has been divided into almost innumerable nations (*populi*), not subject to one another and not sharing the same system of government', and continues by enunciating the following maxims:

1. The laws of every *imperium* have force within the boundaries (*termini*) of its *Respublica*, and bind all subject to it, but not beyond.
2. Those are held to be subject to an *imperium* who are found within its boundaries, whether they be there permanently or temporarily.[11]

Huber explicitly connects these maxims with a conception of the state—*Respublica*: he writes that 'the proposition that all persons who act within the limits (*fines*) of an imperium are to be deemed subject thereto is absolutely certain, for it is in accordance both with the nature of the *Respublica* and the practice of subjecting all persons found therein to its authority.'

On further inspection, however, the situation appears more complex. The basic idea that politico-legal authority is territorial is at least medieval. Of the Holy Roman Emperor it was said both that he

---

[10] T. A. Walker, *The Science of International Law* (London, 1893); cf. T. J. Lawrence, *The Principles of International Law* (London, 1895), 112. For a recent version of the same thesis, cf. R. A. Falk, 'A New Paradigm for International Legal Systems: Prospects and Proposals', in R. A. Falk, F. V. Kratochwil, and S. H. Mendlowitz (eds.), *International Law: A Contemporary Perspective* (London, 1985).

[11] 'The Conflict of Laws' is ch. 3 of vol. ii, bk. 1 of Huber's *Praelectiones Juris Civilis Romani et Hodierni*. The best modern discussion of Huber's work is D. J. Llewelyn Davies, 'The Influence of Huber's *De Conflictu Legum* on English Private International Law', *British Year Book of International Law*, 18 (1937), 49–78.

was a *rex qui superiorem non recognoscit* and that *rex in regno suo est imperator regni suo*; and the second of these two maxims captures well the aspect of the Weberian definition with which I am concerned (just as the first maxim captures the other aspect of it). Admittedly there is not here the recognition of a plurality of *regni*, as there is in Huber, and one might suppose that, given the universalist aspirations of the Emperor, this is an aspect that did have to wait until the end of the medieval period. But Canning has shown that even in the thirteenth century there were jurists ready to question this.[12] For, in connection with the claims of the Kings of Sicily not to be subject to the Emperor, it was argued by the Neapolitan jurists that the King of Sicily and other 'free kings' have the same exclusive authority within their kingdom as the Emperor has within his.[13] Admittedly the Pope's authority on ecclesiastical matters was not thereby called into question;[14] this, I take it, is an issue that did not arise until the Reformation. But it is none the less fair to say the basic conception of the territorial sovereignty of independent kingdoms was clearly delineated (although not widely accepted) well before this time.

Another respect in which the familiar appeal to the Peace of Westphalia needs to be qualified arises from an implication to which it gives rise, namely that the conception of the state to be found in the classic texts of early modern political theory should be of an intrinsically territorial entity. The trouble in this case arises from the fact that if one turns to the classic texts, one finds little, if any, reference to the territorial nature of the state. Thus Grotius introduces the state (*civitas*), in *De Juri Belli ac Pacis* simply as 'a compleat Body of Free Persons associated together to enjoy peaceably their Rights and for their common benefit' (1. 1. 14; this is taken from Cicero—cf. *De Republica* 1. 25). Grotius goes on to say more about the mode of association involved: the state, he says, is the 'common subject' of sovereign power (1. 3. 7), by which he means that we only have a state where people are so associated that amongst them there is some one person, or a group, who, in relation to all others, is supreme, in the sense that 'his acts are not subject to another's *ius*'. Manifestly, there is here no reference to the existence of a territory. Of course, Grotius has a great deal to say about the property rights of individual persons, about their basis in 'a certain compact or agreement, either expressly,

---

[12] J. P. Canning, 'Law, Sovereignty and Corporation Theory, 1300–1450', in J. H. Burns (ed.), *Cambridge History of Medieval Political Thought* (Cambridge, 1987), 454–76.
[13] Ibid. 466 n. 46.   [14] Ibid. 476.

as by a division; or else tacitly, as by seizure' (2. 2. 5); and if we assume
that these property rights are among those which the state exists to
protect, then there will be some vague territorial implications to the
existence of a Grotian state. But these implications fall short of the
conception of an area of exclusive jurisdiction, and they require
assumptions other than those constitutive of Grotius's conception of
the state.

Likewise Hobbes tells us that where human beings covenant with
each other to authorize a man, or group of them, to act on their behalf
on all matters concerning 'Peace and Common Defence', 'the
multitude so united in one Person, is called a COMMONWEALTH, in
latine *CIVITAS*'. Hence, Hobbes says, the definition of a Commonwealth
is 'One Person, of whose Acts a great multitude, by mutual Covenants
one with another, have made themselves every one the Author'
(*Leviathan*, ch. 17). Again, there is no mention here of any territory.
One may feel that Hobbes's artificial person will not be able to secure
the peace and safety of its members unless it has exclusive control over
the area of land where they reside; but, as with Grotius, this is only an
implication of Hobbes's definition given other assumptions, in this
case about the best ways to secure peace and safety. Hobbes's
Commonwealth is not territorial by definition.

In the case of Locke the situation is a bit different. He affirms that
'Where-ever therefore any number of Men are so united into one
Society, as to quit every one his Executive Power of the Law of Nature,
and resign it to the publick, there and there only is a *Political, or Civil
Society*' (*Second Treatise*, para. 89). There is here no requirement that
the Political Society thus created should have control over a territory.
But Locke certainly assumes that many of those who thus create, or
enter into, a political society already have property in land—an 'estate';
for 'the great and chief end of' the creation of political society is 'the
mutual *Preservation* of . . . Lives, Liberties, and Estates' (para. 123).
And Locke is quite explicit in maintaining that those who enter into a
political society with an estate thereby bring their estate under the
jurisdiction of its government in such a way that it comes to form part
of its 'territory'—a word he employs with a clear grasp of its juridical
implications. He writes:

But as Families increased, and Industry inlarged their Stocks, their *Possessions
inlarged* with the need of them; but yet it was commonly *without any fixed
property in the ground* they made use of, till they incorporated, settled

themselves together, and built Cities, and then, by consent, they came in time, to set out the *bounds of their distinct Territories*, and agree on limits between them and their Neighbours, and by Laws within themselves, settled the *Properties* of those of the same Society. (para. 38; cf. 119–20)

So Locke's political societies should be taken to have territories, though this is not a consequence of Locke's definition of a political society itself, but only of that definition in conjunction with Locke's other assumptions. Indeed these assumptions do not warrant the territorial implications Locke draws. For he holds that although those who have rightly acquired (for example by inheritance) an estate within the territory of a political society can emigrate to join another political society, they cannot alienate the estate that they acquired and incorporate it within the territory of their new political society (para. 191). The original act of incorporation of the estate is supposed to bind that patch of land indissolubly within the jurisdiction of the political society within which it is incorporated. Yet this thesis does not follow from his natural law premisses and his account of the origins of political society, since this is supposed to protect antecedent property rights, and not to limit them in the way that Locke actually proposes.

Locke comes as close to an explicitly territorial conception of the state as any of the early modern political theorists I have encountered. The approach more characteristic of these theorists is essentially that of Grotius: the state (the commonwealth, political society . . .) is defined in terms of the unification of a group of people by bonds of power and authority in such a way that the Ciceronian goals of justice and prosperity can be secured. In so far a state thus defined has a territory (*imperium*), it is only in virtue of further assumptions about the antecedent property rights (*dominia*) of the people whose unification constitutes the state. This is the position advanced by Pufendorf in his *Of the Law of Nature and of Nations* of 1688 (cf. 7. 2. 13, 4. 6. 3); and it is again to be found in Vattel's famous treatise on *The Law of Nations* of 1758 (cf. Bk. 1, chs. 1, 18).

I embarked on this quick survey of early modern political theory in discussing the thesis that the territorial conception of the state is a mark of early modern, post-Westphalia, Europe. Although it is doubtless true that this conception does inform much political and legal writing from this time onwards (as Huber's work demonstrates), it does, I think, emerge that political theory had still to catch up with practice in this respect. Now my interest in this matter is not primarily historical; I want to discuss the basis, if any, for the legitimacy of the territorial claims states make. But before taking this up I shall briefly continue the quest for the origin of the Weberian definition, if for no other reason than for the sake of appeasing the curiosity which such questions arouse.

Where, then, do we first find explicit recognition of the territorial nature of states within political theory? Certainly not in Weber himself. The point is discussed by Sidgwick in *The Elements of Politics*, where he writes that 'in modern political thought the connection between a political society and its territory is so close that the two notions almost blend, and the same words are used indifferently to express either'.[15] Yet if one looks back from Sidgwick to the earlier utilitarians, Bentham and Austin, the territorial point is absent.[16] Where, then, does the territorial conception come to the surface of political theory? I am not sure, but I think it belongs within the romantic critique of the abstract rationalism of the political theory of the Enlightenment. A clear, and influential, example occurs in Bluntschli's *Theory of the State*: the state, he argues, is not just an ordered community; in addition 'a permanent relation of the people to the soil is necessary for the continuance of the State. The State requires its territory.'[17] Just where in the tradition of *Rechtsphilosophie* this requirement that a state be rooted in the soil originates, I do not know. It is not a feature of Hegel's conception of the state, though it fits well with his treatment of the state as a concrete universal. But it is not necessary to pursue the matter further here.

I turn now to the substantive issue of the legitimation of the territorial conception of the state. It is easy enough to see the advantages for a political community of exclusive jurisdiction over the areas of the earth's surface occupied by members of the community, including control of the natural resources that fall within these areas (and, as in the case of parts of the sea-bed, extend beyond it). For it is difficult to envisage how political autonomy is to be effectively secured without some territorial rights (just as it is often maintained that individual freedom requires

---

[15] H. Sidgwick, *The Elements of Politics* (London, 1897), 222.

[16] Austin notoriously defines the state in terms of the existence of a sovereign; see *The Province of Jurisprudence Determined* ed. H. Hart (London, 1954), lecture VI, 193–4, 224–6. Bentham in fact rejected the requirement that there be a sovereign; cf. J. Burns and H. Hart (eds.), *An Introduction to the Principles of Morals and Legislation* (London, 1970), 200 n. x. But he mentions no territorial requirement.

[17] J. K. Bluntschli, *Allgemeines Staatsrecht* (Munich, 1851); translated as *The Theory of the State* (Oxford, 1892), 16. Bluntschli sums up his conception of the state as follows: 'the State is a combination or association of men, in the form of government and governed, on a definite territory, united together into a moral organised masculine personality' (ibid. 23).

some private property). But, as with all exclusive rights, what needs to be elucidated is the way in which such exclusiveness is justifiable at all, and the principles according to which such exclusive rights are fairly distributed.

I return first to the account implicit in early modern political theory. It may have been felt that in searching for an explicitly territorial definition of the state in the writings of these theorists I was raising the wrong question. Instead, by not defining the state in territorial terms, but by locating their definition in the context of a natural law theory which includes property rights, perhaps these theorists were able to provide a theoretical legitimation of a state's territorial claims. For what could be more straightforward than the thesis that a state acquires its territorial rights through a social contract whereby the original members of a political society place their individual holdings under the jurisdiction of the state?

Apart from the issue, mentioned before in connection with Locke, of whether this thesis really does provide an adequate foundation for a state's putative territorial rights, the obvious question to which it gives rise is that of how these individual holdings were acquired. Locke famously introduces his theory of property by arguing that there can be private appropriation without the consent of others. The details of Locke's account are much disputed,[18] but only one point need be stressed here: if, as seems to me correct,[19] one takes it that Locke's account implies that all such appropriations of land (past as well as future) are called into question once land becomes scarce (*Second Treatise*, para. 33), then, in that situation appropriations by groups of people, by tribes and other communities, are equally called into question. What is unjust for one single individual is equally unjust for a group of them. Hence Tully, who argues that Locke's theory implies that scarcity invalidates all individual exclusive rights in the state of nature, is quite wrong to infer that 'community ownership of all possessions is the logical consequence of the premises of Locke's theory'.[20] On the contrary, the logical consequence of Locke's theory

---

[18] Recent discussions include: K. Olivecrona, 'Appropriation in the State of Nature: Locke on the Origin of Property', *Journal of the History of Ideas*, 35 (1974), 211–30; id., 'Locke's Theory of Appropriation', *Philosophical Quarterly*, 24 (1974), 220–34; J. Tully, *A Discourse on Property* (Cambridge, 1980), pt. 2; J. Waldron, *The Right to Private Property* (Oxford, 1988).

[19] This interpretation of Locke is disputed by Waldron, *Right to Private Property*.

[20] Tully, *Discourse on Property*, 165.

as represented by Tully is a complete absence of any exclusive property rights, including the territorial rights of political societies.

In my view Locke is not committed to this conclusion in virtue of his thesis that individual appropriation in the state of nature can also be legitimated by 'a tacit and voluntary consent' (*Second Treatise*, para. 50).[21] Since he also holds that political society only comes into existence when land becomes scarce, this, in effect, brings Locke into line with the Grotius–Pufendorf thesis that all natural property rights rest upon consent: that, as Pufendorf put it, 'although after the Donation of God, nothing was wanting, but for men to take possession; yet that one man's seizing on a Thing should be understood to exclude the right of all others to the same Thing, could not proceed but from Mutual Agreement' (*Of the Law of Nature and of Nations*, 4. 4. 4).

As presented by Grotius and Pufendorf, this 'Mutual Agreement' is pre-political, and the position is, therefore, vulnerable to scepticism concerning any such pre-political contract. The case of Rousseau is instructive here. He endorses the sceptical premiss (cf. *Social Contract*, 1. 8); but he equally assumes that states get their territories from the individual holdings of their citizens. Since the sceptical premiss implies that these holdings are not claims of right in the state of nature, there are no property rights to be transferred to the state by the social contract. Hence states do not have the territorial rights that they like to think they have:

This act [the social contract] does not make possession, in changing hands, change its nature . . . but, as the forces of the city are incomparably greater than those of an individual, public possession is also, in fact, stronger and more irrevocable, without being any more legitimate (*légitime*), at any rate from the point of view of foreigners. (Rousseau, *Social Contract*, 1. 9)

It may be felt that the sceptical premiss employed here concerning the existence of natural property rights is one that reflection on the territorial rights of states should lead one to withdraw. For since territorial claims are claims of right which states make to each other, if one holds that some such claims are valid in the absence of any supranational sovereign capable of effective control of the most powerful states, why should one not equally allow that there are rights for individuals in the state of nature? Of course, one can hold that where there is no sovereign there can be no law and no rights; this is

<hr>

[21] Cf. the papers by Olivecrona cited in n. 18 above.

indeed the line of thought which led Austin to deny that international law is 'law, properly so called'.[22] But this seems altogether too cursory a basis for rejecting the territorial conception of the state. As theorists of international law have repeatedly argued, one should instead reject the emphasis on sovereignty characteristic of Austin's conception of law. Since international law is possible, we must get used to the idea of public systems of right that lack a sovereign.

This much may, and surely should, be accepted. But does it really do the natural rights theorist much good? International law is not natural law; in traditional terminology it is the law of nations, not the law of nature. The question therefore is whether it provides a helpful model for the natural rights theorist. I think not. Although international law lacks a sovereign, it certainly does make essential reference to political institutions, in particular to states. Hence it does not provide a model for a system of contractual property rights that obtains in the absence of any such institutions. For this reason it does not help to rebut scepticism about the traditional use of the Grotius–Pufendorf thesis that property rights rest upon an original, non-hypothetical, 'Mutual Agreement' amongst individuals in the state of nature.

Yet if that thesis is transposed from the individualist context of early modern theory to an explicitly political context, whereby the parties to the agreement are not individuals but states, then, perhaps, there is more to be said for it. On this line of thought, there is no attempt at a derivation of territorial rights from pre-political individual holdings; instead the idea is that the territorial rights of states derive from a 'Mutual Agreement' amongst states themselves as to how the earth's natural resources should be divided. This idea can be connected with a familiar view about the significance of the recognition of one state by another. For, within both the practice and the theory of international law, it is recognition by other states that is often held to be crucial in each other's legitimation, including the legitimation of each other's territorial claims. Kelsen's account is typical:

The procedure provided by general international law to ascertain the fact 'State in the sense of international law' in a concrete case, is called recognition; competent to ascertain the existence of this fact are the governments of the other States interested in the existence of the State in question.[23]

It is not clear for how long recognition has been assigned this central role within the practice of international law. Although the duty of

---

[22] Austin, *Province of Jurisprudence*, 141–2.   [23] Kelsen, *Law and State*, 222.

respect for treaties (*pacta sunt servanda*) is as old as history, the idea that third parties might explicitly signal their interest in the outcome of territorial disputes seems to have developed only through the role of the so-called 'Great Powers' in framing the treaties which, during the nineteenth century, transformed parts of the old Ottoman empire into states such as Greece and Serbia.[24] But by 1914 the practice was well established, and it was central to the new order in Europe introduced by the Treaty of Versailles of 1919. By contrast, a theoretical understanding of the role of mutual recognition evolved considerably earlier. Hegel observes in *The Philosophy of Right* that 'A state is as little an actual individual without relations to other states as an individual is actually a person without *rapport* with other persons';[25] hence, he argues, although

the legitimate authority of a state . . . is partly a purely domestic matter . . . it is no less essential that this authority should receive its full and final legitimation through its recognition by other states, although this recognition requires to be safeguarded by the proviso that where a state is to be recognized by others, it shall likewise recognize them, i.e. respect their autonomy. (ibid.)

In the writings of Oppenheim, Kelsen, Lauterpacht, Chen, and other legal theorists, recognition occupies a central position in the theory of the state.[26] However, these theorists are not agreed as to its significance, and for many years there has been a dispute between proponents of the 'constitutive' and 'declaratory' views of recognition. The 'constitutive' view is that international recognition has a creative role in the legitimation of a state's authority. Indeed, something of this kind seems to be essential to any view which assigns fundamental importance to recognition (and thus to non-recognition, as under the Stimson doctrine). But critics have objected to this account that it treats a state's legitimacy in international affairs (and thus its territorial rights) on the model of membership of a club; and just as existing members of a club are not normally under any obligation to admit a new member, so, it seems, on this theory political communities with as good a claim to territorial rights as any other can be denied them through their failure to secure international recognition. Furthermore, it is asked just how the original 'club' of mutually recognizing states

[24] Cf. R. Langer, *Seizure of Territory* (Princeton, NJ, 1947), ch. 1.

[25] Hegel, *The Philosophy of Right*, tr. T. Knox (Oxford, 1942), s. 331.

[26] Kelsen, *Law and State*; H. Lauterpacht, *Recognition in International Law* (Cambridge, 1947); Ti-Chiang Chen, *The International Law of Recognition*, ed. L. Green (London, 1951).

came to be established; there is a suspicion of vicious circularity in a procedure whereby international rights somehow get parcelled out through the activities of a group whose status itself depends upon this parcelling out of rights.

Proponents of the alternative 'declaratory' view, therefore, hold that the significance of recognition is essentially just diplomatic: it signifies the willingness of one state to enter into normal diplomatic and economic relations with another, but does not have a constitutive role in establishing the validity of a community's claim to be a state and thus its territorial rights. These issues are, rather, to be settled by criteria established within international law—such as that a community is a state if its members are subject to an independent government which has effective control over the territory within which the members live.

Where the declaratory view is interpreted to imply that it is just a matter of empirical, non-legal, fact whether or not these criteria are satisfied, it is open to the objection that it permits the issue of statehood to be settled by the use of force; if territorial rights are simply determined by what government actually has effective control over a region, then successful conquest (together, perhaps, with colonization and forced resettlement) will create title. But that is clearly unacceptable, for the reason given by Kant—'reason, as the highest legislative moral power, absolutely condemns war as a test of rights'.[27] Most proponents of the declaratory view in fact interpret it in a different way: as the view that it is for international law not only to determine whether the criteria relevant to statehood are satisfied, but also what they are. Hence as long as it is established within international law that conquest does not create title (as under art. 2 (4) of the United Nations Charter), the objection lapses.

When the declaratory view is understood in this way, it becomes easy to suggest a compromise between it and the constitutive view. For proponents of the latter view precisely hold that international recognition is in some respects decisive within international law in determining whether or not the criteria for statehood are satisfied (cf. the passage from Kelsen quoted above). Furthermore, in order to avoid the accusation that the constitutive view implies the 'club membership' model of international status, its proponents often also hold that there is a duty to recognize when the familiar criteria of an independent government and effective control within a territory are

[27] 'Perpetual Peace: A Philosophical Sketch', in *Kant's Political Writings*, tr. Nisbet (Cambridge, 1970), 102.

satisfied. This then leads to the view, as Lauterpacht put it, that recognition

is declaratory in the sense that, in the contemplation of the law, the community in question is entitled to recognition as a matter of right and that we may safely disregard the objection that, not being recognized, it cannot be 'legally entitled' to anything. On the other hand, recognition is constitutive in the meaning that it is decisive for the creation of the international personality of the State and of the rights normally associated with it.[28]

Lauterpacht's compromise rests on a judicial model of recognition. He takes it that in the absence of any effective international tribunal with compulsory jurisdiction the international community sits as judge and jury to determine whether the criteria of statehood acknowledged within international law are satisfied.[29] This position remains open to criticism; for it is disputed whether recognition is actually accorded the significance within international law that Lauterpacht's account implies that it should have.[30] But I do not propose to pursue further the details of the constitutive/declaratory debate within international law; that debate has tended to focus on the detailed application of doctrines about recognition within disputed cases of international law, and in that context it is often hard to see the point of the debate.[31] What all this omits, however, is the broader context within which the appeal to international law takes place; and I want to suggest that it is here that the constitutive account of recognition still has a proper place. Lauterpacht's judicial model omits the fact that the international community sits not only as judge and jury, but also as legislator.

What underpins this role for the international community, and the significance of recognition in relation to the validity of territorial claims, is just the old Grotius–Pufendorf thesis that all property rights rest upon 'mutual agreement'. This can be agreement either to particular territorial claims or to a general procedure for determining territorial rights and settling territorial disputes. So once it is granted that recognition by the international community is the expression of that agreement, it follows that recognition is indeed constitutive of the territorial rights of all states. Now there were two objections to the

---

[28] Lauterpacht, *Recognition*, 75.

[29] Ibid. 55. Cf. also the passage from Kelsen referred to above in n. 23.

[30] Cf. J. Crawford, 'The Criteria for Statehood in International Law', *British Year Book of International Law*, 48 (1976–7), 104–5.

[31] Cf. I. Brownlie, 'Recognition in Theory and Practice', *British Year Book of International Law*, 53 (1982).

constitutive view of recognition, based on its association with a 'club-membership' model: that there is nothing to rule out arbitrary and unjust refusals to grant recognition; and that there is a suspicious circularity in relying on mutual recognition to legitimate the status of political communities as states. Both these objections point to genuine weaknesses; but the correct response is not to withdraw to a view which relies on a non-consensual division of the earth's surface (for what could this be but a legitimation of past luck and force?), but to see how to handle them within an understanding of international recognition as the expression, however imperfect, of that consent which provides the only possible foundation for territorial claims.

The first objection points to the need for recognition to be granted for reasons which do not just manifest the expediency of powerful states. A remark made by Neville Chamberlain in 1938 shows the position to be rejected: concerning the Italian occupation of Ethiopia, he remarked that 'the question of the formal recognition of the Italian position in Abyssinia was one that could only be morally justified if it was found to be a factor, and an essential factor, in a general appeasement'.[32] I shall return below to the question of what principles should govern the practice of recognition, but in thinking about it one needs also to confront the second objection to the constitutive view of recognition, which alleges a vicious circularity in the process of legitimation through recognition, since the procedure of recognition presupposes the existence of states whose existence, at least on the territorial conception of the state, is supposed to be constituted by the procedure itself.

To avoid this one needs to distinguish between the concept of a political community, which is that of a candidate for territorial rights, and a state itself; the idea will be that political communities acknowledge the legitimacy of each other's territorial claims, and thereby constitute each other as states. But without an account of what constitutes a political community, this is only a verbal move. One suggestion is that one should return to the original Weberian definition minus its territorial aspect; that is, that a political community is a human association which successfully claims the monopoly of legitimate use of force with respect to a given population.[33] But this is too closely

---

[32] Quoted in Langer, *Seizure of Territory*, 139.

[33] Since Weber himself makes territoriality the distinguishing feature of the state, this suggestion is not one that he would favour. Cf. *Theory of Social and Economic Organisation*, 154.

tied to the successful use of force, and in its reliance on the concept of legitimacy threatens to reintroduce the circularity that was to be avoided. Another proposal is that one should rely on the concept of a nation, as in the principle of national self-determination. But, as the subsequent history of that principle shows, the usual criteria of nationality (language, religion, history) do not by themselves define human associations which are appropriate for political recognition.[34] It seems to me, therefore, that one does best to employ the liberal conception of a voluntary human association of those who wish to constitute themselves as an autonomous political group with territorial rights.[35] There is no logical circularity in relying on the aspiration to become a state to pick out those groups which one wants to consider as candidates for recognition as states; and where this aspiration exists it surely constitutes a prima facie basis for a claim to recognition. In practice, of course, the usual criteria of nationality will often be associated with that of a political community thus understood; for it is typically where national groups feel themselves to be systematically disadvantaged by existing political institutions that they begin to press for political autonomy. But it is this latter aspiration, and not their national characteristics, which give rise to their claim for recognition.

Yet powerful states are characteristically unresponsive to seces-sionist movements within their borders, and these movements frequently gain little support from other states unless recognition by them is in the interest of those states (the current situation in East Timor exemplifies both points). So why should one accept that the international community, the collection of mutually recognizing states, can speak for mankind as a whole and express its consent to some one division of the earth's natural resources? The answer to this must be that since states are precisely political communities with both prima facie internal legitimacy and recognition by others, there is no alternative to relying on their judgement. One simply cannot appeal directly, over the head of all existing political institutions, to the judgement of mankind as a whole (including future generations, who are to be committed by present judgements); nor is there any other formal or informal institution, such as the Papacy or the International

---

[34] Cf. A. Cobham, *The Nation State and National Self-Determination* (London, 1969). For a more recent discussion, cf. D. Miller, 'The Ethical Significance of Nationality', *Ethics*, 98 (1988), 647–62.

[35] Cf. H. Beran, 'A Liberal Theory of Secession', *Political Studies*, 32 (1984), 21–31. I am much indebted to this paper.

Court of Justice, to which an appeal can be directed which does not draw its authority from the international community.

In this sense there is, I think, an inevitable element of circularity in the procedure of international recognition. The resulting situation is analogous to that which Quine's epistemology has made familiar;[36] in both cases, the procedure of justification has to take place 'at sea', that is, in the light of our current epistemological or international commitments. There is no 'first philosophy' to which we can withdraw and which could serve as the basis for the reconstruction of a system of certain knowledge or of international justice. Yet just as the Quinean epistemology is not an unyielding defence of common sense, the role of the international community should not become an excuse for a complacent defence of the status quo. In both cases it has to be possible to call each particular assumption into question while leaving the general system intact. Thus in the international case there needs to be a way in which the status of any given state, and in particular its territorial rights, can be called into question and revised in the light of the claims of previously unrecognized political communities that ask for recognition. Otherwise, the objection based on the 'club-membership' model of the constitutive view of recognition would remain unanswered.

To achieve this end, it seems desirable that the international community should constitute itself as an organization with the authority to scrutinize critically the status of each of its members by providing a forum within which communities that seek political independence, and thus their own territory, can make their appeal. This is not a novel thought: Woodrow Wilson's original draft for Article 10 of the Covenant of the League of Nations suggested that the League should perform just this role:

The Contracting Parties unite in guaranteeing to each other political independence and territorial integrity; but it is understood between them that such territorial adjustments, if any, as may in the future become necessary by reason of changes in present racial conditions and aspirations or present social and political relationships, pursuant to the principle of self-determination, and also such territorial readjustments as may in the judgement of three-fourths of the Delegates be demanded by the welfare and manifest interest of the people concerned, may be effected, if agreeable to those peoples.[37]

---

[36] Cf. W. V. O. Quine, 'Two Dogmas of Empiricism', in *From a Logical Point of View*, 2nd edn. (New York, 1961), esp. 42–6.

[37] Quoted by Langer, *Seizure of Territory*, 40.

In the actual Covenant as adopted this clause was watered down; but the League of Nations did none the less initially seek to apply the principle of self-determination along the lines suggested by Wilson's proposal. What then crippled the League was the non-participation of the USA and Germany, and the hypocrisy of the old imperial powers, Britain and France. The United Nations does not suffer from these defects. On the other hand, it is less clearly informed by an ideal of international justice than the League was, and the role assigned in its charter to the 'Great Powers' within the Security Council appears to lay it open to the 'club-membership' objection to the constitutive account of recognition.

Perhaps this is too critical a view of the constitution of the United Nations. But if one holds that the territorial claims of states are legitimate only where there is an effective international organization of states with authority to adjust the territorial rights of existing states, however powerful, and that the United Nations, the only current candidate for such an organization, is not yet one, it will follow that the territorial claims of states are not legitimate. Hence, if the territorial conception of the state is retained, it will follow that there are now no legitimate states, and that a form of international anarchism currently prevails.

In my view this sceptical conclusion over-dramatizes the current situation; and the argument for it is flawed by a sub-Austinian hankering for an international sovereign. There is no need for such a sovereign to legitimate the informal procedures of general international recognition which fix most territorial boundaries, including those which arise from direct treaties between the parties to a dispute and from judgments handed down by the international court. But what the current world system does not incorporate is a fair procedure for settling disputed claims made by communities which wish to secede from existing political arrangements and are prevented from doing so by force. It is for these cases that the 'club-membership' objection to present arrangements is so potent, and it is no accident that for the communities involved there is at present little alternative but to resort to arms in order to establish 'effective control' over the area they seek as their territory, and in that way make their case for international recognition (cf. Eritrea, East Timor, Kurdistan, etc.[38]). Yet trial by combat has for long been abolished within national jurisdictions: and it

[38] The reports of the Minority Rights Group, London, document many cases of this kind.

should equally be abolished in the international sphere as a test of rights. Hence until some other procedure is adopted by the international community the anarchist conclusion stands for these cases.

These reflections have been largely directed to the issue as to how the exclusive territorial rights that states claim for themselves might be justified. I have suggested that, subject to certain conditions, agreement amongst the international community provides such a justification, indeed the only justification available to us. But I have so far said nothing about the considerations concerning the distribution of territory which should inform such agreements. One may indeed feel that there is no need for such considerations. For if the allocation of territory is a matter for mutual agreement, then one need look no further than the terms of actual agreements to settle territorial rights: *pacta sunt servanda*. There will, of course, remain the possibility of speculations concerning ideal distributions of territory, and here general principles of distributive justice will have a place; but the fact that an actual situation is not ideal does not imply that it is not legitimate. Yet although the contrast between what is legitimate and what is ideal is inescapable, it does not follow that general considerations of justice are irrelevant to the process of reaching agreement. For uncoerced agreement on particular cases can only be expected where there is a higher-order mutual agreement concerning the general principles to be applied. Hence there is a dialectical relationship between the process of international legitimation and the acceptance of substantive principles of justice which gives point to reflection on the latter without their satisfaction being treated as a condition of the legitimacy of actual territorial boundaries.

Within the practice of international law the criteria of discovery, occupation, prescription, and cession are well established (conquest having been invalidated by the adoption of the United Nations Charter). Although one can readily see the point of altering past arrangements as little as possible (and there is no merit in seeking to redraw territorial boundaries *ex nihilo*), it is difficult not to feel that these criteria embody too much respect for past good fortune and military success. They also omit any reference to the need to accommodate the outcome of self-determination by political communities which were not previously recognized as states.[39] And as

---

[39] To acknowledge this need is not to imply that in all cases secession should be permitted—e.g. where the group which wishes to secede occupies an area which is

further considerations are introduced, for example concerning the territorial division of unsettled areas of the Arctic, it is worth asking whether theory of justice provides a general perspective which can be usefully brought to bear on this matter.

Current debates within political philosophy on the topic of justice are dominated by the dispute between utilitarians and contractualists.[40] Both of these approaches can be applied to the current issue. The utilitarian approach will be essentially that developed by Hume.[41] Hume held that the institution of property is essential to the welfare of human society, and that its persistence requires that it be regulated by rules which strictly respect past holdings; indeed Hume offers a utilitarian derivation of the familiar criteria of discovery, occupation, etc. While Hume's discussion follows the order of early modern theorists, in that within his utilitarian framework he derives the territorial rights of states from the property holdings of their citizens, utilitarianism is not committed to this individualist framework. Although, for the utilitarian, it is the welfare of individual people that counts in the end, the utilitarian can readily recognize the great value to an individual of membership of a self-governing political community and hold that it is via this communal good that territorial rights are to be justified.

Despite Hume's insistence on the value of stability, there is surely a strong utilitarian case to be made for supposing that human welfare will be increased by a system of rules with a powerful redistributive element as compared with Hume's conservative prescriptions. Even when due allowance is made for the utility of rewarding past efforts and prudence, and of enabling forward planning to proceed within a stable framework, the utilitarian ideal observer will surely prescribe substantial adjustments in territorial boundaries in order to enable human welfare to be increased. She will find in the often grotesque mismatch between natural resources and human needs to which present territorial boundaries give rise a compelling reason for adjusting the boundaries in order to bring the two more closely into line; and it is hard not to share this attitude. But the objection to the utilitarian approach is that it is liable to encourage an excessively

---

essential to the state from which it wishes to secede (the Sudetenland is perhaps a case in point). Cf. Beran, 'Liberal Theory of Secession', 30–1.

[40] Cf. esp. T. Scanlon, 'Contractualism and Utilitarianism', in A. Sen and B. Williams (eds.), *Utilitarianism and Beyond* (Cambridge, 1982), 103–28.

[41] Hume, *A Treatise of Human Nature*, 3. 2. 2, 3, and 4.

redistributive approach: with its emphasis on the *future* welfare of *all* sentient beings, it is prone to undervalue historical attachments to particular territories and to sacrifice the interests of small communities for the greater good of the rest of mankind. Might not a utilitarian ideal observer have prescribed just what Chamberlain did at Munich? And is not the protest of the Czechoslovak government at the time, that their security should not be sacrificed in order to avert the threat of evils for others, of just the kind which contractualists urge against utilitarians at the individual level?

In turning to the contractualist approach, one needs to bear in mind that Rawls introduces this approach when considering the principles of justice that are to apply to a society which is a 'more or less self-sufficient . . . cooperative venture for mutual advantage'.[42] Since it is idle to pretend that mankind as a whole constitutes a society of this kind, it is not at first clear how the contractualist approach is to be brought to bear on the issue of justice in international affairs. But Rawls himself suggests that his approach can be extended to apply to international affairs by supposing representatives of the world's societies to select, behind a veil of ignorance concerning the identity of their own society, principles which are to govern the relationships between states.[43] Rawls then suggests that the principles thus selected would be a pretty minimal set: the juristic equality within international affairs of all states, a principle of self-determination for all societies, and the principle that *pacta sunt servanda*.[44] But his critics have proposed that one need not be so minimalist, particularly concerning the distribution of the world's natural resources. Why should not the contracting representatives adopt an international distributive principle comparable to Rawls's own maximin principle?[45]

It seems to me that Rawls's critics are largely right on this issue. Furthermore one does not need to introduce the pretence of a single world community in order to make the issue of distribution one which

---

[42] J. Rawls, *A Theory of Justice* (Oxford, 1972), 4.

[43] Ibid. 378–9.

[44] It is not altogether clear to which principles of self-determination Rawls subscribes. He employs the terms 'state', 'nation', 'people', and 'society' more or less interchangeably in discussing international justice; but it makes a good deal of difference to which category the principle of self-determination is to apply.

[45] Cf. B. Barry, *The Liberal Theory of Justice* (Oxford, 1973), 130–3; C. Beitz, *Political Theory and International Relations* (Princeton, NJ, 1979), 138–42. But cf. also Barry's second thoughts in 'Humanity and Justice in a Global Perspective', in *Nomos* 24, ed. J. R. Pennock and J. W. Chapman (New York, 1982), 232–3.

properly arises within Rawls's own hypothetical framework.[46] It suffices to recall the modified Grotius–Pufendorf thesis that the territorial divisions between states (which largely determine the distribution of natural resources) rest upon 'mutual agreement' within the international community. For if this is accepted, then surely it is appropriate to consider what principles the parties to Rawls's international original position will adopt concerning the distribution of natural resources and the determination of territorial boundaries. For what is Rawls's hypothetical procedure in this case if not an idealized version of the procedure which actually legitimates territorial rights?

What principles would the representatives then adopt? The following commend themselves:

1. a principle of self-determination, to the effect that political communities which seek autonomy should, as far as is practicable, be allocated a territory within which they can become autonomous states;
2. a principle of self-sufficiency, to the effect that a state's territory should contain sufficient natural resources to enable it to sustain an economy which meets the needs of its members;
3. a historical principle, to the effect that a state's territorial boundaries should be adjusted as little as possible, to enable the state both to take a long-term view of its natural resources and to preserve its culture by keeping in touch with the historical setting (architecture, agriculture, etc.) within which that culture developed.

These principles are to be thought of as lexically ordered, in Rawls's sense.[47] The principle of self-determination for communities is the fundamental principle when the issue of territorial divisions is considered. It is a principle of political liberty whose priority is comparable to that which Rawls assigns to his own principle of individual liberty. The second principle then asserts that a territory has to enable a community to maintain at least a degree of economic independence sufficient for it to preserve its political dependence. The

---

[46] Barry, 'Humanity and Justice', criticizes Beitz, *Political Theory and International Relations*, for interpreting world trade as evidence that mankind form one single 'co-operative venture for mutual advantage', and using this as his reason for thinking that Rawls's principle of distributive justice is applicable within international affairs. But this is unfair to Beitz; for although he does argue in this way (ibid. 144–53), he also argues directly that the distributive issue arises from within Rawls's own assumption that individual states are self-sufficient (*Theory of Justice*, 137–43).

[47] Rawls, *Theory of Justice*, 42–3.

third principle is then a conservative principle whose rationale is self-explanatory and which also provides the basis for the familiar criteria employed in international law.

I do not, of course, pretend that employment of these principles promises an easy solution to territorial disputes and problems of nationality; history is such that there are often no ideal solutions. And, despite principle 3, there may be a need for further principles concerning territorial readjustment to cover the difficult issues raised by migration, population growth, and climatic change. A related point, on which my principles so far differ from those of Rawls's other critics,[48] concerns Rawls's maximin principle itself. The objection to a direct analogue of this principle which would prescribe readjustment of territorial boundaries in order to maximize the situation of the typical inhabitant of the poorest state is that it would violate the conservative principle 3. If there were no other way to accommodate the intuition that the distribution of natural resources is 'arbitrary from a moral point of view', one might think it right to pay this price. But there is another way: if we think of systems of individual property rights, the standard redistributive device within the state is that of taxation, and one can think of versions of that on an international scale. For it is not obvious that the assignment of a territory, as an area of exclusive political jurisdiction, need carry with it an exclusive right to the benefits to be obtained from exploitation of the natural resources located within that territory. It fits better with the perspective of Rawls's international original position to take it, as Barry puts it,[49] that there is 'an equal basic right to enjoy the benefits of the earth's natural resources', and that this should be realized through an international system of redistributive taxation.

There is much more to be said on these questions of international distributive justice; but my chief aim in this essay has been to argue that political theory, the theory of the state, requires an international context. Although this thesis has long been accepted by legal theorists, it has received little recognition in political theory. Much recent writing in this area has been informed by a 'communitarian' reaction against the abstraction of universal theories of justice. Certainly, too, the emphasis on the importance to individuals of their community is valuable. But one's enjoyment of benefits as a member of one's own political community, one's state, is dependent upon that state's

[48] e.g. Beitz, *Political Theory and International Relations*, 141–2.
[49] Barry, 'Humanity and Justice', 235.

existence within the international community. So justice within the community presupposes a system of international justice. Bakunin famously posed the question 'Anarchism or Statism?'; but, as he himself recognized, the question was ill-posed.[50] For the alternative to anarchism is not statism, the view that the state is by itself a self-sufficient domain of right: that view, under examination, collapses back into anarchism. Instead, the alternative which contrasts with anarchism is a form of internationalism which legitimates the rights of states in order that they should be able to enjoy the limited autonomy to which they are entitled. So, having begun with Weber's definition of the state, I end with that of Kelsen:

The national legal order, that is, an order which constitutes a state, can thus be defined as a relatively centralized coercive order whose territorial, personal, and temporal spheres of validity are determined by international law and whose material sphere of validity is limited by international law only. This is the juristic definition of the State.[51]

[50] Cf. *The Political Philosophy of Bakunin*, ed. V. Maximoff (Glencoe, Ill., 1953), 138–9.

[51] Kelsen, *Law and State*, 351. Although I introduce Kelsen's definition because it fits well with my internationalist conclusion, I should acknowledge that Kelsen's actual position on the relative priority of national and international law is obscure. On the one hand he writes that 'It is the basic norm of the international legal order which is the ultimate reason of validity of the national legal orders' (ibid. 368); on the other hand, he insists that the science of law does not have any implications concerning the relative priority of national and international law (ibid. 386–8). This latter view obviously owes much to his general legal positivism. On other difficulties arising from this aspect of Kelsen's position, cf. H. Bull, 'Hans Kelsen and International Law', in R. Tur and W. Twining (eds.), *Essays on Kelsen* (Oxford, 1986), 321–36.

I I

Liberty and Legal Obligation in Hobbes's *Leviathan*

QUENTIN SKINNER[1]

Thomas Hobbes's philosophy of law, especially as articulated in *Leviathan*, presents the reader with a seeming paradox. On the one hand, the liberty of subjects is held to depend in almost every instance on 'the silence of the Law'.[2] But on the other hand, law and liberty are held to be compatible.[3] One of the questions which has always preoccupied Hobbes's commentators has in consequence been whether Hobbes's views on liberty and legal obligation are merely confused, or whether there is some way in which his apparently contradictory statements can be reconciled.

Perhaps not surprisingly, the consensus has been that no such reconciliation is possible.[4] I have come to feel, however, that this

[1] The ensuing discussion draws heavily on my article 'Thomas Hobbes on the Proper Signification of Liberty', *Transactions of the Royal Historical Society*, 5th Series, 40 (1990), 121–51, © the Royal Historical Society. I have greatly abridged and revised my original text, but I am most grateful to the Council of the Royal Historical Society for permission to reprint considerable sections of it. To Raymond Geuss, Susan James, James Tully, and Austin Woolrych I am much indebted for comments on the original version, and to Ross Harrison for help in revising it.

[2] Thomas Hobbes, *Leviathan*, Penguin Classics edn., ed. C. B. Macpherson (Harmondsworth, 1985), 271. All in-text page references to *Leviathan* to follow are to this edition, as well as references in notes except for n. 50 below. I have retained the original spelling, but dropped Hobbes's copious italicization. I have also felt free to modernize punctuation where this helps to bring out more clearly my interpretation of the text.

[3] For this claim see *Leviathan*, esp. 262–3, 269.

[4] See e.g. J. Roland Pennock, 'Hobbes's Confusing "Clarity"—the Case of "Liberty"' in Keith C. Brown (ed.), *Hobbes Studies* (Oxford, 1965), 101–16; A. G. Wernham, 'Liberty and Obligation in Hobbes', in Brown, *Hobbes Studies*, 120–1; David P. Gauthier, *The Logic of Leviathan* (Oxford, 1969), 62, 65–6; Ralph Ross, 'Some Puzzles in Hobbes', in Ralph Ross, Herbert W. Schneider, and Theodore Waldman (eds.), *Thomas Hobbes in his Time* (Minneapolis, 1974), esp. 55–6; D. D. Raphael, 'Hobbes', in Z. Pelczynski and John Gray (eds.), *Conceptions of Liberty in Political Philosophy* (London, 1984), esp. 30–4. But for two defences of Hobbes's consistency see

criticism arguably stems from a failure to come to terms with certain peculiarities in Hobbes's underlying conception of human freedom. Once these peculiarities are clarified, the apparent confusions in Hobbes's analysis of the relations between legal obligation and liberty can, I think, be shown to dissolve.

I

There are two especially striking features of Hobbes's discussion of liberty in *Leviathan*. One is the vehemence with which he insists that his own explication of the concept represents the only possible one. No comparable tone of urgency underlies his earlier discussions either in *The Elements of Law*, first circulated in 1640, or in *De Cive*, first published in 1642.[5] By the time he came to issue *Leviathan* in 1651, however, Hobbes had clearly come to regard it as a matter of great importance to be able to declare that what he was offering was an account of 'the proper signification' (p. 189) of liberty, what it 'signifieth properly' (p. 261), how to understand it 'in the proper sense' (p. 264).

The other striking feature of Hobbes's analysis is its extreme simplicity. He first introduces the topic of human freedom in connection with his discussion of 'the right of nature' in chapter 14. This he defines as 'the liberty each man hath to use his power as he

W. von Leyden, *Hobbes and Locke: The Politics of Freedom and Obligation* (London, 1982), esp. 45–50; and M. M. Goldsmith, 'Hobbes on Liberty', *Hobbes Studies*, 2 (1989), 23–39.

[5] Hobbes's discussion in *The Elements* fails even to provide a formal definition of liberty. See Thomas Hobbes, *The Elements of Law*, ed. F. Tönnies with Intro. by M. M. Goldsmith (London, 1969), 134. The corresponding passage in *De Cive* does offer a definition, but only alludes glancingly to the alleged dangers of failing to adopt it. See Thomas Hobbes, *De Cive: The Latin Version*, ed. H. Warrender (Oxford, 1983), 167. Note that, as several scholars have recently argued, the English translation of *De Cive* issued in March 1651 is almost certainly not by Hobbes, despite Warrender's assertions to the contrary. See H. Warrender, 'Editor's Introduction', ibid. 4–8. Compare the scepticism voiced in M. M. Goldsmith, 'Picturing Hobbes's Politics: The Illustrations to *Philosophical Rudiments*', *Journal of the Warburg and Courtauld Institutes*, 44 (1981), 232–7, and the references there to earlier expressions of doubt. For further and decisive doubts see Noel Malcolm, 'Citizen Hobbes', *London Review of Books* (18–31 Oct. 1984), 22. The point is also taken up in Richard Tuck, 'Warrender's *De Cive*', *Political Studies*, 33 (1985), 308–15, esp. 310–12. Since the 1651 translation is of such doubtful standing—and indeed makes use of a political vocabulary partly at odds with the one Hobbes generally employs when writing in English—I have preferred, when citing from *De Cive*, to make my own translations from Warrender's edition of the Latin text.

will himself for the preservation of his own nature' (p. 189).[6] This freedom or liberty,[7] Hobbes at once stresses, must be defined in negative terms. The presence of liberty is always marked, that is, by the absence of something else. Specifically, it is marked by 'the absence of externall Impediments' (p. 189). And by 'impediments' Hobbes simply means anything that can hinder a man from using his powers 'according as his judgment and reason shall dictate to him' (p. 189).

This analysis is subsequently taken up and elaborated at the start of chapter 21, at which point Hobbes presents his formal definition of what it means to be a free man. 'A FREE-MAN is he that, in those things which by his strength and wit he is able to do, is not hindered to do what he has a will to' (p. 262). As this makes clear, Hobbes sees two essential elements in the concept of human freedom. One is the idea of possessing an underlying power or ability to act. As Hobbes had already observed in chapter 14, it is in relation to 'a man's power to do what hee would' (p. 189) that we speak of his being or not being at liberty.[8] The other is the idea of being unimpeded in the exercise of such powers. As Hobbes explains later in chapter 21, the freedom of a man 'consisteth in this, that he finds no stop in doing what he has the will, desire or inclination to do' (p. 262).[9]

Hobbes's basic doctrine can thus be very straightforwardly summarized. He already hints as much at the start of chapter 14 of *Leviathan*,[10] but he says so most clearly at the end of *The Questions Concerning Liberty, Necessity and Chance*, his final reply to Bishop Bramhall on the problem of free will. A free agent is he who, in respect of his powers or abilities, 'can do if he will and forbear if he will'.[11]

---

[6] Note that, because Hobbes equates human freedom with the freedom of a man, and because I am seeking to explicate his views, I have felt obliged to follow his usage. But I should not like it to be thought that this is an equation I accept.

[7] As Hobbes makes clear at the start of ch. 21 of *Leviathan*—where he speaks (p. 261) of what 'LIBERTY, or FREEDOME, signifieth'—he makes no distinction of meaning between the two terms. I have followed him in using them interchangeably.

[8] Cf. also the earlier discussion of power in ch. 10, esp. Hobbes's definition of 'the POWER of a man' as 'his present means to obtain some future apparent Good', p. 150.

[9] The point is foreshadowed in the discussion of deliberation in ch. 6. See esp. p. 127, where Hobbes claims that deliberation is so called 'because it is a putting an end to the Liberty we had of doing or omitting according to our own Appetite or Aversion'.

[10] See *Leviathan*, 189, where 'right' is defined in terms of 'liberty to do or forbeare'. See also the earlier account of deliberation as the means by which we put an end to our liberty 'of doing or omitting'. Cf. n. 9 above.

[11] See Thomas Hobbes, *The Questions Concerning Liberty, Necessity and Chance* (London, 1656), 301. Cf. also Hobbes's opening formula, pp. 28–9. For the complete bibliography of Hobbes's debate with Bramhall see H. Macdonald and M. Hargreaves, *Thomas Hobbes: A Bibliography* (London, 1952), 37–41.

As Hobbes recognizes, however, this analysis is not yet a very illuminating one. We still lack an account of the kinds of limitations on human action that can count as impediments. To put the point another way, we still lack a criterion for distinguishing between inherent limitations upon our powers themselves, and positive constraints upon our freedom to exercise or forbear from exercising those powers in accordance with our will and desires.

Turning to this further theme at the start of chapter 21, Hobbes distinguishes two ways in which a man's freedom may be said to be hindered or impeded. The first is common to human and inanimate bodies.[12] It occurs when an agent encounters 'the opposition of some externall body' which operates in such a way that the agent is tied—or, as Hobbes also says (pp. 189, 191), is bound—so that 'it cannot move but within a certain space' (p. 261).[13] Hobbes has just laid it down that to be free is to be unimpeded from doing or forbearing from doing something. But these are cases in which the agent is impeded from doing something. An action within his powers is rendered physically impossible of performance. It follows that such agents 'are not at Liberty to move in such manner as without those externall impediments they would' (p. 262).

The other way in which a man can be hindered from using his powers at will is considered in the same passage. This happens when he is physically bound or obliged to act in a particular way by the operation of an irresistible external force.[14] Hobbes assumes that, if we are to describe a man as free, we must not only be able to say that he is free to act; we must also be able to say that, when he acts, he performs his action freely, in that he 'may refuse to do it if he will' (p. 262). If, by

---

[12] See *Leviathan*, 261–2 and 660. At pp. 261–2 Hobbes even claims that the concept of liberty can be applied to inanimate bodies (his own example being a body of water) 'no less' than to rational creatures. If he means by this that the concept can be applied in exactly the same way, this would seem to be a slip: for his definition of human freedom makes essential reference to the idea of the will. In his *Questions Concerning Liberty*, Hobbes explicitly distinguishes human freedom from wider notions of free action when he observes (p. 209) that 'I understand compulsion to be used rightly of living creatures only'. For Hobbes's view of compulsion, cf. n. 14 below.

[13] Hobbes also speaks in the same passage (p. 262) of the agent being 'restrained'. Cf. also pp. 359, 401.

[14] Note that Hobbes distinguishes, with a fair degree of consistency, between being 'forced' and being 'compelled'. I am compelled if my will is coerced. I am forced if it is rendered physically impossible for me to forbear from acting in a certain way. For Hobbes, compulsion is compatible with liberty, although force is not. See esp. the discussion in *Questions Concerning Liberty*, 199–200, 208–9, 216–17. The point is well brought out in Wernham, 'Liberty and Obligation in Hobbes' (n. 4 above), 123.

contrast, he cannot forbear from acting, then his action will not be that of 'one that was free' (p. 262). As Hobbes had already noted in his preliminary discussion in chapter 14, 'obligation and liberty are in one and the same matter inconsistent' (p. 189).

This second type of impediment might seem to be of merely residual significance, especially as Hobbes largely confines himself to illustrating it with such simple instances as that of the man who is 'led to prison by force'.[15] But in fact the category of actions we cannot forbear from performing is of considerable theoretical importance for Hobbes, since he takes it to be the means of defining two forms of human bondage.

One is that of slavery. According to Hobbes's analysis, both in *De Cive* and *Leviathan*, the lack of liberty suffered by slaves is not simply due to the fact that they are 'kept in prison or bonds' (p. 255). It is also due to the fact that 'their labour is appointed to them by another' in such a way that their bodies 'are not in their own power' (p. 667). A slave is thus defined as someone whose lack of freedom is due in part to the fact that he is, literally, a bondsman: someone who is bound or forced to act, and is not at liberty to forbear from acting.[16]

The other way in which human freedom is similarly forfeited is among those who admit God's providence. This too is stressed both in *De Cive* and *Leviathan*, although in this case the earlier analysis is the fuller one. God's power, to those who recognize it, must appear as irresistible.[17] It follows that when God issues a command to those who believe in him—for example through the Scriptures, which many believe to be the word of God—then 'they cannot forbear from obeying him.'[18] They are tied or bound to obey in such a way 'that their

---

[15] See *Questions Concerning Liberty*, 216–17. Hobbes earlier uses the same example in *The Elements of Law*, 63. The reason the category may appear residual, even empty, is that Hobbes sometimes speaks as though an action we cannot forbear from performing cannot be treated as an action: it is a case in which we are acted upon, not a case in which we act. See e.g. the discussion in *Questions Concerning Liberty*, 209, 216–17. But the implication—that all actions are free by definition—is one that Hobbes elsewhere rejects. See e.g. *Leviathan*, 263, where he lays it down that it is only 'actions which proceed from the will' that 'proceed from liberty'.

[16] See *Leviathan*, 667 for the explicit distinction between 'the service of Bondmen' and of 'a voluntary Servant'. Except for discussing enslavement as a result of conquest in war, however, Hobbes does not explain how such bondage can arise. His discussion of slavery is perhaps somewhat in tension with his stress in ch. 13 on the implications of human equality.

[17] See *De Cive: The Latin Version*, 221, and cf. *Leviathan*, 397.

[18] *De Cive: The Latin Version*, 223: 'non potest non obedire'. For a valuable discussion of this difficult passage, see Robert Orr, 'Thomas Hobbes on the Regulation of

bodily liberty is forfeited'.[19] As Hobbes summarizes in chapter 45 of *Leviathan*, all religious believers 'are God's slaves' (p. 668).

The whole of Hobbes's analysis thus depends on his initial distinction between power and liberty. An agent forfeits his liberty if an external force renders him either powerless to act or powerless not to act in some particular way. The distinction is I think clear, but is nevertheless worth underlining. For as Hobbes himself stresses, it is all too easy for the two concepts to become confused.[20] The danger arises from the fact that, if we follow a Hobbesian analysis, we are bound to say of a man who is capable of exercising the power to act in some particular way that he is also at liberty to act in that way. In this case, the man's power and liberty amount to the same thing. This being so, there is a temptation to add—as Hobbes notes in his reply to Bramhall[21]—that if a man analogously lacks the power to act, he must also lack the liberty.

This is certainly a temptation to which 'negative' theories of liberty have fallen prey in the twentieth no less than in the seventeenth century.[22] But as Hobbes rightly observes, it may or may not make sense to claim that an agent who lacks power also lacks liberty. It will not make sense where the impediment to motion lies 'in the constitution of the thing itself' (p. 262). To take Hobbes's own example, a man 'fastned to his bed by sickness' (p. 262) lacks the power to move, but it makes no sense to say that he also lacks the

---

Voluntary Motion', in George Feaver and Frederick Rosen (eds.), *Lives, Liberties and the Public Good* (London, 1987), 58–9. Orr interprets Hobbes as claiming that, although fear of our fellow men does not take away our liberty, fear of God does have this effect. Even in this passage, however, what Hobbes basically seems to be saying is that it is our disbelief in our capacity to resist God's power which forces us to obey and so takes away our liberty. If we turn, moreover, to the corresponding passage in *Leviathan* (p. 397), we find all reference to fear deleted. Hobbes is now clear that the believer is forced to obey simply by the fact that God appears as an irresistible force. Orr is surely right to point out, however, that there is something strange about this argument. As we have seen, Hobbes holds that liberty can only be taken away by external impediments to motion. It is clear that God's omnipotence will constitute such an impediment if it is a fact. But it is not clear how it can be said to do so if it is merely believed to be a fact. For further discussion of the passage from *De Cive*, see M. M. Goldsmith, *Hobbes's Science of Politics* (New York, 1966), 111–13 and Appendix 4.

[19] *De Cive: The Latin Version*, 223: 'libertas . . . corporeis tollitur'.

[20] See *Leviathan*, 262 and cf. *Questions Concerning Liberty*, 211.

[21] *Questions Concerning Liberty*, 209–11.

[22] See e.g. C. W. Cassinelli, *Free Activities and Interpersonal Relations* (The Hague, 1966), 28, for a contrasting discussion of an example very similar to the one Hobbes considers in *Leviathan*, 262. Felix Oppenheim, *Political Concepts: A Reconstruction* (Chicago, 1981), 87, gives a good criticism of Cassinelli's analysis.

liberty.[23] The reason he cannot be said to be unfree is that nothing is impeding him from moving; he is simply incapable of movement. This contrasts with the predicament of someone 'imprisoned or restrained with walls' (p. 262). His plight is similar to that of the sick man in that he is unable to leave. But the sick man would still be unable even if the prison doors were to be opened, whereas the prisoner is only unable because the doors remain locked. He possesses an underlying power or ability to leave which has been 'taken away' from him.[24] So while the sick man merely lacks ability, the prisoner lacks freedom.

If this interpretation is sound, it is worth adding that Hobbes's theory of human freedom seems to have been rather widely misunderstood. Hobbes is often singled out as the classic exponent of what is sometimes called the pure negative theory of liberty.[25] He is claimed, that is, to hold the view that an individual is unfree if and only if his doing of some particular action has been rendered impossible.[26] But this appears to be untrue to Hobbes's analysis in two distinct ways. Although Hobbes agrees that an agent may be said to lack freedom if an action within his powers has been rendered impossible, he does not think that this is the only way in which unfreedom can be produced.[27] The agent will also lack freedom if he is tied or bound to act in such a way that he cannot forbear from acting. The other misunderstanding is that, even if no one is rendering it impossible for an agent to act in a given way, it still does not necessarily follow for Hobbes that the agent is free to perform the action concerned.[28] This is because, as we have seen, the action in question may still be beyond the agent's powers. It is true that, given the lines along which Hobbes analyses the concept,

[23] Cf. also *Questions Concerning Liberty*, 211.

[24] See Hobbes's initial formula in *Leviathan*, 189, and cf. the summary in *Questions Concerning Liberty*, 285.

[25] See Michael Taylor, *Community, Anarchy and Liberty* (Cambridge, 1982), 142. As a paradigm of the pure negative theory Taylor cites Hillel Steiner, 'Individual Liberty', *Proceedings of the Aristotelian Society*, 75 (1974–5), 33–50.

[26] This is to allude to the definition given by Steiner, 'Individual Liberty', 33. I formerly accepted this interpretation of Hobbes's theory myself. See Quentin Skinner, 'Il concetto inglese di libertà', *Filosofia Politica*, 3 (1989), 83–5.

[27] As appears to be assumed e.g. in J. P. Day, 'Individual Liberty', in A. Phillips Griffith (ed.), *Of Liberty* (Cambridge, 1983), 17–29, where Hobbes's analysis is treated as though he is concerned only with being free and unfree to act.

[28] As appears to be assumed e.g. in Goldsmith, 'Hobbes on Liberty' (n. 4 above), who claims (p. 24) that according to Hobbes 'to be unfree is to be restrained from acting as one wishes to act'. This implies that we remain free so long as no one restrains us from performing an action we may wish to perform. As we have seen, however, Hobbes's view is that, if the action in question is beyond our powers, the question of freedom does not arise.

he might be willing to admit that the agent is free to try to perform the given action—although Hobbes does not in fact pronounce upon that question at any point. But what is certain is that, for Hobbes, the question of whether the action is one that the agent is or is not free to perform simply does not arise.

Rather than being an instance of the pure negative theory of liberty, Hobbes's analysis serves to suggest that there may be something amiss with the theory itself. To state it in its most widely accepted form, the theory holds that a man is free unless an action within his powers has been subjected to 'preventing conditions'.[29] This formulation certainly avoids the awkwardness of claiming that a man remains free to perform actions that are beyond his powers. But it still appears to confuse the general concept of social freedom with the more specific notion of being free to act.[30] It overlooks the possibility that a man's lack of freedom may derive not from being unfree to act, but rather from being unable to act freely.[31]

II

So far I have presented Hobbes's theory of human freedom as a simple and unambiguous one. But it must be admitted that this interpretation faces a difficulty. As I intimated at the outset, moreover, it is a difficulty which has caused many of Hobbes's commentators to conclude that his theory is not only more complicated than I have been implying, but is also seriously confused.

The main grounds for this accusation are furnished by the range of examples Hobbes uses to illustrate his theory at the start of chapter 21. One of the cases he considers is that of a free gift. 'When we say a Guift is free,' he maintains, 'there is not meant any liberty of the Guift, but of the Giver, that was not bound by any law or Covenant to give it' (p. 262). Hobbes's point is that the agent is free in the sense of being able to act freely as opposed to being bound or forced to act. But his

---

[29] See e.g. the classic essay by Gerald C. MacCallum, 'Negative and Positive Freedom', in Peter Laslett, W. G. Runciman, and Quentin Skinner (eds.), *Philosophy, Politics and Society*, 4th Series (Oxford, 1972), 176.

[30] See the excellent discussion of this point in Oppenheim, *Political Concepts* (n. 22 above), 83–4.

[31] This distinction is well drawn, however, in F. S. McNeilly, *The Anatomy of Leviathan* (London, 1968), 171. See also J. W. N. Watkins, *Hobbes's System of Ideas* (London, 1965), 120–2, and the valuable remarks on unfree action in Raphael, 'Hobbes' (n. 4 above), 30.

chosen instance seems to presuppose a view much broader than I have so far been suggesting of the range of ties that can properly be said to take away our liberty to forbear from acting. As well as the purely physical constraints of slavery, he now includes the bonds of covenants and of the law.

A further example Hobbes discusses in the same passage is that of freedom of speech. 'When we speak freely', the freedom we exercise 'is not the liberty of voice or pronunciation, but of the man, whom no law hath obliged to speak otherwise than he did' (p. 262). Here Hobbes is making the contrasting point that the agent is free in the sense of being free to act as opposed to being prevented. But again he appears to expand his sense of the range of ties that are capable of stopping us from acting, and hence of taking away our liberty. As well as the purely physical bonds on which he initially concentrated, he again speaks of the bonds of law as another such potential impediment.

In the light of such examples, it is easy to see how the accusation of inconsistency arises. Hobbes first defines freedom as the absence of purely physical hindrances. But he then seems to allow that our liberty can also be limited by moral and especially legal ties. By passing, as one critic has put it, 'from physical impediments to obligations' as his criterion of unfreedom, he leaves his analysis muddled and confused.[32]

It seems to me, however, that this criticism ignores the fact that Hobbes is interested in *Leviathan* in two separate 'conditions of mankind'. One is our natural condition, in which we are free from legal constraints, and at the same time possess our natural liberty to the extent that we are capable of exercising our powers without being physically prevented or compelled.[33] But the other condition in which Hobbes is interested is, in his own phrase, not natural but 'artificial', a condition created by art in which we act as subjects of an 'Artificiall Man' (p. 81), the sovereign author of the 'Artificiall Chains' (p. 263) of the law.[34] It is in relation to this underlying duality—which runs through the whole of *Leviathan*—that we need to assess the coherence of Hobbes's views about legal obligation and liberty.

Hobbes is of course clear that the force of law limits our liberty as subjects. To say that someone is a subject is to say that he has

---

[32] McNeilly, *Anatomy of Leviathan*, 171. Similar criticisms are advanced by several of the commentators cited in n. 4 above. Note that, although *Leviathan* contains an extensive discussion of the concept of unfreedom, Hobbes at no point uses that word.

[33] See *Leviathan*, ch. 13, pp. 183–8.

[34] For the fullest analysis of Hobbes's dichotomy between the worlds of art and nature, see Gigliola Rossini, *Natura e artificio nel pensiero di Hobbes* (Bologna, 1988).

covenanted to give up the condition in which we all naturally find ourselves, the condition of 'meer Nature' in which, apart from our obligation to obey the laws of nature, we have no legal obligations at all (pp. 183, 188, 190). There is therefore a sense in which, in agreeing to quit the state of nature, we must be deciding to give up a form of liberty. By covenanting to become subjects of a Commonwealth, we agree to regulate our behaviour according to the civil law. 'But Civil Law is an Obligation, and takes from us the Liberty which the Law of Nature gave us. Nature gave a Right to every man to secure himselfe by his own strength, and to invade a suspected neighbour by way of prevention; but the Civil Law takes away that Liberty' (pp. 334–5; cf. also p. 240).

It is the fulcrum of Hobbes's theory of the Commonwealth to insist on the rationality of giving up this freedom from any obligation to obey human laws. Because everyone in the state of nature enjoys this freedom, and because 'nature hath made men so equal' in power and strength (pp. 183–4), the state of nature can only be described as a condition of liberty in the most paradoxical sense. It can equally well be described as a condition in which we all enjoy an equal liberty to master and enslave our neighbours, while they enjoy the same liberty 'to make themselves Masters' of our own 'persons, wives, children and cattell' if they can (pp. 184–5; cf. also p. 264).

Nevertheless, there remains a sense in which liberty is forfeited when we take on the role of subjects.[35] Given that a subject is, by definition, someone who is subject to law,[36] it follows that the liberty of subjects must basically depend upon 'the silence of the Law' (p. 271).[37] If there are 'cases where the Soveraign has prescribed no rule, there the Subject hath the liberty to do or forbeare according to his own discretion' (p. 271). But where the law enjoins or forbids a certain course of action, there the subject is tied or bound to act or forbear from acting as the law and sovereign command.[38]

---

[35] As *Leviathan*, 315 puts it, 'the Right of Nature, that is, the naturall Liberty of man, may by the Civill Law be abridged and restrained: nay, the end of making Lawes is no other but such Restraint'. But this summary could perhaps be misleading. As Hobbes has already argued (p. 263), to speak of natural liberty is only to speak of the absence of external impediments. But this is not the form of liberty that defines the state of nature. What characterizes that state is freedom from the obligation to obey any human laws.

[36] For this point see *Leviathan*, 273, 356, 367.

[37] Apart from the exception constituted by 'the true Liberty of a Subject' (p. 268), which 'can by no covenant be relinquished' (p. 272). On this point see n. 39 below.

[38] Hence Hobbes defines a crime (*Leviathan*, 336) as 'the Committing (by Deed or Word) of that which the Law forbiddeth, or the Omission of what it hath commanded'.

As Hobbes makes clear at the outset, however, these considerations apply to us only in relation to our 'artificial' condition as subjects. It remains to ask whether he thinks that the bonds of law serve at the same time to limit our natural liberty as men. For only in that case will it be justifiable to claim that his exposition is confused.

Before turning to that question, it is important to note that Hobbes allows one exception even to his doctrine that the liberty which characterizes our natural condition—liberty from human law—is cancelled by the obligations we undertake when we covenant to become subjects. The exception is grounded on the fact that, when I covenant, 'the motive and end for which this renouncing and transferring of Right is introduced is nothing else but the security of a man's person in his life and in the means of so preserving life as not to be weary of it' (p. 192; cf. also pp. 254, 272). It follows that, if 'the end of obedience is protection', there must be certain natural rights—and hence liberties of action—that 'can by no Covenant be relinquished' (p. 272). Specifically, I cannot consistently agree to relinquish my freedom to act in protection of my life and bodily liberty. For my sole aim in agreeing to the covenant was to assure a better protection for precisely those rights than I could ever have hoped to achieve by my own unaided efforts in the lawless condition of mere nature.[39]

Hobbes's main point, however, is a far more general and challenging one. It is that, even when our freedom from legal obligation in the state of nature is undoubtedly abridged by our duty as subjects to obey the civil law, this does nothing to limit our natural liberty to employ our powers in accordance with our will and desires.

Hobbes of course intends this conclusion to seem paradoxical. But the paradox can readily be resolved if we turn to the account he gives of the distinctive ways in which any system of law operates to ensure the obedience of those subject to it. There are two separate routes, according to Hobbes, by which a citizen can come to feel the force of a law and decide to obey it. First, all rational persons will, *ex hypothesi*, recognize that obedience is in their interests. For the basic aim of law is to seek peace by protecting life and liberty, and these are the goals

---

[39] For this claim see *Leviathan*, 199, and cf. also p. 337. For the things that a subject, 'though commanded by the Soveraign' may 'without Injustice refuse to do', see pp. 268–71. Since these are taken (p. 269) to include actions that the subject may judge to be dishonourable, their range seems at once indeterminate and potentially extensive. It is not altogether clear how this passage is to be reconciled with Hobbes's basic doctrine to the effect that the dictates of conscience cannot be allowed to take precedence over our obligation to obey the law.

that all rational persons seek above all. So the liberty of such agents to act as their will and desires dictate will not in the least be infringed by their obligation to obey the law. The dictates of their will and the requirements of the law will prove to be one and the same.

This expresses a traditional view about the compatibility of liberty and legal obligation, one that John Locke was classically to restate a generation later in his *Two Treatises of Government*. 'Law in its true notion is not so much the Limitation as the direction of a free and intelligent Agent to his proper interests.' Locke draws the inference that, when we submit to the direction of such laws, this will constitute an expression rather than a restriction of our liberty. 'That ill deserves the Name of Confinement that hedges us in only from Bogs and Precipices.'[40] This is not merely a doctrine that Hobbes appears to endorse, but one that he enunciates in the form of a simile later echoed by Locke with remarkable closeness. 'The use of Lawes', as Hobbes puts it in discussing the office of the sovereign in chapter 30, 'is not to bind the People from all Voluntary actions, but to direct and keep them in such a motion as not to hurt themselves by their own impetuous desires, rashnesse, or indiscretion, as Hedges are set, not to stop Travellers, but to keep them in the way.'[41]

As Hobbes stresses, however, this is not the reason why the generality of men obey the law, moved as they are by mere considerations of wealth, command, or sensual pleasure. The only mechanism by which they can be brought to obey is by making them more terrified of the consequences of disobedience.[42] There is admittedly no hope of employing this device outside the confines of the commonwealth. 'Covenants without the Sword are but Words, and of no strength to secure a man at all' (p. 223). But if a 'visible Power' is erected 'to keep them in awe, and tie them by fear of punishment', then there is every prospect of compelling them both to act in line with their obligations and at the same time to forbear from acting as

---

[40] John Locke, *Two Treatises of Government*, ed. Peter Laslett, Student Edition (Cambridge, 1988), ii. 57, 305.

[41] Hobbes puts the point in this way in the course of discussing the extent to which laws are necessary. See *Leviathan*, 388. But the argument is a corollary of his earlier contention that we are bound by reason to obey the laws of nature. Cf. esp. p. 215.

[42] Hobbes occasionally seems to allow, however, that there can also be a more direct mechanism: a citizen may be physically forced to act by an authorized agent of the commonwealth. For passages in which this seems to be envisaged, see *Leviathan*, 196, where the 'common Power' of the state is said to be capable of compelling by force, and p. 269, where the sovereign is described as authorizing assault.

partiality, pride, and revenge would otherwise dictate (p. 223; cf. also pp. 343, 355).

It is of course true that, where the mechanism of using fear to produce obedience works successfully, a subject will elect not to exercise his powers or abilities in various ways. The whole purpose of assigning the right of punishment to sovereigns is 'to forme the wills' of subjects in just this way (p. 227). Hobbes's point, however, is that this does nothing to take away the continuing power or ability of the person concerned to act as his will and desires dictate. 'The Consent of a Subject to Sovereign Power' is such that 'there is no restriction at all of his own former natural liberty' (p. 269).

To see how Hobbes can consistently defend this crucial conclusion, we need only recall his account of the means by which we are alone capable of forfeiting our liberty in 'the proper signification of the word' (p. 189). An external impediment must intervene in such a way that we are either stopped from acting or forced to act contrary to our will and desires. But neither fear nor any other passion of the soul can possibly count as such an impediment. Rather, a man who acts out of fear performs his action because he wills or desires to avoid various consequences which, he fears, will otherwise befall him. Of such a man we may certainly say that he acts as he does because his will has been 'formed' or 'compelled'.[43] But to compel someone's will is only to cause him to have a will or desire to act other than the will or desire for the sake of which he would otherwise have acted. When such a person acts, it will still be because he possesses the will or desire to act in precisely the way in which he acts. It follows that, even if the cause of his will is fear, the actions he performs out of fear will still be free actions.

To illustrate his argument, Hobbes takes the familiar example originally considered by Aristotle at the start of Book 3 of the *Nicomachean Ethics*, the example of a man who 'throweth his goods into the Sea for feare the ship should sink' (p. 262).[44] The man certainly acts out of fear; so we may say if we like that he felt compelled

---

[43] Because Hobbes distinguishes between bodily coercion, which takes away liberty, and coercion of the will, which does not, he has no objection to describing threats of punishment as coercing and compelling us to act, while insisting that the resulting actions will nevertheless be freely performed. For his invocation of this vocabulary, see *Leviathan*, 196, 202, 362, 594, 670.

[44] For Aristotle's discussion see *The Nicomachean Ethics*, 1110a.

to act. But as Hobbes grimly adds—challenging Aristotle's analysis[45]—'he doth it nevertheless very willingly, and may refuse to do it if he will: it is therefore the action of one that was free' (p. 262).[46]

Hobbes's basic argument is thus that 'Feare and Liberty are consistent' (p. 262).[47] It follows that, if we speak of being tied or bound by the laws, we cannot be speaking of natural ties, but only of artificial or metaphorical ones. Hobbes is clearly anxious to underline this point, for he describes the artificial character of these bonds in a memorably grotesque piece of imagery at odds with his usual expository style:

As men for the atteyning of peace, and conservation of themselves thereby, have made an Artificiall Man, which we call a Common-wealth, so also have they made Artificial Chains, called Civill Lawes, which they themselves, by mutuall covenants, have fastned at one end to the lips of that Man or Assembly to whom they have given the Soveraigne Power; and at the other end to their own Ears. (pp. 263–4)

Hobbes is alluding to Lucian's version of the fable of Hercules. According to Lucian, the ancient Gauls thought of Hercules as a venerable and exceptionally prudent orator, and symbolized his gifts of persuasion by picturing him as drawing men along by fetters attached at one end to his tongue and at the other end to his followers' ears.[48] Hobbes's original readers might perhaps have been surprised to come upon this sudden classical flourish, especially as Hobbes was to boast in his Review and Conclusion (pp. 726–7) that he had deliberately left *Leviathan* unencumbered with any such conventional references to ancient authorities. But Hobbes would undoubtedly have expected his original readers both to recognize the allusion and to grasp its relevance, especially as Lucian's claim that men can be 'led by the ears' had already become a favourite humanist topos by the end of the sixteenth century.[49] The moral of the story, as Hobbes makes clear, is

[45] According to Aristotle, *Ethics*, 1110a, the action is 'mixed': voluntary and yet in a sense involuntary.

[46] Hobbes makes the same point in his *Questions Concerning Liberty*, 199, 208.

[47] Cf. *Questions Concerning Liberty*, 209.

[48] See Lucian, 'Heracles' in *Lucian*, ed. and tr. A. M. Harmon, 8 vols., i (London, 1913), 65.

[49] See e.g. the reference to those who are 'subjects a estre menez par les oreilles' in Michel de Montaigne, *Essais*, ed. Jean Plattard, 6 vols. (Paris, 1946), ii. 55, and Montaigne's further reference to the same topos at ii. 230 in his discussion of oratory. Cf. the claim that 'with his golden chaine / The Orator so farre mens harts doth bind' in Sonnet 58 of Philip Sidney, 'Astrophel and Stella', in *The Complete Works*, ed. Albert

that while the chains of the law are of course sufficient to bind us in our artificial role as subjects, these chains 'in their own nature' are 'but weak'. They can only be made to hold 'by the danger, though not by the difficulty of breaking them' (p. 264). They may persuade, but they cannot force. We retain our natural liberty to break through what Hobbes later calls the cobweb laws of our country whenever we choose (p. 339).

I cannot see, therefore, that there is any serious inconsistency in Hobbes's theory of human freedom. He does not contradict himself by first saying that liberty can only be constrained by external impediments and later that it can also be constrained by civil laws. Rather his point is that civil laws form part of an artificial world which supervenes upon, but does not of course abolish, the world of nature. The laws bind us as subjects in such a way that, legally speaking, there are certain things we cannot do, and other things we cannot avoid doing. But these bonds are purely artificial; they leave entirely unimpaired our natural liberty to make use of our powers as we please. Summing up at the end of chapter 21, Hobbes spells out this crucial implication as unambiguously as possible: 'generally all actions which men doe in Common-wealths for feare of the law are actions which the doers had liberty to omit.'[50]

III

I have now tried to lay out what I take to be Hobbes's view about 'the proper signification' of liberty. But I am far from supposing that I have said enough to enable his theory to be fully understood. As I intimated at the outset, one of the most important questions raised by his analysis is why he should have insisted with so much vehemence that it constitutes the only possible way of thinking about the idea of human freedom. Having followed out his analysis, we may now rephrase that question more pointedly. Why should Hobbes have been so anxious to insist on such a restricted account of the circumstances in which we can legitimately claim that our liberty has been infringed?

The answer, I shall argue, is that Hobbes's conclusions—as well as the special emphasis he places on them in *Leviathan*—follow in part

Feuillerat, ii (Cambridge, 1922), 241–301, at p. 265. Lucian's image of Hercules appears as Emblem 181 in Andreae Alciati, *Emblemata*, cum commentariis Claudii Minois [*et al.*] (Padua, 1621), 751.

[50] Here I quote from the first edition of *Leviathan* (London, 1651), 108, since this sentence is garbled in the Macpherson edition.

from his anxiety to confront and overturn two prevailing theories about the nature and especially the limits of legal and political obligation which he had come to regard as particularly dangerous.

It is clear in the first place that, by the time he published *Leviathan*, Hobbes had come to feel an urgent need to respond to the classical republican theory of liberty espoused by so many of his fellow countrymen. This attitude reflects perhaps the sharpest change of direction we encounter at any point in the evolution of Hobbes's political thought.[51] In *The Elements of Law* he had basically accepted the classical republican case, arguing that 'liberty in a commonwealth' can only be said to be truly secured 'in the popular state or democracy'.[52] Aristotle is warmly praised for having stressed this insight: he 'saith well' that 'the ground or intention of a democracy is liberty'.[53] In the *De Cive*, however, Hobbes already begins to change his mind. Aristotle's contention that 'in the case of a Commonwealth governed by its own citizens liberty can simply be assumed' is now dismissed as a vulgar speech, and Aristotle is criticized 'for following the custom of his time in confusing dominion with liberty'.[54] By the time Hobbes published *Leviathan*, moreover, he had come to have a new and far graver reason for wishing to repudiate the classical republican theory of liberty. He had come to believe that 'by reading of these Greek and Latine Authors, men from their childhood have gotten a habit (under a false shew of Liberty) of favouring tumults, and of licentious controlling the actions of their Sovereigns' (p. 267). One of the results, he now felt convinced, had been the civil war itself. The outcome of being 'made to receive our opinions concerning the Institution, and Rights of Common-wealths from Aristotle, Cicero', and other defenders of popular states has been 'the effusion of so much blood, as I think I may truly say, there never was anything so deerly bought, as these Western parts have bought the learning of the Greek and Latine tongues' (p. 267–8).[55]

[51] A point excellently brought out in Gauthier, *Logic of Leviathan* (n. 4 above), 145–6.
[52] *Elements of Law*, 169–70.   [53] Ibid. 170.
[54] *De Cive: The Latin Version*, 176: 'Aristoteles . . . consuetudine temporis libertatem pro imperio nominans. Lib. 6. *Politicorum*, cap. 2. *In statu populari libertas est ex suppositione. Quad vulgo dicunt.*'
[55] Cf. also *Leviathan*, 369, 698–9. The charge is reiterated in *Behemoth*, ed. F. Tönnies with Intro. by M. M. Goldsmith (London, 1969), 3, 23. See also R. MacGillivray, 'Thomas Hobbes's History of the English Civil War: A Study of *Behemoth*', *Journal of the History of Ideas*, 31 (1970), 179–98. James Harrington sought in *Oceana* (1656) to revive the classical theory of liberty—esp. as enunciated by Machiavelli

According to the exposition Hobbes now gives in chapter 21, the classical republican theory of liberty may be said to embody two false and seditious elements. One is the claim—which Hobbes again quotes from Aristotle's *Politics*—that 'in democracy, Liberty is to be supposed; for 'tis commonly held that no man is Free in any other Government' (p. 267; cf. also p. 369). The other is the connected doctrine that Greece, Rome, and modern republics are worthy in some special sense to be described as 'free Common-wealths', whereas 'all manner of Common-wealths but the Popular' can be dismissed as 'tyrannies' (p. 698; cf. also p. 266).

Faced with these contentions, which he now regards as treasonous, what Hobbes does is to deploy his distinctive analysis of liberty in such a way as to try to show that both claims are at the same time arbitrary and absurd. This is obvious, he thinks, in the case of the inflammatory contention 'that the Subjects in a Popular Common-wealth enjoy Liberty; but that in a Monarchy they are all Slaves' (p. 369).[56] As Hobbes has explained in chapter 21, to speak of the freedom of subjects is basically to speak of the silence of the law. But all commonwealths have laws, and no subject is free of them. 'They that live under a monarchy' may deceive themselves into thinking otherwise. But we never encounter this illusion among those who actually live under popular governments. For as Hobbes adds in his most forbidding tones, 'they find no such matter' (p. 369).

No less dangerously absurd, on the analysis Hobbes now gives, is the idea of 'free Commonwealths', the idea 'whereof there is so frequent and honourable mention' in Greek and Roman writings on statecraft (p. 266).[57] Given that freedom merely consists in the absence of impediments, the only sense that can be assigned to this concept is that such commonwealths must be free to act as they will or desire. But this form of natural liberty is obviously common to all states that are 'not dependent on one another', each of which 'has an absolute Libertie to doe what it shall judge' to be 'most conducing to their

in his *Discorsi*—in direct opposition to Hobbes's account. See James Harrington, 'Oceana' in *The Political Works of James Harrington*, ed. J. G. A. Pocock (Cambridge, 1977), esp. 161–3. For the Machiavellian account itself, and for Hobbes's attack on it, see Quentin Skinner, 'The Idea of Negative Liberty: Philosophical and Historical Perspectives', in Richard Rorty, J. B. Schneewind, and Quentin Skinner (eds.), *Philosophy in History* (Cambridge, 1984), 193–221.

[56] *Leviathan*, p. 369. But for a contrasting explanation of Hobbes's rejection of this belief, see Richard Tuck, *Hobbes* (Oxford, 1989), 47.

[57] Hobbes also mocks the absurdity of 'free states' in *Behemoth*, ed. Tönnies, 164.

benefit' (p. 266). It makes no sense, therefore, to speak as though some particular types of commonwealth can uniquely be described as 'free states'. 'Whether a Common-wealth be Monarchicall or Popular, the Freedome is still the same' (p. 266).

I turn finally to Hobbes's other and more immediate reason for insisting so strongly in *Leviathan* on his distinctive analysis of liberty. By doing so, he was able to suggest an answer to the most vexed question of conscience that had arisen during the very years—between 1649 and 1651—when he was completing his masterpiece: the question of whether the new government of the Commonwealth 'without a king or House of Lords' could be lawfully obeyed.[58]

No sooner had the Rump Parliament and its Council of State settled themselves in power after the execution of Charles I in January 1649[59] than they found their legitimacy questioned on all sides. The most strident denunciations came of course from surviving royalists. But the most dangerous opposition arose from a number of groups that had hitherto supported the parliamentary cause. Among these, the most intransigent were the Levellers. But by far the most numerous were those who remained loyal to the authority of Parliament as it had been constituted before its purge by the army leadership in December 1648.

Both these latter groups attacked the government from the same basic standpoint. They agreed that, because liberty is a birthright, any regime must derive its legitimacy from a voluntary act of submission on the part of its own citizens. With the Levellers this took the form of a demand that the new government should receive its powers from a formal Agreement of the People.[60] But among the leading writers in support of Parliament—such writers as Edward Gee, Edmund Hall, William Prynne, and Nathaniel Ward—there was no less emphasis on the claim that any regime which can lawfully call on the allegiance of

[58] The formula used in the Oath of Engagement which, by an Act of 2 Jan. 1650, all males over the age of 18 were required to take. For the oath, and extracts from the Act, see David Wootton (ed.), *Divine Right and Democracy: An Anthology of Political Writing in Stuart England* (Harmondsworth, 1986), 357–8. For the definitive survey of the associated pamphlet literature, see John M. Wallace, 'The Engagement Controversy 1649–1652: An Annotated List of Pamphlets', *Bulletin of the New York Public Library*, 68 (1964), 384–405. See also Margaret Sampson, ' "A Question that hath non-*plust* many": the right to private property and the "Engagement Controversy", 1648–1652' (MA, University of Sussex, 1979).

[59] For the settlement and creation of the Council see Blair Worden, *The Rump Parliament* (Cambridge, 1974), 177–85.

[60] The Levellers issued their third and final *Agreement* in May 1649. For the document itself, together with commentary, see G. E. Aylmer (ed.), *The Levellers in the English Revolution* (New York, 1975), 159–68.

its citizens must originate (as the anonymous author of *The Grand Case of Conscience* put it) in 'the generall consent of the major part of the people'.[61]

As both groups went on to argue, however, the government of the Rump lacked any such basis in consent. The Levellers concentrated on the fact that, with its 'long plotted Council of State erected', as John Lilburne put it, the army leadership now 'threateneth tyranny'.[62] More sweepingly, the supporters of Parliament declared that the entire sequence of events from Pride's Purge to the execution of the king and the abolition of the House of Lords lacked any vestige of consent and hence of legality. As William Prynne declared, the new Commonwealth has been 'forcibly and treasonably erected' by sheer military strength, 'without consent of Kingdome, People or Parliament'.[63]

Having fought for their liberty against the tyranny of Charles I, the people of England have thus been rewarded with a new form of slavery. John Lilburne's major pamphlet of February 1649 is actually entitled *Englands New Chains Discovered*. Scarcely less violent is the language of the tracts written in support of summoning a new Parliament. Nathaniel Ward affirms that 'I believe, while the Parliament of England are the armies Servants, the People of England shall be very Slaves.'[64] William Prynne even feels able to congratulate the late king Charles I for his prophetic insight in seeing that the army would 'subject both King and People, Lawes and Liberties' and 'bring them into perpetuall slavery and bondage'.[65]

There can therefore be no duty to obey the new government. It owes its position, Edmund Hall maintains, to 'bare possession, without any right'. But this 'gives no true title to any power', and no basis in consequence for obligation.[66] Edward Gee goes further, stressing the positive duty of disobedience. The new government has come to power

---

[61] Anon., *The Grand Case of Conscience Stated* (n.p., n.d. [Thomason copy, British Library, gives date of 22 June 1649]), 14.

[62] John Lilburne, *Englands New Chains Discovered* and *The Second Part of Englands New Chains Discovered*, in W. Haller and G. Davies (eds.), *The Leveller Tracts, 1647–53* (repr. Gloucester, Mass., 1964), 157–70 and 172–89, at pp. 165, 167. For the authorship and circumstances of composition, see Aylmer (ed.), *Levellers*, 142.

[63] [William Prynne], *Summary Reasons against the New Oath and Engagement* (n.p., 1649), 3, 13. For a discussion of the tract, and attribution to Prynne, see William Lamont, *Marginal Prynne* (London, 1963), 187–8.

[64] [Nathaniel Ward], *Discolliminium* (London, 1650), 53. For the attribution to Ward see Wallace, 'Engagement Controversy', 398.

[65] Prynne, *Summary Reasons*, 6.

[66] [Edmund Hall], *Lazarus's Sores Licked* (London, 1650), 3. For the attribution to Hall see Wallace, 'Engagement Controversy', 401.

by sheer force, in the manner of a conquering party usurping a lawfully established form of sovereignty.[67] But 'the right and title of Sovereignty is not built upon possession'; it can only be built 'upon the people's consent'.[68] Such 'violent intrusion into, and possession of the Seat of Authority gives no right to it, and consequently neither draws allegiance after it, nor evacuates it in relation to another.'[69] To yield obedience to such a conquering and usurping power is in consequence unlawful, and cannot be justified.[70]

Among supporters of the Rump, the initial response to these outbursts was partly a concessive one. They admitted that the new government was perhaps illegal in its origins, but argued that it ought nevertheless to be obeyed as a power ordained of God.[71] In the course of 1650, however, a much more positive line of defence emerged. A number of writers began to claim that, even though the government may have acquired its powers only as a consequence of the army's victory, this ought not to be regarded as impugning either its legitimacy or its title to obedience.

This suggestion appears to have originated with Anthony Ascham,[72] but was soon taken up in even more forthright style by such publicists as George Wither and especially Marchamont Nedham. The point on which they all agree is that conquest is simply one of the means (and historically the most usual means) by which political authority comes to be lawfully acquired.[73] Bodin and Grotius had already developed this

[67] [Edward Gee], *An Exercitation Concerning Usurped Powers* (n.p., 1650), 5–7, using the pretence that he is describing 'a nation in America'. For the attribution to Gee, see Wallace, 'Engagement Controversy', 394–5. For a yet more explicit reference to the new government as 'a conquering party', see *Grand Case*, 7.

[68] Gee, *Exercitation*, 11–12.

[69] Ibid. 13. For the same claim see Prynne, *Summary Reasons*, 12 and Ward, *Discolliminium*, 8.

[70] Gee, *Exercitation*, 9. For the same conclusion see *Grand Case*, 7, 9; and Prynne, *Summary Reasons*, 3.

[71] For the development of this position see John M. Wallace, *Destiny his Choice* (Cambridge, 1968), 43–7, 51–6; and Quentin Skinner, 'Conquest and Consent: Thomas Hobbes and the Engagement Controversy', in G. E. Aylmer (ed.), *The Interregnum: The Quest for Settlement 1646–1660* (London, 1972), 79–98.

[72] On Ascham see Wallace, *Destiny his Choice*, 30–41, 45–8, 53–8; and Richard Tuck, *Natural Rights Theories: Their Origin and Development* (Cambridge, 1979), 116–17, 123–4, 152–4.

[73] For this claim see [George Wither], *Respublica Anglicana* (London, 1650), 42. (For the attribution see Wallace, 'Engagement Controversy', 401.) See also Marchamont Nedham, *The Case of the Commonwealth of England, Stated*, ed. Philip A. Knachel (Charlottesville, Va., 1969), 15–29. A similarly forthright argument had earlier appeared anonymously in *The Constant Man's Character* (London, 1650), 64–70.

case, as had a number of likeminded writers in England, including John Hayward, Alberico Gentili, and Calybute Downing.[74] Nedham not only quotes both Bodin and Grotius,[75] but proceeds to apply their doctrine (in defiance of common law sentiment[76]) directly to the history of England, claiming that William I and Henry VII both founded their dynasties on the right of conquest.[77]

It is thus a misconception, Nedham argues in his attack on Gee, to suppose that 'only a call from the people' can 'constitute a lawful magistracy.'[78] This forgets that a king may 'by right of war lose his share and interest in authority and power, being conquered'. When this happens, 'the whole right of kingly authority' is 'by military decision resolved into the prevailing party.' This in turn means that 'what government soever it pleases them next to erect is as valid *de jure* as if it had the consent of the whole body of the people.'[79] 'For the sword creates a title for him or those that bear it, and installs them with a new majesty of empire, abolishing the old.'[80] As Richard Saunders more succinctly put it in the title of a sermon published shortly afterwards, 'plenary possession makes a lawful power.'[81]

Hobbes's view of political obligation in *Leviathan* has sometimes been assimilated to that of these defenders of *de facto* powers.[82] While there are important similarities, however, this interpretation overlooks the fact that, in the basic premisses of his political theory, Hobbes stands much closer to Prynne, Gee, and other such enemies of the Rump. He agrees that our natural condition is one of 'full and absolute Libertie' (p. 266). He agrees that, because 'all men equally are by Nature Free', there can be 'no Obligation on any man which ariseth

[74] For the development of arguments about conquest see Quentin Skinner, 'History and Ideology in the English Revolution', *Historical Journal*, 8 (1965), 151–78; and esp. Johann P. Sommerville, 'History and Theory: The Norman Conquest in Early Stuart Political Thought', *Political Studies*, 34 (1986), 249–61.

[75] Nedham, *Case*, cites Bodin, p. 32, Grotius, p. 39.

[76] For common law hostility to conquest theory, see J. G. A. Pocock, 'The Ancient Constitution Revisited' in *The Ancient Constitution and the Feudal Law: A Reissue with a Retrospect* (Cambridge, 1987), esp. 42–55, 293–305.

[77] Nedham, *Case*, 25–9, 48–50.

[78] Ibid. 37.   [79] Ibid. 36; cf. also 40.   [80] Ibid. 38.

[81] Richard Saunders, *Plenary Possession Makes a Lawful Power* (London, 1651). [Thomason copy, British Library, gives date of 28 July.]

[82] I originally argued for this interpretation myself. See the article cited in n. 26 above and also, more fully, Quentin Skinner, 'Thomas Hobbes et la défense du pouvoir "de facto"', *Revue philosophique*, 98 (1973), 131–54. Some of the best recent scholarship on *Leviathan* has continued to uphold this point of view. See e.g. David Johnston, *The Rhetoric of Leviathan* (Princeton, NJ, 1986), 208; see also, more fully, Deborah Baumgold, *Hobbes's Political Theory* (Cambridge, 1988), 124–33.

not from some Act of his own' (p. 268). Finally, he agrees in consequence that conquest and victory can never yield any 'right of dominion over the vanquished' nor any obligation on the part of the conquered (pp. 255–6). The reason is that, where men submit merely as a result of being 'overcome', their obedience will be due to the fact that they have been 'put into prison or chains' and have found it impossible not to submit (p. 256). As we have seen, however, to be physically forced into submission in this way is, for Hobbes, to be in the condition not of a subject but of a slave.[83] If, by contrast, a man's obligation is to be that of a true subject, it is indispensable that his submission should take the form of an act of free consent. Right and obligation can never be derived simply from conquest or victory.[84]

The significance of Hobbes's intervention in the debates about the Commonwealth government is not best captured, therefore, by seeing him essentially as a defender of *de facto* power. The importance of his argument stems rather from the characteristically ironic form in which it is couched.[85] Hobbes accepts the premises of the Rump's leading enemies, but he seeks to show that the wrong conclusions have been drawn from them. Above all, he seeks to show that those who believe the government to be imposing a new form of bondage have simply failed to understand the proper signification of liberty.

In mounting this case, Hobbes develops two distinct lines of attack. The more general is aimed at those who, as he puts it, are clamouring for liberty and calling it their birthright.[86] Given his analysis of human freedom, Hobbes now feels able to dismiss these claims as totally confused. Suppose we take it, he says, that what these agitators are demanding is 'Liberty in the proper sense', that is, 'freedome from chains and prison'. Then it is 'very absurd for men to clamour as they doe' for this form of freedom, since they manifestly

[83] A point Hobbes subsequently corroborates in his Chapter on Crimes by saying (p. 339) that, although in all places and all ages 'Actions have been authorised by the force and victories of those that have committed them', such actions have in all cases been unjust.
[84] See *Leviathan*, 721, on the mistake of those who seek to 'justify the War by which their power was at first gotten, and whereon (as they think) their Right dependeth'.
[85] Several leading arguments in *Leviathan* are presented in a form that Renaissance rhetoricians, following Quintilian, described as dispositionally ironic: familiar premises are adopted, but surprising conclusions are then shown to follow from them. For Quintilian's discussion of this form of irony, see *Institutio Oratoria*, 9. 2. 44–6.
[86] For these phrases see *Leviathan*, 264, 267. For evidence about the clamour for liberty, see Keith Lindley, 'London and Popular Freedom in the 1640s', R. C. Richardson and G. M. Ridden (eds.), *Freedom in the English Revolution* (Manchester, 1986), 111–50.

enjoy it (p. 264). But suppose, he goes on, we instead take them to be calling for liberty in the sense of 'exemption from laws'—what Hobbes has been describing as the liberty of subjects. To ask for complete freedom in this sense is no less absurd. For this is to demand a return to the state of nature. And as Hobbes has already shown, to call for this is to call in effect for slavery, since it is to ask for that form of liberty 'by which all other men may be masters' of our lives (p. 264).

Hobbes reserves his most detailed criticisms, however, for those who had been arguing about the rights of conquest. He mainly focuses on this issue in the Review and Conclusion of *Leviathan*, where he complains that 'divers English books lately printed' make it evident that no one has understood the concept properly (p. 719). But it is in chapter 20 that he first takes up the question of 'Dominion acquired by Conquest or Victory in war', and is thus led to examine the predicament of a man who, finding his sovereign vanquished, submits to his conqueror in order 'to avoyd the present stroke of death' (p. 255).

The first point Hobbes makes specifically about the liberty of a man in such a situation is that he is free to submit. If 'his life and corporall Libertie' are given to him 'on condition to be Subject to the Victor, he hath Libertie to accept the condition' (p. 273). Here in turn Hobbes has two claims to make. The first, which he takes for granted, is that such a man is free in the fundamental sense that nothing is stopping him. Although Hobbes observes in his Conclusion that such impediments can certainly arise, the only instance he mentions is that of someone prevented from submitting by the fact of being abroad at the time when his country is conquered (p. 721). Hobbes's other and principal point is that such a man is also free as a subject. He is under no legal or moral obligation not to submit. The reason is that our obligations as subjects depend, as we have seen, upon our sovereign's capacity to protect us. If our sovereign is conquered, we lose any such protection and the commonwealth is dissolved. We thereupon cease to be subjects, and each of us is left 'at liberty to protect himselfe by such courses as his own discretion shall suggest unto him' (p. 375; cf. also pp. 272–3, 345).

In his Review and Conclusion Hobbes clarifies and expands this account of 'when it is that a man hath the liberty to submit'.[87] He reiterates that 'for him that hath no obligation to his former Sovereign

---

[87] *Leviathan*, p. 719, referring the reader back to the discussion in ch. 21.

but that of an ordinary Subject', the moment comes 'when the means of his life is within the Guards and Garrisons of the Enemy' (p. 719). But he now adds the highly topical observation that, if the man is not merely a subject but a soldier in a civil war, the case becomes more complicated. 'He hath not the liberty to submit to a new Power as long as the old one keeps the field and gives him means of subsistence.' For in that case 'he cannot complain of want of Protection'. But as soon as that fails, he too is at liberty to 'seek his Protection wheresoever he has most hope to have it, and may lawfully submit himself to his new Master' (p. 720).

The other point Hobbes makes about the liberty of a man in this predicament is also brought out in chapter 20, but is particularly underlined in the Review and Conclusion. It is that such a man is not merely free to submit; if he submits, he will also be acting freely.

Here again Hobbes has two points to make. The first and obvious one is that such a man will be acting freely in the legal sense. He is clearly under no legal obligation to submit, since his predicament is such that he has no legal obligations at all. But Hobbes's main point— and the heart of his eirenic reply to the enemies of the Commonwealth— is that such a man will also be free according to the proper signification of the word. If he submits, his act will be that of a free man voluntarily consenting to a new sovereign power.

To see how Hobbes arrives at this crucial conclusion, we need only recall the conditions that would have to be met before it could properly be claimed that such a man's freedom of action had been infringed. He would have to be physically tied or bound to submit in such a way that he could not forbear from submitting. As we have seen, this is of course a possible way of inducing submission. It describes the manner in which a slave, someone 'not trusted with the libertie of his bodie', is forced to obey (p. 273; cf. also pp. 256, 720). It is Hobbes's principal aim, however, to establish that this is not the position of the man who submits to a conqueror in order to avoid imprisonment or death. The reason is that this describes the predicament of a man who, unlike the slave, is offered a condition of submission, and is thus at liberty to accept or refuse that condition 'if hee will' (p. 720). He is not forced to submit by being 'beaten and taken'; on the contrary, 'he commeth in and submitteth to the Victor' on condition that 'his life and the liberty of his body' are spared (pp. 255–6).

Hobbes's fundamental contention is thus that the man he is describing is someone who, far from being forced to submit, freely consents to the terms of his own submission and thereby enters into a covenant with a new sovereign.[88] 'Having liberty to submit to him, he consenteth either by expresse words or by other sufficient sign to be his Subject' (p. 719). He may thus be said to 'contract with the Victor, promising Obedience for Life and Liberty' (p. 721). Hobbes's reason for treating it as an error to suppose that plenary possession makes a lawful power is thus that 'it is not therefore the Victory that giveth the right of Dominion over the Vanquished, but his own Covenant' (pp. 255–6).

In relating his theory of liberty to the debates about the legitimacy of the post-regicide government Hobbes appears to have acted with full self-consciousness. The best evidence lies in the fact that his conclusions are based on not just a clarification but a revision of his earlier arguments. In *The Elements of Law* he still espouses the orthodox position which *Leviathan* repudiates, contrasting the position of a man who 'submitteth to an assailant for fear of death' with that of someone who makes a 'voluntary offer of subjection'.[89] In *De Cive* the discussion is more ambiguous, and undoubtedly begins to move in the direction later followed up in *Leviathan*.[90] But Hobbes still makes a distinction between states 'founded on contracts and on mutually given faith' and states 'acquired by power and natural force'.[91] Only in the former case is he prepared to say that the *civitas* has been 'founded on the consent of many men' who have 'willingly submitted themselves'.[92]

---

[88] Leviathan, 719. But if the man submits only on condition that his life and liberty are spared, this would appear to make the victor a party to the covenant. This would be contrary to Hobbes's basic contention (p. 230) that 'he which is made Soveraigne maketh no Covenant with his Subjects beforehand'. This contention raises no problems in the case of what Hobbes calls (p. 228) 'commonwealth by institution'. For the form taken by the Covenant in such cases is simply that each prospective subject agrees with everyone else who shall be sovereign. Ever since Pufendorf stressed the point, however, critics have complained that Hobbes contradicts himself when he comes to what he calls (p. 228) 'commonwealth by acquisition', and thus to the relationship of victor and vanquished. For in this case he explicitly states (p. 252) that the subjects covenant not with each other but with 'him they are afraid of'. Hobbes's consistency can be rescued, however, if we interpret him as saying not that the conqueror covenants to allow life and liberty to those he has vanquished, but merely that he accepts their covenant by allowing them life and liberty, while remaining free from any obligation to respect those terms. This point is excellently brought out in Gauthier, *Logic of Leviathan* (n. 4 above), 114–15. [89] *Elements of Law*, 127.

[90] Esp. in clearly stating that conquest and consent are at least potentially compatible. See *De Cive: The Latin Version*, 160.

[91] Ibid. 160, contrasting the case of a *civitas* 'pactis & fide mutuo data . . . inita est' with a *civitas* 'quae acquiritur potentia & viribus naturalibus'.

[92] Ibid.: only the *civitas* founded 'pactis & fide mutuo data' can be described as founded 'multorum consensione' by men acting 'volentes'.

In *Leviathan*, by contrast, he unequivocally insists that, when a man submits to a conqueror to avoid the present stroke of death, his act of submission is the willing act of a free man. As a result, he is able to make a novel and dramatic intervention in the debate about conquest and allegiance. As we have seen, many enemies of the Rump had argued that, because the new Commonwealth government had been founded on conquest and usurpation, it lacked any basis in consent and condemned the people of England to a state of enslavement. Many of its defenders had retorted that, although the government had no doubt been imposed without consent, the fact of its being founded on an act of conquest gave it a just title to be obeyed. By contrast with both these positions, Hobbes suggests that there is no need to invoke the supposed rights of conquerors in order to vindicate the present duty of allegiance. By deploying his distinctive analysis of liberty, he is able to insist that the concepts of conquest and consent are not in the least incompatible in the way that all parties to the debate had hitherto supposed.

This in turn enabled Hobbes to draw the polemical conclusion in which he is clearly most interested. Since the act of submitting to a conqueror is based on consent and expressed in a covenant, a man who submits in this way cannot possibly be described as a slave—as the Levellers and supporters of Parliament had both tried to claim. Rather he must be acknowledged to be a true subject with an absolute duty of obedience. The conclusion is first drawn at the end of the chapter on the liberty of subjects. If a man 'hath his life and corporall Libertie given him, on condition to be subject to the Victor, he hath Libertie to accept the condition, and having accepted it is the subject of him that took him' (p. 273). The suggestion that such a man has no obligation to obey, on the grounds that he has merely been compelled to submit out of fear, is scornfully dismissed at the end of the chapter on the dissolution of commonwealths as nothing but a 'fraudulent pretence' (p. 375). Finally, the basic argument is triumphantly reiterated in the closing pages of the Review and Conclusion. A man who finds himself conquered is at liberty to 'submit himself to his new Master' and 'may do it lawfully, if he will. If therefore he doe it, he is undoubtedly bound to be a true Subject: for a Contract lawfully made, cannot lawfully be broken' (p. 720).

12

T. H. Green, J. S. Mill, and Isaiah Berlin on the Nature of Liberty and Liberalism

RICHARD BELLAMY[1]

In his seminal lecture 'Two Concepts of Liberty', Isaiah Berlin examines the work of Mill and Green as exponents of the concepts of negative and positive liberty respectively.[2] Berlin regards the two accounts of liberty as incompatible and opposed to each other. He charges Green with adopting the two cardinal errors of positive liberty: (1) the use of a notion of self-realization which confuses 'freedom from' with 'ability to do'; and (2) the identification of liberty with equality. Mill, in contrast, is praised as an exponent of the 'negative' definition of liberty as freedom from constraints.[3] This paper criticizes Berlin's interpretation by maintaining that the core idea of Mill's *On Liberty* is a defence of that very notion of individual autonomy, as something which society should foster equally for all its members, which Berlin attacks. Moreover, Green believes his political theory is consistent with Mill's. He does not criticize the concept of liberty espoused by Mill so much as the utilitarian terms in which it is framed.[4]

The inadequacy of Berlin's treatment of both Mill and Green puts in doubt the validity of his negative/positive liberty distinction, at least

[1] I am very grateful for the written or verbal comments, often on successive versions of this paper, of Tom Baldwin, Isaiah Berlin, Keith Dowding, Richard Flathman, Caroline Forder, John Gray, David Miller, Ross Harrison, John Morrow, Peter Nicholson, Raymond Plant, Quentin Skinner, Andrew Williams, and the publisher's anonymous referee.
    [2] Isaiah Berlin, 'Two Concepts of Liberty', in *Four Essays on Liberty* (Oxford, 1969), 118–72.
    [3] Berlin, *Four Essays*, pp. xlix n., lxi, 133 n., 150. The view has been very influential, e.g. in the otherwise excellent book by Melvin Richter, *The Politics of Conscience: T. H. Green and his Age* (London, 1964), 24.
    [4] On the political and philosophical influence of Mill on Green see R. L. Nettleship, 'Memoir of Green', in *Works of T. H. Green* ed. R. L. Nettleship (London, 1888), iii, p. xliv; and Christopher Harvie, *The Lights of Liberalism* (London, 1976), 151, 303 n. 35.

as it is applied to them. To establish the unsatisfactory nature of Berlin's view of liberty will be the task of the first section of this essay. The next two sections examine the concept of liberty in the writings of Mill and Green respectively. Again, the argument will be that Green's account complements and completes Mill's version. I shall argue that individual freedom presupposes certain moral commitments on the part of all members of society to the fostering of a particular quality of life—one which values autonomy. An analysis of Mill's writings reveals this thesis to be an implicit component of his utilitarian doctrine. Green's theory, however, makes the social and moral basis of freedom explicit, thereby providing liberalism with solider foundations— a claim defended in the conclusion.

I

Berlin describes positive and negative liberty respectively as '[t]he freedom which consists in being one's own master and the freedom which consists in not being prevented from choosing as I do by other men'.[5] These definitions suggest that the difference between the two concepts rests upon a distinction between internal and external constraints on freedom. Negative liberty consists in freedom from the external hindrances placed in the way of my satisfying my desires. Positive liberty includes the removal of restrictions on my conceiving those desires in the first place. As Berlin concedes, they 'seem concepts at no great logical distance from each other'.[6] Indeed, earlier in the essay he clearly combines the two when arguing that negative liberty is asserted in '[e]very protest against exploitation and humiliation, against the encroachment of public authority, or the mass hypnosis of custom or organised propaganda'.[7] The first three cases are examples of external constraints on individual liberty, but the last two are surely internal.

It is not clear that mixing the two notions of constraints does involve any logical confusion of two different concepts of liberty. Rather, the concentration on purely external constraints makes the concept of negative liberty unacceptably narrow. For if liberty is simply not to be prevented by others from doing what you want, then you could increase your freedom by trimming your desires. The paradigm case is the contented slave, who is conditioned to accept his slavery as natural

---

[5] Berlin, 'Two Concepts', 131.   [6] Ibid.   [7] Ibid. 128.

and whose desires and expectations therefore match the opportunities available to him. Berlin admits committing this error in his reply to his critics, but as he points out this strengthens rather than weakens the concept of negative liberty. If, for example, my agoraphobia (internal constraint) is removed by psychoanalysis, I am not thereby obliged to walk about in open spaces. I merely have the choice to do so or not. This broadening of the concept of freedom to include the removal of internal constraints is entirely consistent with Berlin's view of negative liberty as 'the absence of obstacles not merely to my actual, but to my potential choices . . . due to the closing of such doors or failure to open them, as a result, intended or unintended, of alterable human practices'.[8]

This notion of liberty as the ability to make an autonomous choice without the hindrance of removable internal or external constraints on possible life plans has become accepted in most recent accounts of freedom. It is distinguished from positive freedom on the grounds that there is 'no requirement that an agent actually realise an end for him to be free from all constraints to realise that end'.[9] However, it is not certain that the concept of freedom can be emptied of all normative import. Benn and Weinstein, whose classic article expounds the above notion of liberty as autonomy, remark that 'there is something paradoxical about saying that a person is either free or not free to starve [or] cut off his ears . . . on account of the standard association between "being free" and experiences or activities normally regarded as worthwhile.' As a result, they suggest that one can only be free to do something 'if it is a possible object of reasonable choice'.[10] Baldwin makes a similar point when he argues that the removal of inhibitions or complexes by psychoanalysis is consistent with his revised account of negative liberty. For the therapy aims 'not to determine the patient's life for him but to make it possible for him to determine it for himself'. According to Baldwin, this example clarifies the 'central phenomenon' of negative liberty, namely that an agent's choices be 'carried out in the light of all his reasonable beliefs and desires', a condition he describes as 'weakly normative'.[11] On this account, the difference between

---

    [8] Berlin, Introduction to *Four Essays*, xxxvii–xl.
    [9] Thomas Baldwin, 'MacCallum and the Two Concepts of Freedom', *Ratio*, 26 (1984), 130. A similar point is made by William E. Connolly, *The Terms of Political Discourse*, 2nd edn. (Oxford, 1983), 143–6.
    [10] S. I. Benn and W. L. Weinstein, 'Being Free to Act and Being a Free Man', *Mind*, 80 (1971), 195.
    [11] Baldwin, 'MacCallum and the Two Concepts', 131–3.

negative and positive liberty arises from the belief of the proponents of the latter conception that it would be irrational, and hence not an object of freedom, not to pursue one's real interests once one was free in the negative sense to choose to do so. To employ Charles Taylor's terminology, freedom is not simply an opportunity concept, it is also an exercise concept.[12] The proponents of both negative and positive liberty can agree that individual freedom depends not simply on the quantity of options open to an agent but also on the quality of choice available. However, for the advocates of positive liberty it is only a necessary but not a sufficient condition of freedom to be able to choose in a reasonable manner from a number of worthwhile options. They require that we use this freedom in a way consistent with our status as rational moral agents. This injunction arises from the contention, examined below, that individual freedom can exist only in a certain sort of community, namely one orientated towards the common good.

Berlin's original formulation sought to avoid this conflation of freedom with rationality. He believed that self-consciousness could only be taken so far if the danger of replacing the natural, unplanned web of human needs and desires by a crude, rationalist set of rules, which the individual was obliged to obey, was to be avoided.[13] Those who adopt the autonomy view of negative liberty argue that reason could not determine action in the manner feared by Berlin because the range of possible rational choices is infinitely large. One is always faced with numerous alternatives of equal reasonableness. This plurality of acceptable rational choices, as Baldwin notes, leaves negative libertarians 'with a profound antinomy', and he appositely quotes Sidgwick's conclusion that 'unless we assume or prove a moral order of the world, there is a conflict between rational convictions.'[14] Berlin appears to accept this dilemma as a 'permanent characteristic of the human predicament'.[15] However, even if the problem proves irresolvable at a

---

[12] Charles Taylor, 'What's Wrong with Negative Liberty', in A. Ryan (ed.), *The Idea of Freedom* (Oxford, 1979), 253–70.

[13] John Gray, 'On Negative and Positive Liberty', *Political Studies*, 28 (1980), 518–21, also argues, against Berlin, that even negative freedom requires some notion of self-determination if 'internal' restraints on freedom are to be avoided. But this, despite Gray's disclaimer, must involve conflating acting freely with acting rationally, a view strongly resisted by Berlin in 'From Fear and Hope Set Free', *Concepts and Categories* (London, 1978), 173–98.

[14] Baldwin, 'MacCallum and the Two Concepts', 140, quoting Henry Sidgwick, *Lectures on Green, Spencer and Martineau* (London, 1902), 168 n. 58. A similar dilemma faces Connolly's ideal of autonomy in *Political Discourse*, 157.

[15] Berlin, *Four Essays*, li.

meta-ethical level, practically one cannot ignore it—particularly in those cases where individual rationality seems to conflict with freedom.[16]

An instance of such a conflict is that posed by 'the Prisoners' Dilemma'. Two prisoners are separately faced with the alternatives of confessing to a major crime or of being convicted for a minor one. If both confess they get a reduced sentence of ten years; if neither do they will only be sentenced to two years for the minor crime; if only one confesses he will go free and the other will be sent down for the full penalty of twenty years. If both are rational self-seekers then both will confess rather than risk only their partner doing so. Therefore both go down for ten rather than two years, thereby rendering themselves less free. The dilemma is particularly relevant to the negative/positive liberty distinction because it is related to an atomistic model of society which characteristically underlies the negative liberty thesis. According to this model, society is made up of self-regarding individuals who act rationally by seeking to maximize their want-satisfaction. Individual liberty is assessed in a social and moral vacuum. But our choices and preferences cannot be treated in abstract isolation from those of other people. In a celebrated article, Sen and Runciman have suggested a solution to the Prisoners' Dilemma in terms of Rousseau's conception of the 'general will'.[17] They argue that a prior commitment to a given moral ordering, honour amongst thieves for example, modifies the individualistic assumptions of the game to produce a better overall result.

Whilst Green's positive conception of liberty encompasses such a social theory, Mill's negative version of liberty does not. Both define liberty in terms of individual autonomy and the possibilities it opens up for self-realization in the pursuit of worthwhile ends.[18] However, Green sees individual behaviour as socially and morally orientated. This orientation produces an ordering but not, I shall argue, an imposition of human goals, thereby removing a chief objection to positive liberty—that it defines our 'real interests' for us. Mill, in contrast, attempts to adopt the classic negative libertarian atomistic

---

[16] On this point, see B. Williams, 'Conflicts of Values' in Ryan (ed.), *Idea of Freedom*, 221–32.

[17] W. G. Runciman and A. K. Sen, 'Games, Justice and the General Will', *Mind*, 74 (1965), 554–62.

[18] I discuss the source of these common assumptions in a shared Victorian moral and political language which went beyond their epistemological and conceptual differences in my *Liberalism and Modern Society* (Cambridge, 1992), ch. 2.

model of society and treats collective choices as identical with a neutral utilitarian summation of individual preferences. Although Mill invokes a richer concept of liberty than the classical liberal notion of an absence of impediments to an individual's express wants, he remains perfectly orthodox in seeking to adjudicate between conflicting plans of life on grounds independent of any particular conception of the good life. It will be shown that this thesis is only possible because his utilitarianism presupposes his own moral preferences.

The combination of a rich theory of individuality with the claim that a liberal theory of justice must foster all lifestyles, and hence remain neutral between different concepts of the good, is shared by many modern liberal theorists.[19] The example of Mill will reveal this stance to be ambiguous and ultimately untenable. For the commitment to the central liberal value of autonomy presupposes a particular moral and social context which fosters individual liberty as a collective project. Without this context, freedom neither has meaning nor is possible for individuals.[20] The examination of Green's theory is intended to show that liberalism therefore requires a concept of the good as its foundation.

II

Mill's objections to what we called the 'narrow reading' of negative liberty, as simply the absence of external constraints, are revealed in his criticisms of Bentham. Mill believes that Bentham's definition of freedom, as the absence of obstacles to the fulfilment of human desires, is open to the distortion noted above. It suggests that there is a theoretical limit to human freedom in the satisfaction of a fixed number of wants. As a result, our freedom could be increased by diminishing our desires. For Mill, the values of human freedom derive from the individual's capacity to increase and develop his wants in an infinite variety of ways. The human potential for self-expression is inexhaustible; any limitation of it is hence a restriction of human

[19] e.g. J. Rawls, *A Theory of Justice* (Oxford, 1972); R. Dworkin, 'Liberalism', in S. Hampshire (ed.), *Public and Private Morality* (Cambridge, 1978), 113–43. I examine these theories in detail in my 'Defining Liberalism: Neutralist, Ethical or Political?', in R. Bellamy (ed.), *Liberalism and Recent Legal and Social Philosophy, Archiv für Rechts- und Sozialphilosophie* Suppl. 36, 23–43.

[20] My argument in this respect runs parallel to that of J. Raz, *The Morality of Freedom* (Oxford, 1986).

freedom.²¹ This observation commits Mill to the definition of freedom as autonomy. As Berlin notes, Mill rejects Bentham's psychology because '[f]or him man differs from animals primarily . . . as a being capable of choice . . . the seeker of ends, and not merely of means.'²²

At the same time, Mill wants to retain utilitarianism as an objective standard capable of adjudicating between the conflicting desires of different individuals. He tries to bring the two together by amending Bentham's notion of happiness to include a distinction between those enjoyments which employ the 'higher faculties' and those which merely trade on the 'beast's pleasures'. He links this in *On Liberty* and *Utilitarianism* to a notion of self-realization which connects an increase in human happiness with the development of character in the sense of human capacities:

A being of higher faculties requires more to make him happy, is capable probably of more acute suffering, and certainly accessible to it at more points, than one of an inferior type; but in spite of these liabilities, he can never really wish to sink into what he feels to be a lower grade of existence. We may give what explanation we please of this unwillingness; we may attribute it to pride . . . to the love of liberty and personal independence . . . to the love of power, or to the love of excitement . . . but its most appropriate appellation is a sense of dignity, which all human beings possess in one form or another, and in some, though by no means in exact, proportion to their higher faculties; and which is so essential a part of the happiness of those in whom it is strong, that nothing which conflicts with it could be, otherwise than momentarily, an object of desire to them.²³

As Green, who quotes this passage *in extenso*, points out, Mill has done much more than amend Bentham's conception of happiness.²⁴ He has called into question the whole project of deriving moral axioms from his revised accounts of human psychology. He has done this in two ways. First, he has destroyed the notion of pleasure as a simple unitary concept, which can act as a criterion for making our choices

---

²¹ J. S. Mill, *Autobiography*, in *Collected Works*, general ed. J. M. Robson, i, *Autobiography and Literary Essays* (Toronto, 1969), 139.

²² I. Berlin, 'John Stuart Mill and the Ends of Life', in *Four Essays*, 178.

²³ J. S. Mill, *Utilitarianism, On Liberty and Considerations on Representative Government* (London, 1972), 8–9. (NB References below to *Utilitarianism* are to pp. 1–61 of this edn.; reference to *On Liberty* are to pp. 63–170 of the same edn.)

²⁴ T. H. Green, *Prolegomena to Ethics*, ed. A. C. Bradley (Oxford, 1883), para. 167. All references to paragraph numbers in the text are to this work. Mill's position is arguably more complicated than Green suggests, in that strictly speaking he eschews moral axioms as such for moral guidelines, e.g. his debate with Spencer on this point in *Utilitarianism*, 58–9.

without calling the status of our desires into question. Mill seems to want to suggest that in choosing some immediate pleasure over another higher pleasure an individual may not be making the best of himself. Yet this suggestion is just what Berlin, in criticizing Green, regards as repugnant. The pertinent question to ask in such a case is then, as Berlin points out, 'in whose view' is such a pleasure better than another?[25] Different pleasures are largely incommensurable. The enjoyment to be derived from having a drink is simply different from that of reading a book or going for a walk. Comparing them can only make sense when we discriminate between motivations, and do not take our desires as fixed and all-determining in relation to the goals and objects which we pursue. Berlin's first question, 'in whose view?' is logically related to his second, 'what self?' The sort of discrimination between pleasures which Mill's revised utilitarianism presupposes cannot simply be a matter of doing what you want. It must also be related to your basic purposes or self-realization—a notion Mill slips in under the heading of human dignity. This concession, as Green comments, reveals that 'the real ground . . . of Mill's departure from the stricter utilitarian doctrine, that the worth of pleasure depends simply on its amount, is his virtual surrender of the doctrine that all desire is for pleasure' (para. 167).

Mill's 'sense of dignity' is a moral term in the traditional sense. To quote Green, 'he regards it as a counter motive to desires for animal pleasure' (para. 166). What is involved is a distinction between human beings as we find them, subject to animal desires, and human beings as they could be if all their capacities were realized—a distinction which the language of morals seeks to bridge. Mill has reintroduced this distinction by arguing that some goals are more significant than others, but failed to alter his psychology accordingly. For Mill (formally at least) what is at stake is simply the desirability of different pleasures as defined by *de facto* desires. But the evaluative language he uses to distinguish between these different pleasures goes further, to examine the different possible modes of being of the individual. In this latter

---

[25] See Berlin, 'Two Concepts', 133 n.: ' "The ideal of true freedom is the maximum of power for all members of human society alike to make the best of themselves" said T. H. Green in 1881. Apart from the confusion of freedom with equality, this entails that if a man choose some immediate pleasure—which (in whose view?) would not enable him to make the best of himself (what self?)—what he was exercising was not "true" freedom; and if deprived of it he would not lose anything that mattered. Green was a genuine liberal; but many a tyrant could use this formula to justify his worst acts of oppression.'

instance, motivations and desires do not count simply in relation to the attractiveness of the pleasures we expect from their fulfilment, in which case 'in whose view?', but also in virtue of the kind of life or person that we are or want to be—precisely 'what self?' Berlin does not regard these as legitimate questions to ask. It will be argued below that whilst Mill's solution has many of the dangers Berlin fears, Green's does not.

Mill plays upon the ambiguity of moral language in order to derive a theory of autonomy and self-realization from false psychological premises. He incorporates the ideals of positive liberty into his utilitarianism in order to maintain the appearance of being a negative libertarian. This comes out very clearly in the famous passage of *On Liberty* where he quotes from von Humboldt:

'the end of man, or that which is prescribed by the eternal or immutable dictates of reason, and not suggested by vague and transient desires, is the highest and most harmonious development of his powers to a complete and consistent whole'; that, therefore, the object 'towards which every human being must ceaselessly direct his efforts, and on which especially those who design to influence their fellow-men must ever keep their eyes, is the individuality of power and development'; that for this there are two requisites, 'freedom, and variety of situations', and that from the union of these arise 'individual vigour and manifold diversity', which combine themselves in 'originality'.[26]

Mill has, however, immeasurably impoverished this notion of self-development to mean simply the second-order desire to satisfy the first-order desires. Calculating reason, given the opportunity to experience sufficient pleasures, will work out which most satisfy human desires, and the individual will progressively move up the hierarchy of pleasure from a base animal happiness to the higher happiness of a civilized being. However, there are both internal and external obstacles to human progress which might inhibit our possibility to experience or conceive of fresh pleasures. This leads Mill's interpretation of self-realization into the two problems associated with negative accounts of liberty noted earlier. Mill argues that want-satisfaction is intrinsically good. But desires are reason-dependent; people would not want particular objects unless they believed they were desirable. Mill cannot avoid, as he does, the question of what are to count as 'reasonable beliefs and desires'.

[26] Mill, *On Liberty*, 115–16.

Resolving this issue is a necessary preliminary for tackling the second problem of how to mediate between conflicting desires. Bentham believed that the world could be so arranged that the psychological mechanism underlying human action could be allowed free play to establish a natural order amongst human beings. Such a view is, of course, something Mill is seeking to avoid. It is significant that he did not pursue his plans for a science of ethology and harshly criticized the excesses of Comte's positivism. Instead, he sees the development of the state in terms of a *modus vivendi* which allows, in so far as this is consistent with the liberty of others, individuals to pursue their own goals. He appeals to the necessary moderation which individuals have to practise in pursuing their own desires, seeing this restraint as a product of human sympathy and the experience which a mature society has acquired. Some such assumption was necessary, as Sidgwick was to point out, since both the abnegation exercised by individuals involved in pursuing their own personal happiness and the injunction to cultivate the greatest happiness of the greatest number are logically independent and not derivable from the psychological premisses of utilitarianism.[27] But, as Green remarked, Sidgwick's conclusion that 'As rational beings we are manifestly bound to aim at good generally, not merely at this or that part of it' (a very similar claim to that of Mill in quoting the passage from von Humboldt cited above) plainly involves a more radical rejection of utilitarianism than he allows.[28] Reason in the utilitarian tradition prescribes means not ends. Sidgwick breaks with this in making a distinction between pleasure as defined by *de facto* desires, and the greatest pleasure of the greatest number as something which as rational beings we can see as desirable. Mill admits a similar distinction when he quotes von Humboldt as saying that 'the end of man' is prescribed by 'immutable dictates of reason', not 'vague transient desires'. Yet he cannot consistently hold on to this position without bringing the utility principle into conflict with the negative view of liberty as independent from a notion of what is morally best for human beings on the whole.

John Gray has argued that Mill adopts an indirect form of utilitarianism.[29] The utility principle, according to Gray, is an

[27] H. Sidgwick, *Methods of Ethics*, 6th edn. (London, 1901), esp. concluding chapter.
[28] Green quoting Sidgwick, *Methods of Ethics*, 3. 14. 2, in *Prolegomena*, para. 365.
[29] John Gray, *Mill on Liberty: A Defence* (London, 1983). For a similar view see Richard Wollheim, 'John Stuart Mill and Isaiah Berlin—The Ends of Life and the Preliminaries of Morality', in Ryan (ed.), *The Idea of Freedom*, 253–70.

axiological principle defining the end of human conduct, namely 'that pleasure and freedom from pain are the only things desirable as ends', not a moral axiom that we maximize happiness.[30] The individuality of self-development, which Mill praises so much in *On Liberty*, does not conflict with his utilitarianism, since Mill is not suggesting that we seek to maximize happiness directly. Rather, this is the end-product of the process of character formation, which is so central to his doctrine of liberty. Utility is only maximized, therefore, by allowing individuals the possibility for experimentation and hence self-development.[31]

Whilst Gray's view undoubtedly absolves Mill from the traditional charge of inconsistency, it also reveals the circularity of Mill's solution to the classic utilitarian problem of moving from the pursuit of one's own happiness to the pursuit of the general happiness. For his conclusion is contained in his contentious premiss that we are Millian utilitarians by nature. Thus Mill argues that human nature must be allowed to develop 'according to the tendency of the inward forces which make it a living thing'. Character formation is the development of an 'authentic' self. Only a 'person whose desires and impulses are his own—are the expression of his own nature, as it has been developed and modified by his own culture—is said to have a character.'[32] But he also claims that, given sufficient experience, the rational satisfaction of wants will lead the individual from a 'lower' to a 'higher' self.[33] In this way he is able to dovetail his conception of individual psychological progress, expressed in terms of the increase of individual autonomy, with his moral ideal, as encapsulated in the principle of utility.

At the very least Mill invites the corruption of his liberalism as a result of the poverty of this ethical theory. For his account of human development misses the point that character formation is not a matter of satisfying desires by giving them free play, but of identifying those objects which are desirable. Mill's unwillingness, on liberal grounds, to engage in the identification of human goods, because he believes we should be free to choose, makes the construction of any plan of life highly arbitrary. Once the investigation of the appropriate objects of human action has been laid to one side, then the distinction between

---

[30] Mill, *Utilitarianism*, 6; Gray, *Mill on Liberty*, 19–28.

[31] A good recent restatement of the sort of view Gray and Wollheim are attacking is Ted Honderich, 'The Worth of J. S. Mill on Liberty', *Political Studies*, 22 (1974), 463–70. My own account owes much to the able survey of C. L. Ten, *Mill on Liberty* (Oxford, 1980), chs. 2 and 3.

[32] Mill, *On Liberty*, 117–18.   [33] Mill, *Utilitarianism*, 16.

higher and lower satisfactions, central to Mill's notion of a worthwhile life, is also undermined. Why shouldn't we be satisfied with the lowest type of experience when there is no motivation to change? The nature of human flourishing can only be elicited by the study of the objects of human action, not by the mechanics, biology, or psychology of human impulses and desires.[34] Mill avoids such questions because his revised utilitarianism is but a rationalization of his view of human goods. Mill smuggles into his liberal theory a teleological conception of human fulfilment, framing it in utilitarian terms so that what people desire is identified with the end of humanity which reason enjoins us to realize.

Some interpreters argue that Mill's essay contains two logically distinct doctrines of liberty. The first, encapsulated in Mill's 'very simple principle', limits the reasons which can be adduced to interfere with individual liberty to the prevention of harm to others. The second, the notion of autonomy or individuality outlined above, is a metaphysical doctrine defining what liberty consists in.[35] However, by including 'the moral coercion of public opinion' amongst his list of impediments to 'liberty of action',[36] Mill invokes his fuller notion of freedom when he formulates his principle. This is not surprising, since Mill believes the major threat to freedom in modern societies comes from the pressure to conform arising from the power of majority opinion in democracies and the enervating effects of industrial labour. A society of contented slaves is too real a prospect for Mill to limit political liberty to the narrow negative version Rees and others attribute to him.

The issue of social conformism poses a particularly difficult problem for Mill because of his empiricist theory of personal identity. As we saw, he regards the development of character as deriving from the provision of opportunities to experience new pleasures, not from a willed desire on the part of the individual. As he put it in the *Logic*, 'the will to alter our own character is given us, not by any effort of ours, but by circumstances we cannot help: it comes to us from external causes, or not at all.'[37] Mill is able to counter Owen's fatalistic belief, that we

---

[34] In developing my criticisms of Mill I am indebted to the work of Charles Taylor, especially his essays 'What's Wrong with Negative Liberty', in Ryan (ed.), *The Idea of Freedom*, 175–94 and 'What is Human Agency?', in T. Michel (ed.), *The Self: Psychological and Philosophical Issues* (Oxford, 1977), 103–35.

[35] J. C. Rees, *Mill and his Early Critics* (Leicester, 1956), 48–9.

[36] Mill, *On Liberty*, 72.

[37] J. S. Mill, *System of Logic*, in *Collected Works*, general ed. J. M. Robson, viii (Toronto, 1974), 840.

are necessarily products of our social environment, only by assuming that we have a natural desire for self-development.[38] This optimistic view of human nature allows him to pass as a conventional liberal in most circumstances. But a difficulty arises should social conditions inhibit our desire for self-improvement. Mill admits:

Capacity for the nobler feelings is in most natures a very tender plant, easily killed, not only by hostile influences, but by the mere want of sustenance; and in the majority of young persons it speedily dies away if the occupations to which their position in life has devoted them, and the society into which it has thrown them, are not favourable to keeping that higher capacity in existence.[39]

Such circumstances, Mill argues, require the state to intervene to provide the conditions suitable for human self-development or freedom. This argument could still be consistent with the broader definition of negative liberty outlined in section I. For he need not impose a set of interests upon the individual to place him in a position to choose between higher and lower pleasures. The difficulties begin when conflicts between different conceptions of the good life arise. Mill appears to resolve this question without imposing any 'real' will upon the actual preferences of individuals. He maintains that social legislation simply provides the necessary co-ordination of different individual wants and preferences commensurate with their maximum satisfaction. I shall argue below that Mill achieves this solution by a sleight of hand. He can only provide a coherent ordering of different individuals' preferences because he assumes a hierarchy of pleasures within the individual. For a calculation on the part of various agents as to how to satisfy a number of contingently arrived at wants can provide no rules by which to arrive at a common interest—their preferences would be too unstable to allow a consistent ranking. His concept of a common interest is therefore parasitic upon a theory of the good. The pursuit of certain objects, of poetry rather than pushpin, constitutes our true freedom because it realizes our capacities, giving us 'power over our character' and hence rendering us 'morally free'. Only 'a person of confirmed virtue is completely free',[40] because the virtuous alone have the stamina and conviction to resist the temptations and enervating effects of industrial society.

Mill's position is clearest in the *Principles of Political Economy*. Here

---

[38] Mill, *Logic*, 836–43. For a fine analysis of this passage see G. W. Smith, 'The Logic of J. S. Mill on Freedom', *Political Studies*, 28 (1980), 238–52.
[39] Mill, *Utilitarianism*, 9–10. [40] Mill, *Logic*, 841.

liberty is viewed in a classically negative manner, as 'acting according to one's own judgement of what is desirable', but is subject to numerous limiting conditions. Some, like the bar on entering into irrevocable contracts (including marriage), are against external constraints on autonomy—that is, the ability to enter into new relationships in the future.[41] Others, concerning the care of lunatics or children, reflect internal restraints.[42] However, the most interesting example, as Martin Hollis has shown, focuses on Mill's own version of the Prisoners' Dilemma discussed in section I.[43] According to Mill, 'the practical principle of non-interference', that 'individuals are the best judges of their own interests',[44] is undercut by the observation that

[i]n the particular circumstances of a given age and nation, there is scarcely anything really important to the general interest, which it may not be desirable, or even necessary, that the government should take upon itself, not because private individuals cannot effectively perform it, but because they will not.[45]

Mill realizes that there are certain forms of collective action, analogous to the type examined earlier, which are unlikely to be performed without a prior commitment on the part of all concerned to the goal it seeks to achieve. Thus, to quote Mill's example, the reduction of factory hours from ten to nine would be for the advantage of all working people, but 'will not be adopted unless the body of operatives bind themselves to one another to abide by it'.[46] A worker who refused to work ten hours when others continued to do so would be sacked. Moreover, without the sanction of law it might always be in the immediate interest of the single individual to increase his or her wages by working an extra hour, thereby eroding the long-term advantage of the reduction of hours since all would be again obliged to work the tenth hour to be on a par with everyone else. The fact that in such a situation the individual's immediate self-seeking will ultimately be worse for everybody (the blackleg included) gives, as Sen and Runciman have shown, 'an immediately and plausible sense to Rousseau's notion of the members of a society being "forced to be

---

[41] J. S. Mill, *Principles of Political Economy*, in *Collected Works*, general ed. J. M. Robson, iii (Toronto, 1965), 5. 11. 2, p. 938; 5. 11. 10, p. 953.

[42] Mill, *Principles of Political Economy*, 5. 11. 9, p. 951.

[43] Martin Hollis, 'The Social Liberty Game', in A. Phillips Griffiths (ed.), *Of Liberty* (Cambridge, 1983), 31–44.

[44] Mill, *Principles*, 5. 11. 9, p. 951; 5. 11. 10, p. 953. Mill adopts this formulation in most sections of this chapter.

[45] Ibid. 5. 11. 16, p. 970.   [46] Ibid. 5. 11. 12, p. 957.

free" '.[47] Agreement between individuals is only to be achieved by a prior commitment. Formally, Mill rejects the positive libertarian solution of a common good shared by all individuals. Instead, he deploys his theory of self-development and argues that such agreement would naturally develop as an ontogenetic process. Whilst this solution enables him to remain in form a negative libertarian, it has the potential for just the sort of tyrannical manipulation Berlin fears from Green.

In *Utilitarianism* Mill argues 'that the happiness which forms the utilitarian standard of what is right in conduct, is not the agent's own happiness, but that of all concerned'. He implies that this is necessarily true for purely procedural reasons requiring that you 'do as you would be done by'. But he ends his discussion by considering what would be needed to make 'the nearest approach to this idea'. The principle of utility, he believes,

would enjoin, first, that laws and social arrangements should place the happiness, or (as speaking practically it may be called) the interest, of every individual, as nearly as possible in harmony with the interest of the whole; and secondly, that education and opinion, which have so vast a power over human character, should so use that power as to establish in the mind of every individual an indissoluble association between his own happiness and the good of the whole.[48]

The identification of what these interests are, however, is extremely difficult for Mill without subverting the individual's freedom of choice. Neither utility nor social norms are particularly attractive candidates, since both could be used to override individual life-plans on grounds Mill seeks to avoid. More recently Gray and Wollheim have argued that Mill's account of interests is similar to Rawls's 'thin' theory of primary goods.[49] Mill can argue on these grounds, for example, against an individual voluntarily choosing to become a slave, since this would necessarily deprive him or her of the opportunity to frame and execute any plan of life. Yet even if this reading is correct, it still leaves Mill with the intractable problem of how to decide between conflicting interests without appealing to a strong theory of the good.

Mill's harm principle, for example, cannot mediate between conflicting freedoms in a neutral manner. The exclusion of moral

[47] Runciman and Sen, 'Games, Justice' (n. 17 above), 556–7.
[48] Mill, *Utilitarianism*, 16.
[49] Gray, *Mill on Liberty*, 88; Richard Wollheim, 'John Stuart Mill and the Limits of State Action', *Social Research*, 40 (1973), 12; and Wollheim, 'Mill and Berlin', 267.

offence alone provides proof of its value-laden nature. In general, Mill seems to avoid the problem by assuming that the higher pleasures are essentially complementary. His view of marriage as the union of male reason and female intuition provides a particularly striking instance of his social ideal in this respect.[50] He never appears to have contemplated that different liberties might clash. In any case, his indirect utilitarianism saves him from attempting to weigh incommensurable freedoms, such as the right to free speech and the right to privacy, against each other in order to show which combination produces less harm on balance. Rather, he assumes that the refinement of human pleasures brings with it 'the better development of the social part of [the individual's] nature' with the result that society becomes increasingly consensual— a view curiously at odds with his praise of diversity![51]

In the *Principles* Mill apparently rejects the notion of a natural harmony of interests between rational actors, in all circumstances at least. As we saw, this conclusion led to a justification of state intervention which would certainly infringe a prima facie reading of his defence of liberty. However, Mill resolves this problem in *On Liberty* by assuming the revised account of individuality given above, in which our wants and the 'true' interests of humanity are identified. This stratagem is evident in the manner in which he refers both to 'higher' and 'lower' pleasures and the consequences and effects of our acts in the same breath as he talks of human interests. Unless he can prove humans to be Millian utilitarians by nature, this commits him to trying to rank within a common system of values goods which are strictly speaking incommensurable. It is this difficulty which Mill's progressivism seeks to obviate. In the passage quoted above, for instance, he achieves this result by identifying interest and happiness. The interest of the individual and society are united in a common desire to maximize happiness. Since this goal might be interpreted differently by different people, Mill defines it in terms of self-realization. To avoid the philistine Benthamite utopia of contented pigs, he appeals to 'utility in the largest sense, grounded on the permanent interests of man as a progressive being'[52]—just the sort of 'objective' concept of human ends Berlin explicitly attacks. Thus Mill neatly resolves the conflict between liberty and utility by asserting that our true freedom inheres in our maximizing utility. Whilst liberal in spirit and inspiration, Mill's

---

[50] J. S. Mill, *Subjection of Women*, in *Collected Works*, general ed. J. M. Robson, xxi, *Essays on Equality, Law and Education* (Toronto, 1984), 306, 336.
[51] Mill, *On Liberty*, 121.   [52] Ibid. 74.

theory is therefore based on the assumption 'that in some ultimate, all-reconciling, yet realizable synthesis duty is interest', a doctrine Berlin equates with positive liberty.[53] Although Mill begins from premisses not inconsistent with negative liberty, he ends up by smuggling in a supposedly objective notion of human flourishing which is the trademark of theories of positive liberty. He supplements his principle of liberty with a doctrine of individuality or self-realization and frames them in utilitarian terms. Individual and social liberty are thereby identified by just the sort of imposition of a 'real' interest upon an individual's empirical interest Berlin most fears. This does not mean that all conceptions of liberty which invoke a theory of self-development, and in particular Green's, need involve such a 'monstrous impersonation' as Mill's requires to render them coherent.[54]

III

Green begins his *Prolegomena* by noticing a disjunction in the minds of his contemporaries between the high aspirations for humanity which they acknowledge when reading poetry or engaging in religious worship, and the base view of human nature which had emerged from the developing natural science of humanity (para. 1). Mill, as we have seen, tries to reconstruct the former in terms of the latter. Green's first task is to submit this whole enterprise, and naturalism generally, to a harshly critical assault. In these theories actions are conceived as deriving partly from natural impulses and wants, partly from experienced pleasures and pains. Human development is a natural sequence of events in which reason, acting on the basis of antecedent pleasures and pains, seeks ever more complex forms of happiness by satisfying *de facto* desires. Green, however, notes that human desire is quite different in quality to animal impulse or appetite. Human beings have a capacity to evaluate desires which is in turn related to their power of self-evaluation. Such judgement is impossible in naturalistic terms, since 'it is obvious that to a being who is simply a result of natural forces an injunction to conform to their laws is unmeaning' (para. 7).

It is not sufficient to regard knowledge as the outgrowth of a process of natural evolution, for how would it be possible for a being which is merely a product of natural forces to form a theory of those forces

---

[53] Berlin, 'Two Concepts', 171.
[54] The phrase is from Berlin, 'Two Concepts', 133, and is used against doctrines of positive liberty generally, rather than Mill's theory.

(para 8)? Knowledge must rather presuppose the presence in humans 'of a principle not natural, and a specific function of this principle in rendering knowledge possible' (para. 8). Green argues, in Kantian manner, that the view of the world, essential to science, as a related series of objects and events, is not a product but a presupposition of knowledge. But he goes beyond Kant to regard the relation of objects in the manifold of experience not simply 'as fictions of our combining intelligence', but as explicable only on the assumption of the existence of a divine consciousness present in both mind and nature and guaranteeing their ultimate unity. 'Consciousness is therefore not just the basis of our knowledge of uniform relations between phenomena, but of there being those uniform relations' (para. 33).

Green links this account of the metaphysical basis of knowledge to his criticism of naturalist ethics. To see actions as the product of antecedent impulses and desires, explicable by natural laws analogous to those of physics, is to make morality redundant. But, Green argues, natural laws are themselves a product of human consciousness, which in turn reproduces the divine consciousness. Morality is to be accounted for in a similar manner. Calling into question our animal wants and passions is to relate the idea of the object of desire to the self, which in turn presupposes Green's theory of knowledge and of consciousness. Desire, intellect, and will interact in the framing of motives for actions. Natural instincts and impulses are transformed into desires for self-satisfaction through the relation of consciousness of the object of desire to a possible self. Thus:

[e]ven those desires of man . . . which originate in animal want or susceptibility to animal pleasures in the sense that without such want or susceptibility they would not be, yet become what they are in man, as desires consciously directed to objects, through the self-consciousness which is the condition of those objects or any objects being presented. (para. 125)

Self-realization or self-development, even of the most minimal kind, involves the individual in conceiving his or her life as an end in itself and framing goals for which s/he seeks to live. This is only possible for beings who can distinguish themselves from the manifold of their experience, actual and possible. Moral experience is thus only conceivable for a self-conscious subject, capable of acting in an autonomous manner as outlined in section I. Morality and freedom are inextricably linked. By freedom Green means 'the primary or juristic sense of power to act according to choice or preference', without internal or external constraints. He then extends the argument and maintains that 'such freedom is precious to [us] because it is an achievement of the self-seeking principle'. We can only attain freedom in the 'juristic' sense if we have overcome our conflicting desires and natural conditioning by seeking moral freedom. Virtue similarly implies the ability to act in an uncoerced manner, to choose freely to behave morally.[55]

We are now in a position to assess Berlin's criticisms of Green's notion of positive liberty.[56] Berlin's comments carry some force, for Green appears to place a transcendent self over and above an empirical self and this is only possible if one accepts his metaphysics. Section I of this essay discussed the similarities between positive and negative liberty ignored by Berlin's distinction. Both concepts relate the freedom of agents to the ends they choose. For Green, and for most advocates of positive liberty, choosing between ends implicitly prescribes certain types of self-satisfaction as being more important for humans than others. However, this reasoning does not entail the imposition of a 'real' self upon an 'empirical' self, but forms part of the process of critical evaluation which we all employ when seeking to choose between possible courses of action. Green asks us to seek the realization of a *telos* within humankind, not that we substitute a new 'higher' self for an old base self. The language of morals is precisely the language of this transition from 'is' to 'ought'. It is not imposed upon the individual, but emerges out of common human practices.

As a result, Green's positive conception of liberty is compatible with many of the attributes of individual liberty praised by Mill and his admirers. In *On Liberty* Mill attacks a world in which custom turns human thoughts and action into 'ape-like imitation':

The human faculties of perception, judgement, discriminative feeling, mental activity, and even moral preference, are exercised only in making a choice. He who does anything because it is the custom makes no choice. He gains no practice either in discerning or in desiring what is best. The mental and moral, like the muscular powers, are improved only by being used.[57]

[55] T. H. Green, 'On the Different Senses of Freedom as Applied to Will and to the Moral Progress of Man', in *Works*, ii, paras. 17–18.

[56] For a parallel defence of Green to my own, see Peter Nicholson, *The Political Philosophy of the British Idealists: Selected Studies* (Cambridge, 1990), Study IV. I provide a more historical account of Green's political theory as a whole in 'T. H. Green and the morality of Victorian liberalism', in Richard Bellamy (ed.), *Victorian Liberalism: Nineteenth Century Political Thought and Practice* (London, 1990).

[57] Mill, *On Liberty*, 116–17.

It is just such a conception of the exercise of human faculties which Green is attempting to articulate. But what is 'best' can only arise from individuals challenging the satisfaction of their desires in the circumstances in which they find themselves and seeking higher forms of satisfaction which, to refer back to an earlier quote from Mill, fulfil their 'higher faculties'. This end Green describes as a higher realization of our moral capabilities. This sort of reasoning leaves open the question of what these capabilities are. As Green points out, we have no picture of the fully developed human being before us, nor can we ever have. Yet in engaging in any activity we are forced to ask, 'How can I carry this practice out in such a manner that I do it well?' This enquiry involves the further question, 'What does this activity develop in me?' In other words our 'mental and moral . . . powers' are 'exercised'. What both these questions imply is a conception of the common good of humankind. The search for the good is what gives human practices their unity with respect to the 'end of man'. For, to quote von Humboldt once more, this goal is not 'suggested by vague and transient desires' but is 'the highest and most harmonious development of [man's] powers to a complete and consistent whole'. Accordingly, as Green writes, it is 'the practical struggle after the Better, of which the idea of there being a Best has been the spring' (para. 172) which generates human self-realization. This process, as has already been shown, cannot be explained naturalistically as an evolution of self-regarding desires. Rather, it is by virtue of consciousness that 'man . . . is determined, not simply by natural wants according to natural laws, but by the thought of himself as existing under certain conditions, and as having ends that may be attained and capabilities that may be realised under those conditions'—a way of thinking Green describes as the manifestation of a 'self-objectifying principle' within the moral agent (para. 175). What is all-important, therefore, is the will to contribute in some form or other towards human fulfilment. That will cannot by its very nature be imposed upon people. Its development is made possible only by an openness to the idea of human self-realization, which is the operative ideal in any liberal society.

Green grounds his theory of knowledge, and by extension his theory of morals, in a conception of God. A 'divine principle' is said to realize itself in human beings through their consciousness and will, leading humanity to perfection and harmonizing conflicting human wills. There would appear, then, to be some basis for Berlin's fear that a single 'real' self can be imposed upon independent 'empirical' selves by conceiving of the 'true' self as some entity, such as spirit or the state or the notion of humanity as a collective subject, which realizes the potential of its members. Green, however, explicitly counters such a perversion of his doctrine:

Our ultimate standard of worth is an ideal of *personal* worth. All other values are relative to value for, of, or in a person. To speak of any progress or improvement of a nation or society or mankind, except as relative to some greater worth of persons, is to use words without meaning. (para. 184)

For Green, individual self-development is necessarily something one does for oneself. It involves conceiving oneself as an end to be realized. Green's denial of naturalism implies this human ability to act autonomously by being conscious of the forces affecting us, and to transcend them as far as possible. But such acts are not without purpose, since they involve the development of those specific capabilities which define what we are. Self-realization involves recognizing that there is a hierarchy amongst human satisfactions, that we value some more than others. This does not mean that individuals transcend their animal selves to become totally spiritual beings, or that there is a 'higher' self dictating continuously to a 'lower' self within each of us. Human beings live on several layers of existence and the lower imply, but are not cancelled out by, the higher.[58] Personal identity is constituted by the choices made at all levels of one's existence: from a liking for a particular type of food, to religious or political beliefs. Personal freedom consists of being an autonomous agent in all levels of existence, as far as that is possible for finite beings such as humankind. Yet there is an implicit *telos* in such activity too, implied in the very notion that we have capabilities which are refined through being exercised in specific practices. The activities which an individual engages in cannot be separated off from his or her personality and explained either by external factors, internal impulses, or a combination of both. For it is precisely through such activity that we realize ourselves. Our different acts are no longer to be regarded as disparate and unconnected events, but have a unity in the self which defines them. Self-realization is thus the development of human capacities through engaging in activity. In so doing individuals are

[58] T. H. Green, *Lectures on the Principles of Political Obligation*, in *Works*, ii, paras. 134, 141.

seeking a personal good, bettering themselves by conceiving what their best self could be like.

The above might be accepted as having established the ideal-regarding nature of desire, that to have wants requires some notion of human fulfilment. It need not imply that there can be any agreement on what those ends are. This point is obviously central to a doctrine of positive liberty, and needs to be justified if Berlin's accusation of its tyrannical implications is to be countered. Green's answer is that we never realize ourselves solely as individuals, but in the context of society. Part of my identity is constituted by the social role I adopt, a role which has many facets to it, involving my membership of a particular professional group, my friends and family, the city and country I live in, etc. There is a certain contingency about many aspects of this identity. I frame my plan of life within limits. But the essential point is that my effort of identification, or seeking a personal good, will inevitably be expressed in social terms. I am not, as in the negative libertarian theory, an abstract individual, defined simply by a number of psychological features which determine my behaviour. Instead I find my self involved in a society which inevitably defines an aspect of what I am and want to be. A community consists of a number of shared ways of experiencing and interpreting the world, from which we cannot cut ourselves off without ceasing to engage in relationships with other people. Even if we did so we would necessarily retain part of this cultural baggage to think and act at all—Robinson Crusoe is very much an eighteenth-century English gentleman even on his island. Thus, as Green puts it: 'The individual's conscience is reason in him as informed by the work of reason without him in the structure and controlling sentiments of society' (para. 216).

These shared concepts and practices involve a socially embodied pursuit of the good life analogous to that which we have described in isolation for the individual. Indeed, the individual's search for a personal good is both constituted by and creates the wider search by society as a whole of which he or she necessarily forms a part. All societies, to some extent, conceive themselves as realizing an idea of the good life which all their members, to some greater or lesser degree, participate in promoting. It provides the necessary framework behind all individual actions, given that they occur within a social context. Negative libertarians deny this, noting that theories of negative liberty evolved when social cohesion had broken down to a radical degree, and the clash of opinion demanded that large areas of life be defended from political or religious fanatics. But in defending a pluralist view of the world, the negative libertarian must nevertheless trade on just the sort of framework which she denies in principle. As we saw, Mill treats each individual as naturally unique and regards custom and tradition as a block to our individuality. Green, in contrast, appreciates that the liberal commitment to autonomy is a product of Western civilization. Mill's value-laden utilitarianism enabled him to neglect the vital role social conventions play both in shaping our identity and in enabling individuals to coexist without a constant resort to coercion. However, without the assumptions built into his theory of self-development, a Millian society of rational experimenters would quickly degenerate into a Hobbesian state of nature. For Green, pluralism involves an equality of respect for individuals to realize themselves. This self-realization of autonomous individuals is necessarily done in conjunction with others on the basis of a conception of what is best for human beings which is held in common by virtue of membership of a given society, rather than a mutual interest to protect one's neighbours safety lest someone invades one's own. This conception of the good is not a static ideal or custom which individuals mechanically obey. It is the living force within all communities, stimulating and being stimulated by the activities of their members. It is not an ideal completely relative to the particular society you find yourself in, for it is grounded on a notion of the fully realized individual. That is an eternal ideal, not fully attained in any particular society, but which all societies in history attempt to make real.

Green illustrates this thesis by tracing the development of the Western moral tradition from its Greek and Judaeo-Christian origins to the present day. He does not see history as a process of inevitable development, or as an endless series of events, but as the realization of the ideal as it has appeared in human history. It is thus possible for societies to vary in the extent they embody the ideal of human perfection. It is not a unilinear development since there can be a regression away from the ideal, such as Green believed to be happening in his own day. But it is a tradition capable of surviving even the dark ages, for it lives eternally in human minds as the foundation for all meaningful activity in society. There are three components of positive liberty:

1. that it involves self-development towards a personal good;
2. that this personal good is inextricably linked with a social good;

3. that the notion of the fully realized individual—of society as 'the individual writ large'—is the operative ideal throughout history.

All three are inextricably linked and lead human beings to call into question their desire for satisfaction in an immediately attractive pleasure in the first place (para. 232).

The common good, which is logically connected with Green's idea of freedom, has often been misinterpreted as a number of particular goods which individuals desire in common. This interpretation is obviously a misrepresentation. Rather, the 'common good' is the common pursuit of the self-realization of human capabilities by members of a given society. Society is not therefore the fully realized individual in the sense Berlin claims—'the "true" self which, by imposing its collective (or "organic") single will upon its recalcitrant "members", achieves its own, and therefore their, "higher" freedom'.[59] Instead, it represents—as an ideal, not as empirical fact—the universal development of all human capabilities of which the individual is a unique and particular synthesis. Individuals contribute to the common good in seeking their own personal good whilst at the same time asking what is good for humankind as a whole, that is, what all searches similar to their own must have in common. Society is the expression of this dual search as embodied in its laws, customs, morals, and institutions.

It is important to stress the tripartite nature of this enterprise, for it prevents anyone taking any single individual will or collective entity or religious belief and imposing it as the fully realized self on others. Green's theory entails not only having equality of respect for other individuals pursuing their own personal good but also, what is perhaps more important, some notion of what this requires of us as members of a particular society. Equality of respect involves enabling all members of society to participate in it on equal terms. This is both a relative and an absolute doctrine of equality. It is relative to the particular community individuals find themselves in, but it is absolute with regard to both the integrity of the individual as a unique synthesis of human capacities and faculties—as an end in himself or herself—and in the sense that it is grounded in an ideal of the ultimate good as what is good for human beings on the whole. It is the equal right of each

---

[59] Berlin, 'Two Concepts', 132.

individual to realize his or her potential via participation in the goods basic to human fulfilment.[60]

Whilst Green's view of liberty is not incompatible with individual liberty, it is not personal freedom in Berlin's negative sense of simply doing what you want to do at any particular time. Baldwin believes that Green's definition of 'freedom in the positive sense', as 'the liberation of the powers of all men equally for contributions to a common good',[61] 'surely requires that the subject of this freedom be a society and not an individual person'.[62] But Green's argument, as we saw, is that individual freedom requires that society recognizes an equal freedom for all. Liberty and equality go together because my opportunities for self-development are a product of society as a whole, and not simply my individual will. They are not confused, therefore, but stand together in the creation of a society providing the optimal conditions for self-development.

Weinstein suggests that Green's interpretation of freedom can be taken as relating to the conditions under which liberty can be exercised, rather than as a positive definition of what liberty is.[63] These conditions, as we have seen, involve the absence of both internal constraints, such as being of sane mind, and external constraints, such as a number of basic material resources. The distinction between negative and positive liberty would then disappear, since both define liberty in terms of the removal of constraints on freedom rather than the goals achieved. This aim is clearly part of Green's argument when, in his famous 'Lecture on Liberal Legislation and Freedom of Contract', he claims that the regulation of hours of work is not incompatible with *laissez-faire* liberalism. But Green goes further to equate being free with being virtuous. As he points out: 'Moral freedom is not the same thing as a control over the outward circumstances and appliances of life. It is the end to which such control is a generally necessary means, and which gives it its value.'[64]

---

[60] A similar concept of equality is to be found in Bernard Williams, 'The Idea of Equality', in P. Laslett and W. G. Runciman (eds.), *Philosophy, Politics and Society*, 2nd Series (Oxford, 1967), 110–31.

[61] T. H. Green, 'Lectures on Liberal Legislation and Freedom of Contract', *Works*, iii, 372.

[62] Baldwin, 'MacCallum and the Two Concepts' (n. 9 above), 133.

[63] W. L. Weinstein, 'The Concept of Liberty in Nineteenth-Century British Political Thought', *Political Studies*, 13 (1965), 146, 151.

[64] Green, *Political Obligation*, para. 219.

Individual freedom has moral value only to the extent that it is orientated by the common good. Whilst the possession of certain material goods and capacities is necessary for human action, Green specifically excludes the possibility of identifying the common good with a particular set of such goods—the sort of argument favoured by welfare rights theorists, for example (para. 245). The common good provides the basis for a common morality. It offers criteria for deciding what constitutes a rational or reasonable choice, namely, that it must necessarily be a moral choice taking the tripartite form suggested above. Such reasoning produces:

on the one hand an ever widening conception of the range of persons between whom the common good is common, on the other a conception of the nature of the common good itself, consistent with its being the object of a universal society co-extensive with mankind. The good has come to be conceived with increasing clearness, not as anything which one man or set of men can gain or enjoy to the exclusion of others, but as a spiritual activity in which all may partake, and in which all must partake, if it is to amount to a full realisation of the faculties of the human soul. (para. 286)

Hence, Green's theory of liberty is undeniably 'positive', requiring us to uphold the common good and acknowledge our duties to others as a condition of being free. It remains for us to see whether this preserves freedom, or is a metaphysical ruse to destroy it, as Berlin claims.

IV

The distinction between positive and negative liberty hinges on the former's insistence that an autonomous life is possible only under social conditions provided by a collective allegiance to the common good. Negative libertarians, like Berlin, argue that such agreement is incompatible with individual liberty. It is inconsistent with offering people the possibility to choose how they should live. We cannot oblige people to pursue a given course, because we cannot know what is truly best for people beyond what they express a preference for. For Green, however, the social nature of human life means that an absolute moral individualism, of the sort Berlin espouses, ultimately undermines freedom. It can provide no grounds for going beyond the *bellum omnium contra omnes* except the 'force of the sword' of Hobbes's *Leviathan*. Green argues that the exercise of freedom presupposes the existence of certain options; these can only be provided by a respect for the common good which furnishes the social morality necessary to mediate between conflicting individual plans.

Green's notion of the 'common good' is similar to what Joseph Raz has called an 'inherent public good'.[65] That is a good the benefits of which are under the sole control of each potential beneficiary and which by their nature could not be voluntarily controlled and distributed by any single agency. Raz's example is tolerance, which benefits all to the extent that their behaviour warrants it but which cannot, like friendship, be controlled by anyone but the individuals themselves. Such a good cannot be regarded as instrumentally, as opposed to intrinsically, beneficial, because its existence is constitutive of the ultimate good of the quality of life derived from living in a tolerant society. If tolerance was interpreted as instrumentally beneficial, then an individual could justify being intolerant in order to gain a personal advantage (for example when racialists claim that expelling coloured immigrants increases job opportunities). It might be argued that such intrinsic common goods nevertheless infringe human liberty, since they ascribe value to something independently from the interest particular individuals have in it.

However, it was noted in section I that liberty, defined as freedom from constraints, entails a number of normative conditions. These include internal states of mind, that the individual can make rational decisions, and external circumstances, that a reasonable number of options are open. If autonomy is intrinsically valuable, which it is presumed most liberals believe to be the case, then so are the goods which provide the necessary options for it to be a workable ideal. Some of these conditions will be social rather than purely individual in character. For key opportunities can only be provided by certain 'inherent public goods' like tolerance. Take the earlier example of factory hours. It was noted that the collective action needed to obtain the reduction from ten to nine hours required a sense of worker solidarity to be achieved. Without such shared feelings the common interest could always be undermined by short-term individual gain. The instrumental reasons for combining with others are not in themselves sufficient to oblige each person to do so. The other elements turn on a deeper commitment to the ideal of freedom itself and the possibilities for others to enjoy the increased opportunities that will come from working less for the same pay. The commitment within

[65] J. Raz, 'Right-Based Moralities', in J. Waldron (ed.), *Theories of Rights* (Oxford, 1984), 187.

Green's schema stems from the requirement to pursue those goods necessary in a given society for human fulfilment generally, and not simply my own.

What these goods are will of course reflect our view of human nature and society. Green does not commit the error, usually associated with positive liberty, of asserting that our 'real interests' reside in certain specified goods. His point is that goods are not identified, pursued, and distributed, in a social and moral vacuum. As Michael Walzer points out, even staple goods—bread for example— take on different meanings in different contexts, as the body of Christ, the staff of life, etc.[66] The 'common good' consists of a set of common meanings about what are worthwhile goals of freedom and of how they should be shared. These objectives cannot be separated from the goods people actually do desire but, Green argues, through being desired by individuals in communities, rather than in isolation, they take on a definite normative structure. Goods are common because they are rooted in shared practices. This contention forms the real contrast between Green and Mill. Green attempts to provide a framework within which we may equally and freely debate the moral commitments involved in acting in an autonomous manner as real individuals, with the tastes, desires, and beliefs that we achieve through living in society. This debate takes the triadic form outlined above. Mill, on the other hand, assumes a narrowly conceived and excessively individualistic human agent who perforce must live in an 'iron cage' of rational rules derived from an assumed set of humanity's 'real interests'.

Mill and Green agree that freedom can only be exercised on the basis of reasonable choices. Since the definition of what is reasonable implies some notion of the end of human endeavour, their differences derive from divergent conceptions of human nature. Whilst for Green human beings seek the good, Mill believes they desire happiness. Yet in Mill's theory individuals think they are only pursuing their own interests and self-development. It is this element which provides grounds for Berlin's view of Mill as the champion of negative liberty. But since Mill relates this process to the development of both an 'authentic' and a social self he, rather than Green, is guilty of covering 'self-deceit' under a 'metaphysical blanket'.[67] Green, in contrast, regards the agent as consciously framing a plan of life which

[66] M. Walzer, *Spheres of Justice* (Oxford, 1983), 8.
[67] Berlin on positive liberty in 'Two Concepts', 171.

contributes to the common good in its three aspects and as such fulfils the requirements of practical reason.

If liberalism was simply a set of procedures for maximizing the want satisfaction of self-seeking individuals, then a neutral method for aggregating preferences akin to utilitarianism would provide its most adequate defence.[68] But we have already disputed the possibility of generating either coherent preference orderings or the institutional arrangements necessary to secure optimal satisfaction from self-interest alone. Nor can a narrow individualism provide the motivation for agents to act in a socially responsible manner. Mill could only resolve these problems by imposing a putative real interest upon the conflicting empirical interests both within and between different individuals. He appreciated, no less than Green and Berlin, that the rationale of liberal institutions stems from their fostering a particular lifestyle—that of the self-developing and morally responsible individual. But he was wrong to suppose that a commitment to it could be derived from an individualistic, interest-based conception of society. Respect for autonomy, which I take to be the central value of liberalism, emerges from a process through which each person relates to others in the course of developing his or her personality. They value their goals and purposes as part of a number of common goods which, taken as a whole, make for a valuable social life. Relations with others depend on shared meanings and upholding those goods necessary for self-development generally, regardless of whether one has the taste or ability to pursue them all personally. For the availability and respect for such goods provide the social conditions necessary for liberty. To cut liberalism off from the common good, therefore, is to deprive it of its foundations.[69]

---

[68] As advocated e.g. by R. Dworkin, *Taking Rights Seriously*, 2nd edn. (London, 1978), 276.

[69] This conclusion may seem to contradict the argument I have presented in *Liberalism and Modern Society* and elsewhere. I should point out that this piece was written before most of my other articles on liberalism, and it is only an accident of the publishing trade that it is the most recent to appear in print. Nevertheless, I would still maintain that liberalism as traditionally conceived requires a theory of the common good for its coherence. What I now doubt is that such a foundation is socially plausible within modern complex societies. As a result, liberal categories must either be abandoned or drastically rethought.